THE WIDE WORLD OF WINEMAKING....

How many different kinds of wine are there? The bottles in your local store don't begin to tell the story. For while commercial wineries stick pretty much to grapes and a few other fruits for making their products, the home winemaker has at his command the whole delicious range of flavors found in nature. Fruits such as dates, gooseberries, pineapple ...flowers such as roses, daisies, dandelions ...even such esoteric flavorings as comfrey root, cowslip, vervain, walnut leaf...these are just a few of the over 200 delightful kinds of wine that can grace your table when you follow the simple, clear instructions in this book.

And for devotees of the noble grape, expert winemaker Homer Hardwick describes no fewer than eighteen different ways to make grape wine of classic finesse and distinction!

WINEMAKING AT HOME
was originally published by
Funk & Wagnalls Publishing Company, Inc.

Winemaking at Home

Homer Hardwick

PUBLISHED BY POCKET BOOKS NEW YORK

WINEMAKING AT HOME

Funk & Wagnalls edition published 1954

POCKET BOOK edition published July, 1973

This POCKET BOOK edition includes every word
contained in the original, higher-priced edition. It is printed
from brand-new plates made from completely reset, clear, easy-to-read
type. POCKET BOOK editions are published by POCKET BOOKS, a division
of Simon & Schuster, Inc., 630 Fifth Avenue, New York, N.Y. 10020.
Trademarks registered in the United States and other countries.

L

Standard Book Number: 671-78603-2.
Library of Congress Catalog Card Number: 68-13032.
This POCKET BOOK edition is published by arrangement with
Funk & Wagnalls Publishing Company, Inc.

Printed in the U.S.A.   Cover photograph by Ed Eng.

contents

Picture insert appears between pages 140–41

illustrations

Winemaking at Home

1

home is a place to make wine

THERE ARE few things in life which can afford the individual more pleasure and satisfaction than making his own wine in his own home. Wine is fun to make, it is a great natural food, and it is legal for the head of a family to make up to 200 gallons per year.

Most of the world's wine is made at home, not in the winery. Throughout Europe, from one end to the other, wherever the grape is grown, the farmer would no more neglect laying down his year's supply of wine than he would fail to provide bread for his family or fodder for his flocks. Likewise, from the Biblical lands of the Near East to the farthest reaches of the Orient the householder makes, and has made for centuries, his own wine from grapes and other fruits, from herbs, from grains, or from the juices of trees and plants.

There is no good reason why the American head of a family should not imitate his foreign brother. Doubtless one of the reasons that he does not do so is that the centuries-long failure to produce wine in Colonial America forced its inhabitants to turn to the more readily made distilled liquors, with the result that today America is a hard-drink nation. Another factor, operating especially at the present time, is the excessively high price being asked for marketed wine, a price which puts this healthful beverage beyond the reach of the average American as an article of daily consumption. Partly responsible for the prevailing exorbitant prices are the attitudes of the national and state governments, which seem to consider wine a luxury or a sin or both, and insist on placing heavy taxes upon it. Wine is an important food and most of the world's wine is consumed as food, appearing on the table as regularly as bread. To tax wine is, indeed, like taxing bread. "I think it is a great error," said Thomas Jefferson, "to consider a heavy tax on wines, as a tax on luxury. On the contrary, it is a tax on the health of our citizens." And since not in the foreseeable future will taxes or manufacturers permit wine to be sold at a price that will allow it to become a common article of consumption in the American home, this book goes forth with its many recipes to help the ordinary citizen to take wine out of the luxury bracket and to achieve by himself what others will not allow him to realize, namely, to have wine in his home at all times and in sufficient quantity.

Though the United States is not a wine-conscious nation in the sense that the nations of Europe are, there are, nevertheless, millions of Americans who do make wine and millions of others who would like to do so, but are deterred by the lack of know-how. Many of the latter live in sections of the country where grapes are not readily had, or where, because of the absence of commercial wine manufacture, there is no wine awareness. They do not know that wine, and very good wine indeed, can be made from scores of different fruits, berries, vegetables, flowers, grains, and tree saps. In fact, there is no place in the entire country where the head of a family may not, at any time of the year, make for himself and his family a supply of wine from one or several of nature's gifts to man which are to be found in his own field or garden, or are to be had from his local market.

The following list indicates the wide choice offered to the home winemaker. It includes ninety-five types or kinds of wines for which there are one or more tested recipes in this book.

1. Apple
2. Apple and Plum
3. Apricot
4. Balm
5. Barley
6. Beet
7. Birch
8. Blackberry
9. Blueberry
10. Boysenberry
11. Cantaloupe
12. Caraway
13. Carnation
14. Celery
15. Cherry
16. Chokecherry
17. Cider
18. Clary
19. Clover Blossom
20. Coltsfoot
21. Comfrey
22. Cowslip
23. Cranberry
24. Currant (Black)
25. Currant (Red)
26. Currant (White)
27. Daisy
28. Damson
29. Dandelion
30. Date
31. Dewberry
32. Elderberry
33. Elder Blossom
34. Fig
35. Flower
36. Fruit
37. Ginger
38. Gooseberry
39. Gooseberry and Currant
40. Grape
41. Grape Leaf
42. Greengage
43. Hock
44. Honey
45. Huckleberry
46. Jerk Wine
47. Lemon
48. Lime
49. Loganberry
50. Malt
51. Mango
52. Marigold
53. Mint
54. Molasses
55. Mulberry
56. Muscadine
57. Muskmelon
58. Oat
59. Onion
60. Orange
61. Orange and Raisin
62. Parsnip
63. Peach
64. Pear

65. Pineapple
66. Plum
67. Pomona
68. Potato
69. Primrose
70. Prune
71. Quince
72. Raisin
73. Raisin and Elderberry
74. Raspberry
75. Rhubarb
76. Rice and Raisin
77. Rose
78. Rue and Fennel
79. Sage
80. Sarsaparilla
81. Scuppernong
82. Sloe
83. Sorghum
84. Spice
85. Spruce
86. Strawberry
87. Sugar
88. Sycamore
89. Tomato
90. Turnip
91. Verbena
92. Vervain
93. Violet
94. Walnut Leaf
95. Wheat

The Home Winemaker and the Law. The United States Government supervises, in one way or another, the legal production of all alcohol or alcoholic beverages made in this country. In the case of wines, this supervision is sometimes done directly, as when a government inspector is present at the factory when wine is fortified; at other times it is done indirectly, as, for example, when the commercial producer of wines is required to place a bond and make reports on his product, or when he pays taxes.

Government control likewise extends to production of wine in the home. But the Government's consideration for the home winemaker is extremely liberal: *It allows him to make up to 200 gallons of still wine tax free each year,* requiring of him only that he obtain from the Assistant Regional Commissioner, Alcohol and Tobacco Tax Division, a permit issued on request to the head of a family who wishes to make wine at home for consumption by himself and family. The permit, known as *Form 1541,* must be filed in duplicate with the Assistant Regional Commissioner at least five days before commencing the production of wine. The Assistant Commissioner will stamp one copy and return it to the applicant who, when the wine has been made, simply writes on his copy the number of gallons, the month of manufacture, and the kind of wine he has made. The form is kept so that it may be shown on demand to any duly authorized agent of the Department of Internal Revenue.

That's all there is to it; nothing could be more simple. But this requirement should be observed, and failure to observe it is to break the law just as surely as the mountain moonshiner breaks it when he operates his hidden still in some scrub-oak thicket. The Code is so generous—200 gallons is a lot of wine!

Form 1541 is reproduced in Appendix I and a list of all the Regional Offices of the Alcohol and Tobacco Tax Division of the Bureau of Internal Revenue is given in Appendix II.

America Is Wineland. America is preeminently the land of the grape. Numerous varieties dot its shores, line its streams, climb its mountains, and sprawl across its plains. It grows everywhere in the land, withstanding the severe cold of the north and flourishing to lushness in the humid heat of the south. There is no more fascinating chapter of American history than that which tells of the discovery and cultivation of the grapes and the long, and finally successful, efforts to make the United States a wine-producing country.

In the year 1000 A.D. Leif, son of Erik the Red, left Greenland with thirty-five hardy men and sailed west to the shores of what is now America. In that part of the country we today call Massachusetts, a German member of the expedition named Tyrker took his small skiff and went exploring along the shore. He found quantities of grapes everywhere. Filling his little boat, he returned to exhibit this new treasure to his companions. Their delight at the discovery inspired many later excursions in search of the fruit. In such great abundance was it found, that their leader, Leif Ericson, pondering a name for the new land, could find none more fitting than Vinland, the Land of the Vine. Thus was America named five hundred years before the arrival of Columbus!

And it is today the greatest natural grape-growing country in the world. Considerably more than half of all known species are native to America. In spite of this, however, the cultivation of the grape in the United States has been sadly neglected during most of the country's history. It is true that many of the early colonizers attempted the growing of grapes for the purpose of making wine. The first formal proposal in this direction came from Lord Delaware in 1616. His suggestions were later tried in a serious manner in Virginia, Massachusetts, Georgia and other colonies. When he was in public life, Thomas Jefferson was much concerned with viticulture (the cultivation of grapes for wine production). But failure attended all efforts to produce wine in the colonies. This was due chiefly to the insistence on establishing here vineyards of Old World grapes, the *Vitis vinifera,* neglecting the development and culture of the many native varieties which were already adapted to the soil and climate. The Old World grape simply would not thrive in eastern America. Later sane heads discovered that certain native grapes would produce good wine, but the nineteenth century was already upon the nation when this discovery was made.

West of the Rocky Mountains, however, the story is different. There the climate and the soil offered conditions more nearly like those of Europe, and there certain varieties of *Vitis vinifera* introduced by the Spaniards flourished as well as at home. In the nineteenth century other varieties were brought from Europe, notably from Hungary, Germany, and France, and today all California wine is made from the same grapes as in the Old World.

And the bulk of American wine is now made in California—about eighty-five percent of the total. Second in importance of the wine-growing states is New York, which provides fine wines in its Finger Lakes region and along the southern shores of Lake Erie. In third place stands Ohio, particularly the area around Sandusky and the islands of Lake Erie. Viticulture is practiced with varying degrees of success in numerous other states of the Union; among the most important of them from a commercial point of view are Arkansas, Delaware, Michigan, Missouri, New Jersey, New Mexico, Oregon, Texas, and Washington. In addition to these, there is hardly a state where some grape does not grow and where grape wine cannot be made.

2

apparatus

THE TOOLS needed for the manufacture of wine at home are not many; it would be possible to get along with two: a container for the fermenting juice and something to put the wine in after it has finished working. But, just as extra care and attention will improve the quality, so will the proper equipment make it easier to produce the wine.

In a time of changing prices it would be meaningless to detail the cost of equipment. Suffice it to say that for a moderate outlay the home winemaker can acquire all the tools he will ever need. But whatever he spends, the first fifty gallons of good wine he makes will repay in satisfaction the cost of the apparatus.

Appendix III contains the names and addresses of suppliers of all items mentioned in this chapter. Some are not so readily obtainable in the local market now as formerly, but it may be worthwhile to inquire at farmers'-supply or hardware stores. Drugstores and chemical-supply houses can probably provide some of the smaller articles.

A glossary of all terms used in this chapter and elsewhere in the book will be found in Appendix VIII.

FIGURE 1. FERMENTING VAT (BARREL)

Fermenting Vat. A 50-gallon barrel with one end removed makes an excellent fermenting vat. Barrels are not so universally available as formerly; however, anyone living in or near a large city should have little difficulty in obtaining one. Look in the yellow pages of the telephone directory under "Cooperage" or "Barrels." (A metal drum should never be used.) Companies serving metropolitan areas often sell used whiskey barrels for a few dollars. These are usually charred inside, but this makes no difference if they are used only as fermenting vats and not to store, age, or contain the wine when finished. (See Figure 1.)

Somewhat easier to keep clean, though more expensive when new, is a large crock or stoneware jar. The 30-gallon size is large enough. Crocks and stone jars are not nearly so common these days as formerly. Still, they can be found, especially in rural areas and often at farm sales and auctions.

As the difficulty in obtaining good clean barrels or stoneware has increased, another article has come on the market to take their place among the home winemaker's tools—the plastic "trash can." These receptacles are available in various capacities from 5 to 32 gallons. Relatively inexpensive, light in weight, easy to clean, they can be stored by nesting. They come equipped with a tight-fitting lid (which is not of much use in making wine). There is no evidence that initial fermentation in a plastic container in any way affects the finished wine. (See Figure 2.)

FIGURE 2. FERMENTING VAT (PLASTIC TRASH CONTAINER)

If a crock or plastic container is used, the juice will have to be dipped or siphoned out of it after fermentation. On the other hand, if a large cask or barrel is the fermenting vat, it can be equipped with a spigot fitted in a hole drilled a few inches above the bottom end. In this case, the barrel should be set high enough above the floor to permit a receiving vessel to go under the spigot. Since a barrel of liquid is very heavy, make sure that the supporting stand or platform is of rugged construction.

In addition to two or more large containers for making substantial quantities of wine, it is a good idea to have handy two or three smaller ones of 5-, 10-, or 15-gallon capacity to be used in experimenting, and especially or making the heavier sweet wines from flowers, vegetables, or from fruits other than grapes.

Measuring Stick. If the fermenting vat is a plastic trash container, a convenient accessory is a measuring stick, which can be made at home. It ought to be 1 or 2 inches wide, approximately ½ inch thick, and a few inches longer than the height of the container in which it is to be used. To make this an accurate instrument for measuring the must, it should be carefully graduated or marked off. Since the plastic containers slope outward toward the top, the markings on the stick must be made for each measured gallon poured into the vat. Make the graduations by using water. Obviously a measuring stick that serves for a 5-gallon container will not be accurate for one of 32-gallon capacity. (See Figure 3.)

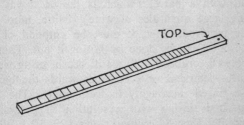

FIGURE 3. MEASURING STICK

Stirring Paddle. Another handy accessory that can be made at home is a long-handled paddle for stirring the must in the fermenting vat. It should be cut from ¾-inch hardwood. The paddle end ought to measure 6 to 8 inches in length and 4 to 6 inches in width. Like the measuring stick, over-all length of the stirring paddle should be several inches greater than the depth of the container; a 36-inch handle will suffice for any home fermenting vat smaller than a 50-gallon barrel. (See Figure 4.)

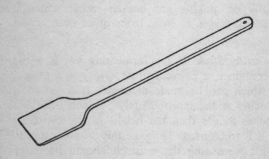

FIGURE 4. STIRRING PADDLE

The fermenting vat, whether it be a "trash can" or a barrel, should be cleaned at once after use. This is no problem with the plastic container, which may be washed out simply by rinsing under a faucet or with a hose. But with a barrel (which is the ideal vat for fermenting large quantities of wine) a little more attention is required. First, it must be emptied of all settlings, which can be done by hosing it out. Then it should be well scrubbed with a stiff brush, using water with a little detergent or soap. Afterwards the barrel should be rinsed thoroughly in fresh water. The last step is a final rinsing with a solution of potassium metabisulphite. (See *Sulphiting,* pages 129–30.) When it is at last clean, allow it to dry in the open air and sunshine. A barrel or wooden tub must be completely dry before being put away. Store only in a dry place, for a wooden container stored in a damp place may grow a fungus (mold) between the staves that will spoil future batches of wine.

Press. For red wines it is convenient, but not necessary, to have a press. The juice is fermented on the skins of the crushed grapes instead of being pressed off. On the other hand, in making white wine either from white or dark grapes, a press is indispensable, for the grapes require pressing, since the juice is never fermented on the skins.

In making red wine the fruit is crushed and placed in the fermenting vat. When fermentation has subsided the juice must be removed from the hulls and seeds. This can be done by squeezing them through a bag with the hands; but if any quantity of wine is being made, a press becomes almost necessary.

A small hoop or basket press (see illustration section at page 140) will answer the demands of the small-scale winemaker. In it small quantities of grapes or other fruits can be crushed. It also serves very well for extracting the remaining juice from skins and seeds left over after the red wine has been drained or siphoned from the vat following the first fermentation.

Still better is common cider press, much stronger and sturdier than the small basket press just described, though built on similar principles. The basket, however, is larger and rests on a platform set in a heavy frame. This press will stand about all the pressure the average man can give it.

Perhaps the best of the presses for the domestic winemaker is the ratchet press. It will cost somewhat more than the simpler basket press and is less cumbersome than the cider press. With proper care it should last a lifetime. The advantage of this press is that it can exert a constant and steady pressure for a long period of time, thus extracting more juice from the fruit being crushed. It is available in various sizes, with either a two-band or three-band basket. The purchaser may also have his choice of a single or double ratchet. (See Figure 5.)

FIGURE 5. RATCHET PRESS

Pressing Bags. When making white wine, and using any of the presses described above, the grapes should be put into a well-sewed bag made of strong cloth. The average bag made of muslin or similar cloth will not do, for it will burst under the tremendous pressure of the plunger plate as it is forced downward by the turning of the screw shaft. A clean, new burlap bag is one of the best pressing bags that we have found; it should be washed or rinsed before using. Another excellent bag can be made of canvas sewed and resewed at the seams with stout thread. Its size should be about that of the burlap bag.

The best way to extend the life of a pressing bag is to press only a relatively small quantity of grapes at a time. If too many are put in it, the bag will suffer great strain. (For description of the pressing process see the section in Chapter 4 entitled *Making White Wine*.) Another disadvantage of trying to press too many grapes at one time is that the fruit will not be pressed dry; that is, not all the juice will be extracted.

After each day's pressing, the bag should be washed with soap and water, rinsed well, and hung up to dry. A bag put away while still damp with fruit juice may develop a mold that will spoil the juice from future pressings.

Fruit Crusher. Grapes, even sizable quantities of them, may be crushed by hand or with a potato masher; but this can be a slow process. Much easier and faster is a fruit crusher. Several kinds are on the market. The best for the home winemaker is also one of the least complex. Although difficult to get at one time, this simple machine is again available. (See Appendix III.) It consists of a wooden hopper over rollers which are set slightly apart and turned by a handle. (See Figure 6.) The whole structure rests on top of the fermenting vat, so that crushed grapes fall directly into it. An electrically operated crusher is also available.

FIGURE 6. FRUIT CRUSHERS WITH WOODEN HOPPER

Two other fruit crushers, both available, are illustrated in Figures 7 and 8. Figure 7 is something like a meat chopper or sausage grinder with an attachment that separates pulp and juice from skins and seeds. It clamps on any table and is usually obtainable in two sizes: family size and farm size.

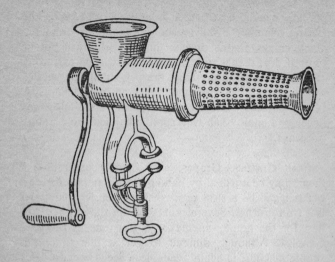

FIGURE 7. FRUIT CRUSHER

The other machine (Figure 8) comes in one size only and is designed to extract juices from vegetables and fruits. Both these extractors are heavily coated with tin, which guards the juice from contact with the iron of which the machine is made.

A third apparatus that will serve the amateur wine-maker is the Squeezo Strainer, sold by Milan Laboratory and Semplex of U.S.A. (see Appendix III.) A hand-operated machine weighing about five pounds, it comes equipped with a hopper and a wooden plunger for feeding the fruit into the grinder. It is made of noncorrosive metal and is therefore safe for winemaking. The Squeezo Strainer can be used in preparing many fruits for initial fermentation, but when used for grapes, it should be restricted to those from which red wine is to be made.

Cask. The term cask is used here and hereafter to refer to any hooped wooden container, closed at both ends and having a bung-hole in the center of its side. Casks are still widely available and can be bought in metropolitan areas from cooperage firms. (See the Yellow Pages of the telephone directory; also Appendix III under *Barrels, Kegs, and Casks.*)

The cask should be made of white oak, and if only one is used, it should be large enough to make a supply of wine that will last throughout the year. However, as in the case of fermenting vats, it is advisable to have several sizes. Since there is always some evaporation of wine standing in casks, it is well to keep in mind

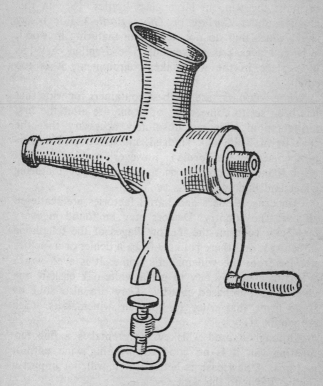

FIGURE 8. JUICER AND FRUIT CRUSHER

that there will be proportionately less in a large cask than in a small one. From a 5-gallon cask one may expect to bottle perhaps 3½ gallons of finished wine. Compare this with the 22 or 23 gallons that may be obtained from a 25-gallon cask, or the 44 or 45 gallons to be had from a 50-gallon one.

For the winemaker who wants to make enough of a certain wine for a full year's use, the 50-gallon cask is the best size. The next smaller are the 35- or 25-gallon sizes, especially useful if one wishes to make different kinds of wine. If lesser quantities are desired, it is best to make the wine in large glass bottles. (See in this chapter under *Carboy or Glass Bottle.*) For heavy sweet wines that do not need long maturing in wood, a 10-gallon cask is convenient. The 5-gallon cask has little place in the winemaker's equipment; it is too small.

White-oak casks are the best containers for wine that has been set to come clear or to mature after the first fermentation. It is not absolutely necessary that the cask be of white oak (indeed, much redwood is currently used in California); however, nothing has yet been found to equal it as a container for maturing wines and liquors.

Cooperage dealers and barrel factories are scattered all over the country. Dealers may be found in every large city (consult the Yellow Pages of the telephone directory), and there is likely to be a dealer or a factory not far from the winemaker's home. It is even worth a trip to a nearby city to get a white-oak cask if one cannot be purchased nearby. They are also sold by some firms that cater to amateur winemakers. (See Appendix III.)

Although a used whiskey barrel makes a fine fermenting vat, it is no good for keeping wine until it matures. A new cask is better, for it will not impart a foreign flavor to the wine.

For anything larger than a 30-gallon cask, it is wise

to make a trip to the factory or visit some cooperage house in a city.

Carboy or Glass Bottle. The carboy is a large bottle, usually of blown glass, that will hold from 4 to 20-odd gallons. It may be used instead of a cask for the secondary fermentation and for the maturing wine. Amateur winemakers are turning more and more to the use of glass containers; in fact, many will use nothing else. And it is true that the carboy has definite advantages over the cask. First, it is transparent and permits the wine to be seen at every stage of its development. Second, there is no shrinkage due to evaporation. Futhermore, the carboy is easier to clean and store.

On the other hand it has certain handicaps. A single carboy is too small to be used for anything except relatively small-scale manufacture—though several may be used at the same time. Futhermore, there is always the likelihood of breakage.

A better buy for the home winemaker is the 5-gallon glass bottle in which distilled water is sold. A superior quality of glass is not necessary and these bottles are quite satisfactory. If they are broken, there is no great loss, while it is usually expensive to replace a genuine carboy. Five-gallon glass bottles can be obtained from any firm that distributes distilled water and from many supermarkets. It is a good idea to buy several, including the water, if necessary. Even if the winemaker uses a cask, it is a good idea to have two or three large glass bottles and jugs handy for holding surplus wine or for experimenting with small quantities.

Finally, there is the plastic bottle, made of unbreakable polyethylene coming in the 5-gallon size fitted with a water-seal. It is obtainable from Herter's, Inc. and Leslie Edelman, Inc. (See Appendix III.) The only advantages over glass bottles are that it is unbreakable and can be collapsed and stored in a small space. A disadvantage is that it is not transparent and does not, therefore, permit the candle-flame test for fitness of the wine (described on page 83).

Water-Seal. This is also known as water-valve, water-bung, or fermentation lock. It is a device for sealing the wine in the cask or glass container, allowing the carbonic gas produced during fermentation to escape but preventing air from reaching the wine. Many "old-timers" will have nothing to do with it, preferring to trust to their experience and luck to tell them when to bung up the cask. However, with the water-seal, the air is always excluded from the wine, the escaping gas passes out freely, and the winemaker is spared a lot of trouble and the risk of having his wine turn to vinegar through overcontact with the air.

An excellent water-seal, devised by Milan Laboratory of New York City (see Appendix III), consists of a water-filled double-ball air trap. It can be used either in glass containers with a number 16 cork, or in barrels with a number 28 cork (Figure 9).

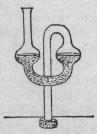

FIGURE 9. DOUBLE-BALL AIR-TRAP WATER-SEAL

Another type of water-seal is a plastic device distributed by Herter's, Inc., of Waseca, Minnesota, and Leslie Edelman, of Horsham, Pennsylvania (see Ap-

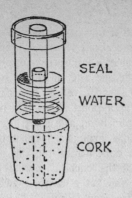

FIGURE 10. FERMENTATION-LOCK WATER-SEAL

pendix III). They call it a "fermentation lock" (Figure 10).

Several water-seals are offered by Semplex of U.S.A. (see Appendix III), including the double-ball type, and the Fisher air lock (Figure 12, A); also a large German water-seal called Giant Hobby 2 (Figure 11), with a fitted bung which tapers from 2¼ inches to 1¼ inches. It can be used with either carboy or barrel.

FIGURE 11. GIANT HOBBY 2 WATER-SEAL

If the winemaker prefers, he can make his own water-seal for just a few cents. A piece of glass tubing ⅛- or ¼-inch bore about 18 inches long can be bought at the drugstore or at a laboratory-supply house. About seven inches from one end, heat the tube over a hot flame. When soft, bend carefully at a right angle. Then heat once more at a point about five inches from the other end and again bend at a right angle. Drill a hole the size of the tube through a large cork an insert the long end. Fit the cork firmly into the bunghole of the cask or mouth of the carboy; seal all junctions with wax or paraffin and set a tumbler two-thirds full of water under the free end (Figure 12, B).

A second home-fashioned water-seal can be made of

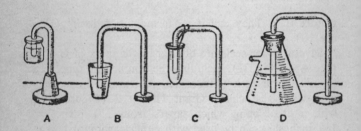

FIGURE 12. FOUR TYPES OF WATER-SEAL

glass tubing (treated as above) and a test tube fastened to the glass tubing by adhesive tape or a piece of string. Since it holds less water, this is a second-choice article, for it needs frequent refilling (Figure 12, C).

The best home-made water-seal will cost a little more, but it is worth the small extra expense because evaporation of the water is reduced. Buy from the local drugstore or from any laboratory-supply house a half-pint Eherlenmeyer filtering flask, a kind with a narrow mouth and a small side tube to permit the escape of gas. Prepare glass tubing as described above, bending it carefully. Then sink the longer end into a large bung cork. Run the shorter end through a cork (preferably of rubber) fitted firmly into the mouth of the flask, allowing the end to go well toward the bottom (Figure 12, D).

The simplest of all water-seals is fashioned from a length of rubber or plastic tubing inserted into a bung cork. The free end is dropped into a glass or jar of water. Care must be taken to prevent the tube from kinking or bending at a sharp angle, which can hinder the escape of gas.

All of the homemade water-seals have one minor disadvantage—they sometimes permit the water to be sucked into the wine. In the cask, this may be due to slow evaporation and the creation of a vacuum; in the case of the carboy, to contraction of the wine caused by a change in temperature. If this happens, the water should be replaced at once to keep the air from lengthy contact with the wine. The quality of the wine is not affected by the addition of such small amounts of water unless it occurs too frequently.

Spigot. Suppliers of equipment for the home wine-maker sell spigots, or wooden faucets. The spigot is a device for withdrawing liquids from casks through a hole drilled in one end near the bottom. Wine should never be poured through the bunghole of a cask; always use a spigot. If possible secure one with an air-valve in its underside. This little device serves two purposes: The wine can be aerated, and fermentation enhanced, by pumping air through the spigot with a bicycle pump. Similarly, if the spigot becomes clogged by lees or dregs, it may be cleaned by forcing air through the valve.

Bottles. Wine should always be stored in bottles. To the beginner it may not make much difference what kind of bottle is used, but as he grows in experience, he will see the advantage of putting his product in bottles es-

pecially made for holding wine. And this is their great
advantage: they are made for holding wine; they are
round, they are uniform in size, and their necks are
made to receive long wine corks. Usually brown or very
dark green bottles are used for red wine and light-
colored bottles for white wine, although many produc-
ers bottle their white wine in green bottles.

The best size for wine bottles is that holding one-
fifth gallon. Some commercial wineries manufacturing
inexpensive wines bottle them in half-gallon and one-
gallon glass containers.

Some bottles, not made for corks, take screw caps.
Really superior wines should probably rest under cork,
but there is no other valid reason for the home winemaker not to use caps. Indeed, many American wines
of good quality are commercially put up in bottles with
screw caps. The amateur must decide for himself
whether to use caps or corks, but he should make the
decision before ordering his bottles.

The procurement of suitable wine bottles may be one
of the home winemaker's most difficult problems. Probably the best first step would be to write one of the
manufacturers listed in Appendix III, asking where
wine bottles in quantity can be purchased locally. Most
of these manufacturers have indicated their willingness
to have their names retained in this book, thereby
implying readiness to cooperate with the domestic
winemaker. When requesting information or ordering, be
sure to specify one-fifth-gallon size and whether the
bottles are to take screw caps or corks.

It is economical for the winemaker to save suitable
bottles from year to year. He can also persuade his
friends to put their unwanted bottles aside for him.

Stoppers. Corks for wine bottles are longer and
straighter than ordinary household corks. They are far
safer to use because they fit the inside of the bottle
neck for a considerable length, thus making leakage

and consequent spoiling of the wine less likely. Buy number 9 or 10 corks one and one-half inches long.

Corking Machine. It is not easy to insert wine corks by hand. Hence, a corking machine becomes necessary. A simple one, made of wood, can be bought for a very modest figure. It consists of a chamber to hold the cork and a throat the size of the inside of the bottle neck to compress the cork as it is driven home with a plunger. A good one is made by the American Wood Working Company (see Appendix III).

Milan Laboratory and Semplex of U.S.A. also offer simple wooden hand corkers as well as a metal one that requires even less effort to use.

Siphon. Another winemaker's tool that comes in handy when using either a cask or a carboy is the siphon, sometimes called the siphon pump. It can be obtained from the addresses given under "Siphon" in Appendix III.

A length of rubber or plastic tubing (hot-water-bottle size) will serve the beginner. However, as he grows more experienced in the business, he will want a more efficient instrument, such as those sold commercially. Or he can make himself a very good one at home as follows: Purchase two lengths of glass tubing of 3/8-inch diameter: one piece 8 to 10 inches in length; the other long enough to reach to within 1 or 2 inches of the bottom of the cask or carboy that is being used and to extend a foot or so above the opening. Heat the shorter tube over a hot flame and bend once at a right angle about midway. Heat the longer piece and bend slowly into a curve at the upper end. Insert both through a cork (preferably of rubber), as shown in Figure 13. The cork should be a number 28 if used for a cask and of appropriate size (to be determined) if used with a glass bottle. Attach a length of rubber or plastic 3/8-inch hose to the curved end of the long glass tube. The

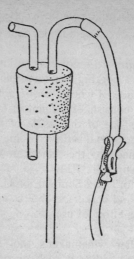

FIGURE 13. HOME-MADE SIPHON

hose must be long enough to hang below the cask or carboy containing the wine. To the free end of the hose attach a pinchcock or shut-off clamp. Rubber and glass tubing, rubber corks, and shut-off clamps may be bought at a well-stocked drugstore, or at a laboratory- or chemical-supply house; or the local druggist may be willing to order them for a customer. (A shut-off clamp can be borrowed from the common syringe found in most homes.)

Saccharometer. This is an instrument for measuring the amount of sugar in a liquid. Many millions of gallons of wine have been made at home and on the farm without a saccharometer, but for the winemaker who wants to be sure of his product, it is an essential piece of equipment. And for the making of dry wine it is indispensable. It can be obtained from any of the suppliers given in Appendix III. Since the saccharometer's function is the measuring of sugar and not the density of a liquid, the Brix scale with a range of 0° to 30° is recommended.

Hydrometer Jar. A saccharometer makes necessary the purchase of a hydrometer jar, a tall slender beaker especially made for holding liquids whose specific gravity is to be read. Its tall straight sides of clear glass make it easy to take a reading from the saccharometer, which cannot be used satisfactorily in bottles or jars because of the imperfections in the glass. This jar is sold by houses that handle saccharometers and should be purchased along with the sugar-meter.

Funnel. A funnel will find many uses in the hands of the winemaker. The most important one is, of course, to make it easier to fill the bottles with the finished wine. It should be of glass, plastic, or enamelware, not of metal or any corrosive material.

Labels. Every bottle of wine laid down should be labeled with the name of the fruit from which it was made and the date of its bottling. Gummed labels can be purchased in a stationery store or five-and-ten-cent store. Labels sometimes come off the bottle because of humidity, careless application, or insufficient mucilage. Glass needs a strong adhesive.

The home winemaker who takes pride in his wine can have lots of fun using his own "personalized" labels. Illustrations in the center insert in this book offer a number of suggestions and the imaginative amateur can invent others. An artist friend may be enlisted to design still more. Any of them can be taken to a job printer or offset lithographer for reproduction. Every job printer has in stock a supply of gummed paper on which the labels should be printed.

Some suppliers of accessories for the home wine-maker offer ready-made labels of interesting design. (See under "Labels" in Appendix III.)

Miscellaneous. As the amateur becomes more experienced, he will decide to include in his equipment many articles not mentioned above. Some of these can be found in every well-supplied kitchen. A few may be suggested here, such as measuring vessels; glass, plastic, or enamel receptacles for transferring liquids from one container to another; large corks and rubber stoppers; thermometer; glass stirring rod; strainer; dipper (glass, plastic, or enamel); bottle brush; food grinder; potato masher; large spoons and small; jelly bag; absorbent cotton; clean cloths; paraffin and a brush for applying it; and candles.

It should be repeated that only a minimum of the utensils mentioned in this chapter is absolutely necessary, but with short experience the amateur will find some of the others becoming important to him.

Essential Equipment. It has already been stated that is is possible for the home winemaker to get along with two items of equipment, a container for fermenting the juice and something to put the finished wine in. But many other tools are so useful that they must properly be classified as necessary. Here is a list of essential equipment for a beginner's 25-gallon winery:

1 30- or 35-gallon vat (barrel, trash container, or crock)
1 25-gallon white-oak cask or 5 glass or plastic 5-gallon bottles
1 saccharometer
1 hydrometer jar
1 spigot (if cask is used) or 1 siphon (if bottles are used)
1 to 5 water-seals

For the sake of economy the smaller fermenting vat and cask have been listed here instead of the 50-gallon size, though the latter will save time and effort when larger quantities are being made. However, several large carboys or a number of 5-gallon glass bottles can always replace a large barrel or cask as a container for the maturing wine, and two 30-gallon fermenting vats will do as well as one of 50 gallons.

The initial cost, though not great, may seem a bit high to one who is making wine for the first time, but if he plans to continue producing wine for himself and his family, he ought to consider the purchase of these items as an investment. It should interest him to know that when he bottles his first 25 gallons of wine, he will have 125 fifth-size bottles. It would cost him about $100.00 at present market prices to buy the same number of bottles of even the cheapest wines at a supermarket or discount store. Hence, the first purchase of equipment becomes an investment that need not be repeated in after years. The expense may even be recouped with the first batch of wine.

Optional Equipment. Many of the smaller items listed above as miscellaneous equipment are common to every household and need not go into a reckoning of the cost of the winemaker's tools. However, as the amateur grows in experience, or if he wishes to increase the capacity of his home winery, he will want to add additional accessories. Whatever he adds, it will be obvious with a little calculation that any equipment purchased will soon pay for itself, to say nothing of the added pleasure and convenience in making wine. Still, the beginner may not wish to make the whole investment at once, but rather spread it over a period of two or three years. If so, he may want to add the items listed below, keeping in mind that once they are his, they will, if handled with care, last him a lifetime.

Extra fermenting vats (number and size desired)
Extra white-oak casks or glass (or plastic) bottles (number desired)

1 fruit press (ratchet type preferred but not necessary)

1 fruit crusher (hopper type preferred)

1 siphon

Several water-seals (several lengths of glass tubing if water-seals are to be homemade)

Supply of large bung corks

Extra spigots (if casks are used)

1 large funnel (of glass or plastic)

1 small funnel (of glass or plastic)

1 stirring paddle (home-made)

Prices are not given for any of the above items because costs are in a state of flux and are likely to be meaningless by the time the winemaker is ready to purchase. But whatever their direction, whether it be up or down, the apparatus suggested will help him to make his own wine more cheaply than he can buy it, and in the process he will experience a pleasure, and perhaps a pride, he has not felt before.

3

grapes of the united states

A GOOD potable wine can be made in the home from any fruit or berry and from many vegetables and grains. But most of the country's wine comes from grapes, and since it is probable that the amateur, after some experience, will wish to turn to grapes as the fruit from which to make his wine, there is given below a list of the country's most available grapes with brief comment on the wine value of each.

The grapes of eastern America present more of a problem than do those of California and the regions west of the Rocky Mountains. The prohibition era caused the destruction of many large wine-producing vineyards and their replanting with other fruits or with entirely alien crops. It was also responsible for the planting and cultivation of large areas of grapes more suitable for the table and for juice than for the manufacture of wine. Much of this vast acreage still remains under cultivation today, for it is an expensive matter in both time and money to replace large extensions of market grapes with types better suited to wine. Consequently in the grape regions of the eastern United States, the Concord and many of its cousins, which are not very good for wine, dominate viticulture and yield much of this region's wine, both red and white.

However, viticulturists, especially the experts of the enterprising New York Experiment Station at Geneva and its branches, have for the past several years been at work developing varieties of native American grapes more suited to specific purposes. Some of these new varieties are extremely promising for both the table and the winery. In fact, many hybrids have been successfully developed and are now established and planted in the vineyards of grape-growing areas. Some are in the lists that follow; others of still uncertain promise are omitted. But the home winemaker, wherever he may live, should not overlook the wine possibilities of any grape available to him. If he is fortunate enough to have several choices, the notes that follow may help him to make a selection.

In that part of the United States which extends east of the Rocky Mountains most of the productive vineyards are planted with grapes that are pure American species or hybrids of native species with some blood of the European grape. Some of these native varieties also grow successfully in the Far Northwest, in Washington and Oregon. The European grape, *Vitis vinifera,* produces well in this country only west of the Rockies, though it is grown with a degree of success in limited areas of Texas, Arizona, and New Mexico. It is *the* grape of the great wine-producing regions of California.

The pleasure of making wine from one's own grapes is not to be denied. Several of the varieties listed may be grown in the garden or in one's own field. A few words will be said later in the chapter about what vines to plant.

SOME GRAPE VARIETIES
THE EASTERN UNITED STATES

America	Not widely grown, but has good qualities. Makes a good red wine.
Athens	A grape of the Concord type, but ripens earlier. About the same as Concord in the quality of its wine.
Bacchus	Not widely grown yet, but makes a red wine which is good and which improves with age. Also good for blending.
Beacon	Grown more extensively in the South than in the North, Beacon yields a wine with a pronounced "foxy" flavor.
Berckmans	The fruit of this grape has many of the superior qualities of the marvelous Delaware. Better than average for white wine.
Beta	A cold-climate grape of the North Plains states. Yields a strong, acid wine which needs to be aged before drinking. A valuable grape for those regions that have short summers.
Brocton	A sweet, nicely flavored grape which will make a very pleasant white wine.
Buffalo	A sweet grape which ripens early and from which a pleasant red wine may be had.
Catawba	One of the queens of native American grapes. Outstanding for dry white wines and champagnes. It also makes a good sweet wine. Has a heavy acid content, as a result of which its wines have good body.
Clevener	At the present time this grape is grown mostly in New York and New Jersey. It produces a heavy-bodied red wine

which needs aging before it can be drunk. A good blending wine.

Clinton
Its wine is rather harsh, but improves considerably with age. A good wine for blending.

Concord
This is the famous "blue grape" so widely grown east of the Rocky Mountains. Though not a good wine grape, it is still the grape most extensively used in the red wines of eastern America.

Cynthiana
A Southern variety from which a good red wine, dry or sweet, may be made.

Delaware
The undisputed and supreme sovereign of native American grapes. It yields the best white wine of the eastern United States. To be at its peak, this wine should have a little aging.

Diamond
This grape is found chiefly in the Finger Lakes region. It makes one of the superior native white wines.

Diana
A superior white wine grape found in the Finger Lakes region of New York, and only occasionally elsewhere. Its wine is excellent.

Dutchess
A fine grape for white wines, in fact, one of the three best, in the opinion of many, standing after the Delaware and the Catawba.

Eden
One of the few early grapes which make a good white wine. Eden ripens by the middle of September.

Elvira
A popular New York grape for the manufacture of white wine. Sugar and acid should be added. It is good for blending.

Etta
Makes a better-than-average white wine which is rather free from "foxiness."

Eumelan	One of the better American red wine grapes. It ripens fairly early, a little after the middle of September.
Flowers	A Southern grape especially known in the Carolinas. Good for red wine.
Fredonia	A standard dark grape in the East. Widely used in the manufacture of red wine.
Gold Coin	A Southern variety which is very good for making white wine.
Golden Muscat	An excellent grape for home use. Its juice has a muscat aroma and its wine is pleasant.
Grein Golden	Once grown rather widely in the Missouri area, this grape remains only in limited acreage. It yields a pretty fair white wine.
Headlight	Found mostly in the South, Headlight is a grape of good quality and produces a nice white wine.
Herbemont	Another Southern grape, found especially in the Gulf States. Makes an excellent red wine.
Hungarian	Like Beta this grape is well-suited to the northern limits of the central West. Yields a fair wine.
Iona	A delicious grape for eating, Iona is also one of the better white wine grapes.
Isabella	Once a favorite Eastern white wine grape. Will give both red and white wines. The latter are better.
Ives	A top-notch red wine grape which is still grown in certain regions. Its wine requires some aging, but is of better-than-average quality. Good for blending, especially with Norton.
James	A Southern Muscadine type of grape which yields a red wine.

Lenoir	Widely grown east of the Rockies, especially in the South, for it does not like the cold. It makes a good red wine.
Mish	This grape is common in North Carolina and produces a very potable red wine.
Missouri Riesling	A good grape for white wine. Though not grown so much now as formerly, there are still some plantings in Missouri and northwest Arkansas.
Montefiore	Most likely to be found in Arkansas and Missouri, it is suitable for red wines.
Muscadine	One of the best-known Southern grapes. Makes a strong red wine that is rather harsh to the palate.
Niagara	The commonly grown white (or green) sister of the Concord. Not of the best quality, but has been known to yield acceptable white wines.
Noah	Good for white wines. Like Grein Golden and Missouri Riesling, it is grown a little in Missouri and Arkansas.
Norton	The best of the Eastern red wine grapes. It thrives best below the Mason-Dixon Line. Its juice blends well with that of Ives.
Ontario	An early green grape, the Ontario is not superior fruit, but is commonly used in Canada, near Niagara Falls, for making white wine.
Scuppernong	With the Muscadine this is the best known of the Southern varieties. Makes a sweet white wine.
Seneca	Not very widely planted, but, where obtainable, it will give a nice white wine.

Triumph	A finicky grape which wants only certain soils and which ripens late, but which yields an extremely good red wine.
Worden	A pure-blooded native variety which was widely grown several years ago. Many home winemakers prefer it to Concord because it has more sugar. However, it is an inferior wine grape.

Most of the varieties listed above are now grown in limited areas. Commercial nurseries are turning more and more to easily grown table grapes. The home wine-maker will do well to stick to the more easily obtainable good wine grapes, such as Catawba, Delaware, Diamond, Diana, Dutchess, Elvira, Fredonia, Iona, and Isabella. Most of these are found in the Finger Lakes region of New York State, though the Ives is still grown on a small scale in northern Ohio. If the State Agricultural Experiment Station cannot advise where these grapes can be found, the amateur should address one of the several local Stations in the State of New York.

Good quality wine grape vines can be obtained from the Henry Leuthardt Nurseries, Inc., Montauk Highway, East Moriches, Long Island, New York 11940.

As a last resort, the Concord or Niagara must serve. The wine from them will give the beginner great pleasure and satisfaction.

THE FAR WESTERN UNITED STATES

Alicante Bouschet	A productive and extensively cultivated grape. It produces a good and drinkable juice, but yields an inferior wine.
Barbera	An Italian variety which yields a pretty fair red wine.
Black Hamburg	A hot-country grape which can be made to give a good dessert wine.

Burger	This is a leading raisin grape, but much of California's white wine is made from it.
Cabernet	A Bordeaux variety, this is one of the very best of the Western grapes, yielding a claret-type wine.
Carignane	A widely planted grape much used in making a potable, but not superior, red wine.
Charbono	Grown in California vineyards and often confused with the Barbera, it makes an ordinary wine.
Chasselas	Often caled the Chasselas Doré or Golden Chasselas, this grape produces a light-bodied wine. (The Napa Golden Chasselas is another grape, the Palomino.)
Chauché Gris	Miscalled the Grey Riesling in California. It makes an acceptable Chablis type of wine.
Chénin Blanc	Often miscalled a Pinot. The wine from this grape is one of the superior white wines of the West.
Colombard	Also called Sauvignon Vert in California, this should not be confused with the Sauvignon Blanc, which gives a much finer white wine.
Duriff	See Petit Sirah.
Folle Blanche	Used in France mostly for cognac, its wine is a fair-quality white.
Freisa	An Italian variety gives a rather nice red table wine.
Gamay	In some soils and climates this produces an excellent red wine; in others its product is poor.
Grenache	A Western hot-country grape, it has been made to yield a pretty fair *vin rosé*.
Grey Riesling	See Chauché Gris.

Grignolino	Another Italian variety which can produce a better-than-average red wine.
Hamburg	See Black Hamburg.
Mataro	A variety from southern France and northeastern Spain. Its juice yields a fair red wine.
Mission	Very extensively cultivated. The wine of this grape is red and of mediocre quality.
Muscat de Frontignan	A good grape for making a heavy red sweet wine.
Muscat of Alexandria	A rather widely grown hot-country grape. It is good for raisins but poor for wine.
Nebbiolo	A fine Italian variety for making excellent red wines. They are heavy bodied and need time to mature.
Palomino	Incorrectly called the Napa Golden Chasselas. It is a good hot-country grape for making sherry-type wines.
Petit Sirah	Though called by this name, many think it to be the Duriff. Makes a very good red wine.
Pinot Blanc	Though not so good as the other Pinots mentioned here, it yields a better-than-average white wine.
Pinot Chardonnay	This is the grape from which Chablis is made in France. In this country it makes an excellent white wine.
Pinot Noir	The best grape for making top-notch Burgundy-type red wines.
Refosco	Another grape imported from Italy that produces a good Burgundy-type wine.
Riesling	When the true Riesling can be found, it makes the best wines of the Rhine and Moselle types.
St. Macaire	A warm-country grape which produces a full-bodied red wine of good quality.

Sauvignon Blanc	A queen of the Western vineyards, this grape yields one of the finest white wines grown in the United States.
Sauvignon Vert	See Colombard.
Semillon	Another member of the royal family, this is one of the best grapes for making sweet white wines. In France it produces some of that country's noblest vintages and in California some of the U.S.A.'s finest whites.
Sylvaner	Cultivated extensively in California, this is a superior grape for white wines.
Traminer	An excellent grape for the making of white wines of the Rhine type.
Trebbiano	This is the grape from which white Chianti is made in Italy. In California it makes a good light-bodied white wine.
Ugni Blanc	Same as Trebbiano.
Valdepeñas	A Spanish variety from La Mancha, the land of Don Quixote, where it produces a wine that is sometimes amazingly good and at others, amazingly poor. In California it gives a pleasant red wine.
Zinfandel	Known as the "poor man's grape," the Zinfandel is widely planted and produces a sound red wine.

Vines for the Home Vineyard. The question of what grapes to plant in the home vineyard is a very complicated one because the success with which a given variety may be grown will depend upon so many different factors, such as length of summers, severity of winters, amount of rainfall, average temperature, whether grown upon high or low land, drainage of the vineyard, nature of the soil, and prevailing vine diseases.

Whole books have been writen on this subject and others will be written in the future.

It is safe to say that the home winegrower who lives east of the Rocky Mountains ought to avoid trying to cultivate most of the *Vitis vinifera* varieties. He will do well to limit his efforts to vines that have been developed for this area; for example, those offered by the Leuthardt Nurseries. (See under "Grape Vines" in Appendix III.)

For most of the eastern United States north of the Mason-Dixon Line the safest bet for the home vineyard is the Concord among dark grapes and the Niagara among the white. These are not the best for wine, but they are the grapes most likely to succeed with the least attention. Many of the superior wine grapes are fussy about the soil they grow in (Catawba, Dutchess); others, like Diana, are temperamental even when grown under the best of circumstances, while still others, such as Diamond, are good growers and prolific bearers but easily subject to disease. Perhaps among the top wine grapes Delaware offers the greatest likelihood of successful cultivation. It will grow wherever native grapes grow, in all kinds of soils and under the most varied conditions. Other varieties to consider are America, Brocton, Buffalo, Clinton, Elvira, Eumelan, Fredonia, Golden Muscat, Ontario, Seneca, and Triumph.

In the far north of the country, up near the Canadian border in northern Wisconsin, Minnesota, the Dakotas, and Montana, the winters are too severe for even the Concord to produce reliably. This, too, rules out any of the superior wine grapes. The best that can be done is to fall back upon grapes which originated in that region, in Minnesota, to be exact, and are among the very few grapes that can be successfully cultivated in any of the states just mentioned. These grapes are Beta and Hungarian, both of which have good sugar content and lots of acid, and make red wines which are very potable after the aging required by the acids. A third and poorer grape is Dakota, also of Minnesota origin.

The home grower in the South has a wider choice of good wine grapes which are less finicky than their Northern sisters. Consequently he is more likely to meet with success for less expended effort. Beacon produces a wine whose foxy flavor is disliked by some people. Flowers is another Southern grape whose wine is marked by foxiness. But better wines can be had from Cynthiana, Gold Coin, and Headlight, while really superior native vintages are yielded by some of the finest of American grapes, Herbemont, Lenoir, and Norton. Delaware will grow in much of the South, as will another good grape, Ives, though neither of these wants a lush, tropical environment.

To secure good plants for his vineyard there are certain steps the inexperienced winegrower may take. He may write his State Agricultural Station, which will be glad to give him precise information about the types of grapes, if any, suited to his locality. He may also consult the nursery or seed company that supplies the area in which he lives, although most companies are likely to deal especially in table grapes.

Grape vines are easily started by rooting cuttings, and the amateur who lives where good grapes are grown can obtain a batch of cuttings either from his neighbor or from a vineyard when the vines are pruned in late winter or early spring.

The home viticulturist will save himself much time by buying young plants. Since the average vine requires five years to come into full production, it is advisable to purchase two-year-old vines. The Henry Leuthardt Nurseries, Inc. (see Appendix III under "Grape Vines") can supply young vines of the following superior Eastern varieties: Fredonia, Delaware, Catawba, Golden Muscat. It also sells the widely grown Concord variety as well as a grape with which the author has no experience, the Portland, an early white grape.

In the last several years much progress has been made in the production and establishment of hybrids, that is, of crosses of the California grape *Vitis vinifera* with the native Eastern grape. Some of these now flourish and produce an excellent fruit for the table and for wine. Leuthardt Nurseries offers the following hybrids for the table: Seibel 9110, Seibel 13047, Seyve Villard 12375, Steuben; and these hybrids for winemaking: Seibel 7053 (red wine), Seyve Villard 5276 (white wine). Seibel 5279 is good both for the table and for wine.

Write the company for their brochure and, when vines are ordered, ask for cultivation and pruning instructions; most of the above hybrids will do well with spur pruning and should even be grown in rich soils and fertilized with manure, neither of which is to be thought of with most Eastern varieties.

4

making the wine

THE FIRST STEP in making grape wine may turn out to
be the most difficult. For some it will be no problem,
for grapegrowing areas spread over broad stretches of
the United States. The Eastern, or native, grapes especially the Concord and its lighter sister, the Niagara,
are grown in quantity from New England through New
York, Pennsylvania, Ohio, Indiana, Michigan, Illinois,
Wisconsin, and Iowa to Oregon and Washington. They
flourish in Missouri, northwest Arkansas, and parts of
Texas. They do not do well in the lush, rich soils of the
Central South or in the Southeast, but there the
muscadine and the scuppernong thrive, and in parts of
the Carolinas there are still some good plantings of the
Catawba.

The real problem, however, is the procurement of
quality grapes. Residents of New York who live in the
Finger Lakes district are surrounded by vineyards producing the best of the native varieties. In other parts of
the state the winemaker would do well to address a
letter of inquiry to the State Experiment Station at
Geneva. In Ohio, those who dwell along the shores of
Lake Erie, from Toledo to Ashtabula, may be able to

persuade grape growers to sell them some of their quality grapes before the wineries gather them in. If they live elsewhere, inquiry should be made of the state's Department of Agriculture. Also, a note sent to the Sandusky, Ohio, Chamber of Commerce, which supports periodic grape and wine festivals, should bring helpful information. Sandusky is one of the centers of the Ohio wine industry.

Every large city has a host of amateur winemakers who create a demand for California grapes. Each fall the wholesale produce markets in or near the larger cities bring in grapes from California to meet this demand. Anyone desiring to join the ranks of those who use the Western grapes should make inquiry regarding the types imported and place his order early in order to assure himself a supply. It ought to be remembered, however, that wine grapes from the West Coast are likely to be more expensive than even the better Eastern varieties.

There is a last recourse. Some houses that cater to the home winemaker offer juice concentrates made from the *Vitis vinifera,* the European (or California) grapes (see Appendix III under "Concentrates"). These produce red and white wine and should ferment out to 12 percent of alcohol without the addition of sugar.

Making Red Wine from Superior Grapes. Let it be assumed that the home winemaker has decided to make red wine from grapes and that he is fortunate enough to live in a part of the country where good grapes are available to him.

The grapes must be ripe. If it is possible to visit the vineyard, an eye can be kept on the progress of the fruit, which should be picked when the stems are losing their greenness and beginning to look dry. At this time the sugar content is at its greatest and the tannic, tartaric, and other acids are in better balance than at any other moment. In harvesting the grapes, pick stems and all, taking care not to shell or strip the berries from the stems. It is usually a good practice to let the picked fruit stand for a day or so; this produces a further concentration of sugar.

In preparing the grapes for the press, do not wash them unless they have lain in wet earth and are dirty. The bloom of the grape, that fine whitish dust on the skins, is not a chemical spray, but yeast, which must go into the vat to help fermentation. But pick out and discard all culls, worm-eaten, shriveled, decayed, or green fruit.

If a yeast starter is to be used, it should be in the making by this time and ready to be dumped into the vat the moment the grapes are crushed. A yeast starter is not necessary, for the grapes are covered with yeast, as has just been indicated; but there are good reasons for considering the use of one. The whole question of the yeast starter and its making is discussed and explained in this chapter in the section entitled *The Yeast Starter*.

The next step is the crushing of the grapes. Unless a large quantity of wine is being made, this is no great problem even though one does not have a crusher at hand. The easiest way to work without a crusher is to mash small quantities at a time in a separate receptacle and transfer them to the larger fermenting vat or crock. The crushing may be done with the hands or with a potato masher. After a year or two, and especially if one is short of time, the crushing of considerable quantities of grapes with the hands or with a potato masher becomes a tiresome chore, and the winemaker will find it worthwhile to invest in a fruit crusher.

If he is lucky enough to have, or be able to find, a crusher of the wooden hopper type mentioned in Chapter 2, all his crushing problems are over. He simply sets the crusher astride the vat and feeds grapes into the hopper just as fast as the turning of the rollers will permit. The broken grapes fall into the vat to begin their fermentation almost at once.

A bit more laborious, but much faster than by hand, is the first of the commercial fruit crushers made of metal, also described in Chapter 2. If a board is fastened across one edge of the vat, the crusher can be clamped onto it and the juice allowed to run directly into the vat. Otherwise, the crusher is clamped to a table and the juice received in a small receptacle first and then transferred to the vat. In either case, the extension of the crusher that receives the skins and the seeds must be emptied frequently. Its contents go into the vat, because, in the making of red wine, the juice is fermented on the skins and the seeds and from them derives some of the properties (tartaric and tannic acid) which help to give it body and character as it matures.

It is always a good idea to make certain that several handfuls of stems are in the vat, to assure that the fermenting juice will pick up a good supply of tannin.

The vat containing the crushed grapes ought now to be kept in a fairly warm place, with the temperature preferably between 60 and 70 degrees Fahrenheit. Cover with a cloth or paper, and allow to stand for from five to ten days. The contents should be stirred twice a day during this time, an important procedure which brings the yeasts at the top into contact with the liquid at the bottom of the cask and which aerates the whole, thus recharging, so to speak, the yeasts and making the fermentation complete.

During this period occurs the first, or primary, fermentation, and it is at this stage that the new wine obtains from the skins its color and much of its quality, not to mention the fact that most of the wine's alcoholic strength is determined by the activity of the yeasts at this time.

When the fermentation has quieted down, which will almost always be by the end of ten days, the juice is ready to be transferred to the cask. At this time it will be noticed that the skins have risen to the top of the vat where they form a thick crust. This crust should be skimmed off and placed in a separate receptacle. The juice remaining in the vat is drawn off and strained, in order to remove the seeds and other matter which may have settled to the bottom. To this strained liquid add the juice obtained from the crust of skins by running them through the wine press or by squeezing them in a cheesecloth or cotton flannel bag with the hands.

The liquid which has been obtained should now be turned into a clean cask or barrel, filling to the top of the bunghole. The surplus wine should be put in a jug, or jugs, to be used later in refilling the cask. (It is usually important to have a surplus. See under *Racking* in this chapter.) Place the filled cask where the thermometer hovers between 60 and 70 degrees Fahrenheit. If it is not possible to find a place where the temperature is constant, the amateur need not worry, for a fluctuation of twenty degrees, from 60 to 80, is not likely to do the wine any harm, though a constant temperature of from 65 to 70 degrees is best because it permits rapid fermentation, and rapid fermentation is good for the wine. It should be kept in mind, nevertheless, that although the wine will ferment at higher and lower temperatures, it does not ferment well below 49 degrees, and wine allowed to remain for any length of time at a temperature much above 80 degrees may spoil, because certain harmful organisms thrive best at high temperatures. If a room tends to be chilly, the container may be raised to a table to gain a few degrees; if it is too warm, a few degrees may be lost by lowering the container from a high support to the floor.

The wine, having been aerated when turned into the cask, may work again for a while, "boiling" through the bunghole, which must be left open for two or three days, to permit the discharge of impurities and insoluble matter which are cast off in this way. Each day the cask must be refilled to the top of the bunghole from any wine that may have been left over, as mentioned above, or if there was none, with warm water, provided of course, that not too much is added—a total of three or four pints will not noticeably affect ten gallons of wine, though it is not likely that even this much will be needed.

After the "boiling over" (if it occurs) has subsided, which will be recognized by the absence of the thick discharge that characterized it earlier, the cask should be water-sealed. This is not absolutely necessary, but it is so easy to do, and will save so much trouble and prevent so many headaches, that it can hardly be dispensed with. To seal properly, draw off enough wine to lower the surface within the cask one and a half or two inches below the bottom of the bunghole, affix the water-seal, or water-bung, and then cover all cracks and junctions with melted wax or paraffin. The wine will now be assured of protection from spoilage due to over-contact with the air, its most deadly enemy at a certain period of its life.

If a carboy is being used instead of a cask, there is no difference in procedure. When the wine is transferred to it from the fermenting vat, the carboy should be filled to the very mouth. As the insolubles are thrown off by the working wine, it must be refilled to the top daily until the most active stage of fermentation has subsided or until no more waste matter rises. Now pour off, or draw off with a siphon, enough of the wine to bring the surface an inch or two below the bottom of the neck, and water-seal, covering all junctions with wax or paraffin.

Making Red Wine from the Concord Grape. While the choicest wine grapes of the United States are still restricted to limited areas and limited acreage, the "old blue grape," that is, the Concord, is available to almost everyone not living in the northernmost sweeps of the

Plains States or the Southern and Southeastern regions mentioned in the opening section of this chapter. It is a safe assumption that the average amateur winemaker who turns to grapes for wine will have at his disposal only the Concord or one of its close cousins. But let him not scorn this grape, for much of the red wine from numerous Eastern wineries, if not the bulk of it, is made from the Concord or has Concord juice in it. Therefore, it is necessary to say something about making wine from the Concord. The procedure is exactly the same as that described in the foregoing section for making wine from superior grapes except in one important detail: Concord juice is deficient in sugar and must therefore be treated so that in fermenting it may be made to yield the right amount of alcohol, 11 percent.

If the juice of the Concord grape is tested with the saccharometer (sugar-meter), it will be found to contain from 12 to 17 percent of sugar. Hardly ever will it run as high as 18 percent, and then only under the most favorable conditions. As this amount of sugar is too low to guarantee the health and lasting qualities of the wine, it is necessary to strengthen the juice with additional sugar. If no saccharometer is at hand, the amount of sugar will have to be estimated. A good estimate for the average Concord juice is an addition of 6.4 ounces per gallon, since that is the amount necessary for a juice containing 17 percent of sugar (see Table I). The sugar is carefully measured out and thoroughly dissolved in the juice just as it is being transferred from the fermenting vat to the cask for its secondary fermentation. "Thoroughly dissolved" means that when the sugar is added to the juice, the whole must be stirred for about fifteen minutes. After the "boiling over" has subsided and the heavy discharge has given way to the light, foamy bubbles of escaping carbonic acid gas, water-seal as described above.

One more pause is necessary before proceeding to the next step in the winemaking process. There is another method of dealing with the juice of the Concord and its close relatives, a method that not only will not hurt the finished product, but will usually improve it. Also, it will double the quantity of wine. And that is the dilution of Concord juice with equal parts of water. (The value of dilution is discussed later in this chapter.)

Concord juice is heavy with tartaric and tannic acids, and when allowed to spend the period of its primary fermentation on the skins, it picks up a larger supply of these acids than it really needs. Consequently, the addition of equal parts of water to the juice will produce a double amount of wine, one that is still sufficiently high in acid content, but which, unless treated, is going to be short in alcoholic strength. It is necessary then to add more sugar than would otherwise be the case, for the finished product must not have less than 11 percent of alcohol. Therefore, at the time the juice is turned into the cask for its secondary fermentation, it should be mixed with an equal amount of water, and sugar should be added in the proportion of 17.3 ounces per gallon of mixture. The way to add sugar is first to dissolve it in a portion of the liquid itself—the juice, the water, or the mixture—and then add it to the whole. It is of the utmost importance that the sugar be thoroughly dissolved, for sugar that settles thickly to the bottom of a cask or carboy is likely to remain unused, thereby leaving the wine with less alcoholic strength than it should have to remain healthy. It is important, therefore, to stir the mixture for about fifteen minutes before putting it in the cask, and then to stir for five or ten minutes more after it has been put in the cask, or in the carboy, if this is used.

The figure of 17.3 ounces is only an estimate based on an average Concord juice diluted with equal parts of water. But the sugar content of the juice of any grape may vary, not only from season to season and from region to region, but from field to field as well.

Therefore it is wise to invest in a saccharometer so that exact tests of the amount of sugar in a must (unfermented grape juice) may be made. (The manner of using the saccharometer is described in detail later in this chapter.) It is important to keep in mind here that the time to test for the sugar content of any juice is *just after the grapes have been pressed and before any fermentation has set in.* After the sugar content of a juice has been read, calculate from Table I the amount of additional sugar to be added to each gallon and record the figure for use when the time comes. The best time to add the sugar is not at the time it goes into the vat for its primary fermentation, but just before it is turned into the cask (or carboy) for the secondary fermentation.

If the grape juice is to be diluted, it is important to read the sugar content, not of the juice, *but of a mixture of equal parts of juice and water,* the juice being taken just after pressing. Calculate from Table I the amount of sugar to be added to the mixture, and record this figure for use when the wine is put in the cask for its secondary fermentation. All care must be taken to make sure that the sugar is thoroughly dissolved.

Once again, the cask, or carboy, should be filled to the top and kept filled until the "boiling over" has ceased, at which time the surface of the wine must be lowered a couple of inches before the water-seal is put in place to protect the contents from the air.

Value of the Water-Seal. The importance of protecting maturing wine from the air can hardly be exaggerated. Air is, at certain stages of the winemaking process, a great asset, but at others it can be a multiple curse. The acetic acid or vinegar germ must be avoided at all costs if the wine is to be any good, and since exposure to the air is the surest way to invite its entry into wine, especially if the alcoholic content is not very high, water-sealing saves time and trouble and gives ease of mind on this score. It is a process which consists of nothing more than allowing the carbonic acid gas which is formed and discharged during fermentation to pass off through water, while at the same time the air is forbidden contact with the wine. (See Chapter 2 for various types of water-seals.)

Waiting It Out. Once the wine is in a container and sealed against the air, there is little to do but wait until it is perfectly fine (clear). It is at this time that patience is required and perhaps a little faith, for the looks and taste of the wine as it passes through this secondary fermentation are anything but promising to the neophyte. He can little know how beauiful and palatable the murky, bubbling liquid is going to be after the passing of a little time. This secondary fermentation may last from two weeks to two months, depending on the type of wine, the amount in the container, the quantity of sugar in the must, the temperature of the room, and other factors.

The subsiding of active fermentation can be observed as the bubbles of carbonic acid gas pass through the water-seal with diminishing frequency, until at last they stop completely. Now the wine is through fermenting, but it is not yet ready to be bottled. It must fine first, or clear up; all the microscopic particles which make it cloudy must settle to the bottom. It should not be put in bottles until perfectly transparent, until it has that brilliant, sparkling clearness that tells the eye that all is well.

The best way to achieve this, if the wine has been properly made and is of good alcoholic content, is by natural fining, that is, by allowing the wine to clear itself. The winemaker can help this process by racking (transferring the wine to a fresh container) at proper intervals. When it has been determined that the last bubble of gas has come through the water-seal, let the wine stand for ten days or two weeks longer. Then remove the water-seal and fill to the bunghole with the surplus wine mentioned earlier, or, if the necessary quantity is small, with warm water. Now drive in the bung and, if the container is not large, let the wine stand four to five weeks longer, or until late November or early December if it is a large amount of 35 or 50 gallons. Now is the time for the first racking. (See later in this chapter for discussion of racking in detail.)

Only undue impatience can lead to bottling at this time. As experience is acquired, the home winemaker is going to set himself higher standards and is going to strive for better wine. This will call for leaving the wine in the cask and for a second racking during the first week in March (by the middle of February in the South).

Very often wine undergoes a spring fermentation, especially if there is any sugar in the wine which was not used up in the earlier fermentation. When this occurs, the wine is racked for the third time in June.

A fourth and final racking may be given the wine in October. By this time most dry wines made from American grapes will have become perfectly fine and need not remain in the cask any longer. It is now that the wine is ready for the bottle.

Using the Saccharometer. The whole question of adding sugar is hotly debated by connoisseurs and purists on the one hand and the defenders of the practice on the other. It is today an established practice in much of the winemaking world. In spite of all that may be said either way, the fact remains that a grape juice of low sugar content, when fermented out, will give a wine that is dry, often sour, and with too little alcohol to permit it to keep long enough to age properly. Wine of this sort is made extensively in homes and on farms, and though it has the headiness of new wine, it often turns to vinegar in the second year or soon after. The juices in our country of low sugar content normally ferment into a wine of not more than 7 or 8 percent alcohol, which is insufficient to preserve it long enough to mature. Also, a low alcoholic content leaves the wine liable to many diseases, for a weak wine, like a feeble constitution in human beings, is easily subject to illness. These diseases can often be treated, but a "cured" wine can seldom, if ever, be as good as a healthy one. Thus it becomes imperative, before the wine is set aside for its secondary fermentation, to take steps to assure its later health and well-being. This is best achieved by the addition of sugar to a must that is short in this respect. A proper amount added to a juice that needs it will produce a wine strong enough to stand on its own feet, so to speak, and grow old with dignity, fearing no sickness and improving with age.

The wine, then, should have an alcoholic content of not less than 11 percent, and with weak juices this percentage can be got only by the addition of alcohol or sugar. The use of alcohol for this purpose is not legal; therefore it is necessary to add sugar, preferably cane sugar, though beet sugar will do quite well—the difference between them resides in their complicated molecular arrangement.

If a saccharometer is being used, the hazard of not having enough sugar in the must is eliminated. To test for sugar with this instrument, fill the hydrometer jar to within an inch or two of the top with fresh must which has previously been strained through several thicknesses of cheesecloth. Take the temperature of the must with a floating thermometer. Sixty degrees Fahrenheit is the point at which its specific gravity can be taken with greatest precision. But since absolute exactness is not necessary, a fluctuation of temperature between 55 and 65 degrees Fahrenheit may be allowed. If it is cooler than the minimum given here, it may be easily warmed up; if its temperature is higher than the allowable maximum, it can be cooled by placing it in the refrigerator.

Hold the jar level, or better yet, place it on a level table or shelf and insert the saccharometer. Let this ride until it has become perfectly still, then take the reading at the surface of the must and not at the top of the meniscus, which is that part of the liquid that climbs slightly up the side of the instrument. (See Figure 14.) Once the reading is taken, it should be recorded at once, for with the passing of just a few hours, the grape juice changes its composition and the sugar reading will vary.

Once the sugar content of a juice has been determined, the maker of wine will know at once how much sugar, if any, must be added to bring his product up to 22 percent. Or, as occasionally happens, the sugar

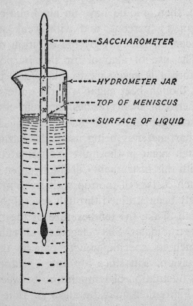

FIGURE 14. SACCHAROMETER AND HYDROMETER JAR

content may in some juices be too high to ferment out to dryness (the quality of being not sweet), in which case it may be desirable to correct the must before fermentation by the adition of water in order to bring the sugar percentage down to 22.

Correcting the Must. No juice with less than 18 percent of sugar should ever be put to ferment alone, for its wine will be thin and sour and will not keep. If the sugar runs higher than 26 percent, the wine is likely to remain sweet and its fermentation will be difficult to carry through to completion. It becomes important then to see that the sugar content is no lower or higher than certain percentages—22 percent is the minimum and 24 percent the preferred maximum. It should be remarked here that it will be easier for the amateur to ferment through to dryness a must with 22 percent of sugar than one containing 24 percent, and for this reason he will do well to consider a percentage of 22 as a desideratum. Consequently, if the sugar content is lower, sugar must be used to raise it; if it is higher, reduction must be made through the addition of water.

The supplying of sugar or water to correct a must can be done experimentally by working with a small quantity (a quart, say) and keeping a close record of the amount of either which is added, until the norm of 22 percent is reached; but the use of the following tables makes the matter much simpler. In Table I the first column represents the percentage of sugar in the must by saccharometer reading, and the second tells in ounces how much sugar is to be added to one gallon of must to bring the sugar content up to 22 percent, a quantity which must be multiplied by the number of gallons which it is desired to correct.

Table II tells how much water in ounces must be added to each gallon of a heavily sugared must or liquid in order to reduce it to a 22 percent content.

TABLE I

(Percentages 0 through 4 are omitted from this table because they have no applicable function.)

Percent of sugar in must %	Sugar to be added to each gallon Ounces
5	21.7
6	20.4
7	19.2
8	17.9
9	16.6
10	15.3
11	14.0
12	12.8
13	11.5
14	10.2
15	8.9
16	7.6
17	6.4
18	5.1
19	3.8
20	2.5
21	1.2

With 22% of sugar add no water; 23–24% will ferment to dryness, but requires more time than 22%; 25–26% will be difficult for the beginner to ferment out; 27%+ will remain a sweet wine of varying degrees of sweetness.

It is important to remember that in raising the sugar content of a must, the addition of sugar is made to the juice which has been tested. If a new quantity of juice has been mixed with that from which the saccharometer sample was taken, the calculation will be thrown off. This new mixture must be tested again. Also, after the total amount of sugar necessary is

TABLE II

Percent of sugar in must %	Water to be added to each gallon Ounces
35	75.5
34	69.7
33	63.9
32	58.1
31	52.2
30	46.4
29	40.6
28	34.8
27	29.0
26	23.2
25	17.4
24	11.6
23	5.8

added and dissolved, a final reading should be taken, in order to correct any error in previous calculations.

Sugar when fermented gives one-half its amount of alcohol by volume. Thus, when completely, fermented, a must having 24 percent of sugar will give a wine with 12 percent of alcohol, and one of 22 percent sugar will yield a wine with an alcoholic strength of 11 percent. It is not out of place to call attention once more to the fact that a sugar content higher than 24 percent is likely to prevent regular and complete fermentation within a reasonable time, and if there is too much sugar in the juice, it will be impossible to ferment it out and the wine will remain sweet, It is impossible for yeasts to continue their function of changing sugar into alcohol when the percentage of the latter has reached 14 or 15. Hence any sugar in excess of 28 percent is going to remain in the finished product, resulting in a sweet wine. But it requires the very best of conditions, and years of time to convert 28 degrees of sugar into 14 of alcohol. And although the production of wine with an alcoholic content of 15 percent is known to be possible under very particular circumstances, the home wine-maker will be wise to eschew the attempt to achieve a percentage of alcohol greater than 11 percent. Let the amateur console himself, if consolation is needed, with the knowledge that a wine with 15 percent alcohol is too strong for the pleasantest use with food.

Once the added sugar has been thoroughly dissolved, the wine is treated exactly as has already been described. When the violent working and the discharge of impurities from the liquid have ceased, the surface of the wine is lowered and the water-seal is put in place.

The Place of Dilution in Winemaking. If the wine-maker has the juice of a top-notch grape to work with, there must be no question of dilution with water. On the other hand, the addition of water to certain juices can be justified on two accounts. The first is that it is an economy measure—it makes more wine; the second is that it improves the wine made from these juices. It is true that the juice of any grape may be diluted with water and made into wine, but there are reasons why dilution is more to be preferred with the juice of some grapes than with that of others. For example, among the finer American grapes, Berckmans, Delaware, Diana, Diamond, Dutchess, Eumelan, Iona, Ives, Lenoir, Norton, and Triumph give a juice which is not improved in any way by the addition of water. On the other hand wine made from Concord, Athens, Isabella, Niagara, and Worden can be materially improved if diluted with water in the making. Two superior grapes can also take an addition of water: Diamond when it is grown on limy soils, which tend to make its juice very "foxy" (a term applied to the characteristic odor and flavor of many Eastern grapes); and Catawba, whose high acid content can stand dilution. This not to say, however, that either Catawba or Diamond wine is improved by diluting with water, as is true for some other grapes. Futhermore, the juice of the *vinifera* varieties of the Far West should never be diluted at all.

Sugar is not the only ingredient of grape juice, which contains much water, certain free acids (tartaric, tannic, etc.), bitartrate of potash, mineral salts, essential oils, and certain albuminous, mucilaginous, and starchy substances. Under the protection of a sufficiently high percentage of alcohol, all these contribute to the character of the wine as it ages, giving it flavor, body, and bouquet, and making it smooth and mellow with the passage of time. Dilution of those juices which have these ingredients, especially the free acids, in low proportion can only produce a wine inferior to that which might otherwise be obtained. And since some of the most extensively planted native varieties are heavily endowed with free acids, dilution does have its place, especially in the work of the home winemaker.

Since the Concord is the grape most likely to be encountered by the average beginner, it is not out of place to list some of its faults. Among its most objectionable traits are two, low sugar content and "foxiness" of flavor, that is, a certain wild pungency of taste which is easily recognizable in wine made from its juice. The matter of sugar deficiency can be correced by the addition of sugar. The "foxy" flavor, which so many wine drinkers find objectionable, cannot be got rid of altogether, but it is possible to remedy it to no small degree. And it is here that dilution plays its role. The addition to the juice of equal parts of water at the time sugar is added will cut this flavor appreciably, in fact, to such a degree that it may become, with experience in drinking, a rather attractive quality of the wine, provided, of course, that one does not try to make it compete, on the palate, with the great wines of the world.

The home winemaker need not turn up his nose at the Concord. It is recommended here because it is the grape most readily available. Of course, if it is possible to get better grapes, by all means get them. In the meantime it should be kept in mind that Concord properly handled can be made to yield a good, healthy, and palatable wine.

Niagara, among the white varieties, like the Concord can stand dilution. Here, too, a dilution with equal parts of water accompanied by a raising of the sugar content of the mixture can help this grape to produce a remarkably pleasant wine.

Among other grapes which can stand dilution, the most debatable one is the Catawba, a grape of the highest quality which produces a superior white wine. The only excuse for diluting the juice of this grape is that more wine can be had by so doing. The addition of water will not improve the quality of the wine as is the case with the Concord grape, but Catawba does have a heavy free acid content, a fact which will assure that diluted juice will make a good wine. Many winemakers dilute Catawba juice up to 100 percent, that is, they use equal parts of juice and water. A considerably better wine can be had, however, by using only half as much water as juice. Whether diluted or not, Catawba wine requires from two to three years of age before it is at its best for drinking.

Making White Wine. The manufacture of white wine has been held until this point because the process involved has certain complications which must not be confused with the making of red wines, and the differences in the methods of manufacture must be carefully observed.

If it is at all possible, obtain a grape which is regularly used in the manufacture of white wine. Among the best are the following, which repeat some of the names already given: Berckmans, Brocton, Catawba, Delaware, Diana, Diamond, Dutchess, Eden, Elvira, Etta, Golden Muscat, Iona, Ontario, and Seneca. With the exception of Delaware and Catawba, most of these grapes cannot be found in quantity outside of New York State. There are very limited plantings in northern Ohio. Two good Southern grapes for white wine are Gold Coin and Headlight, both of which yield a better-than-average product. In parts of Missouri and north-west Arkansas there are three good white wine grapes, though they are planted in limited acreage: Grein Golden, Missouri Riesling, and Noah.

Elsewhere the home winemaker should look for Catawba, Delaware, and Niagara. If none of these is to be found let him take any white grape he can get.

However, it is worthwhile to make an effort to obtain some of the finer white grapes mentioned, for the wines made from these native varieties are very fine wines indeed and will fully repay any extra effort or cost. If the amateur lives where grapes are grown, a spring or summer trip through the countryside accompanied by inquiries may discover for him some grapes that will make his autumn work very rewarding.

In the making of white wine, the important first step is to press the juice off the grapes, for regardless of the type of grape used, *the juice must not be fermented on the skins*. If the winemaker is fortunate enough to live near a commercial press, he can have his grapes pressed there; if not, he must provide himself with a smaller press.

The great hydraulic presses can extract all the juice from a large quantity of grapes in a very few minutes, and this is desirable, for it is important that the juice be removed from the skins as quickly as possible. If the work is done at home, it can be done efficiently but more time and effort are required.

To press the juice from grapes with a small hoop or basket press, put about one-half peck of grapes in a strong cloth bag which has previously been washed well and thoroughly rinsed. If a larger press, say a cider press, is used, double this quantity of grapes may be pressed at one time, that is, a peck. (A good ratchet press is more effective than either of the above.) Place the bag containing the grapes in the crate of the press, spreading the fruit out as evenly as possible within the bag, and fold the surplus cloth so that it will not form lumps that can interfere with the pressing. Now press slowly and with as much force as the crate will stand until the juice ceases to run. Release the pressure, take out the bag, stir up the mashed grapes with the hand, and return the bag to the crate, folding the cloth as before. Press again. Repeat this process at least a third time, and if the marc (the mashed grapes) still appears to contain some juice, do it again. Usually several pressings are required to extract all the juice. When all the grapes have been taken care of in this manner, strain some of the juice through several thicknesses of cheesecloth or through cotton flannel and test with the saccharometer. If the juice needs additional sugar, now is the time to add it (see Table I).

Turn all the extracted juice, or the juice treated with sugar, into a clean cask, filling to the bunghole. (If a carboy is used, fill to the mouth of the neck.) Allow the wine to work until all impurities and insolubles have been discharged from the container. Do not forget to fill the cask or carboy daily until the violent working of the wine has diminished to the point where there is no longer any discharge but white bubbles of carbonic acid gas. Now lower the surface of the wine an inch and one-half or two inches below the bunghole and affix the water-seal, covering all junctions with melted wax or paraffin. If the wine is in a carboy, lower it an inch or so below the bottom of the neck and seal the junctures.

Now comes a step which is very important in the making of white wines. Not having been fermented on the skins and seeds, the juice is lacking in tannin, a very important substance for the preservation and the proper aging of wine. It is also an aid in the fining or clearing of the wine. This must be added in proper proportions: one gram of tannin (dry tannic acid) for each five gallons of wine. Dissolve it first in a quart of wine and pour into the cask, stirring thoroughly, that is, a good ten minutes. Dry tannic acid can be purchased in any drugstore.

The wine may now be sealed and allowed to ferment itself out. Since white wine usually requires more time in which to clear than does red wine, there must be no haste about getting it into bottles. Three to twelve months may be required before it is ready to be put away for keeps. A full year with its repeated rackings will assure a maturer wine. Only undue impatience in the first year of experience can be an excuse for putting the wine into bottles by the end of November. After this first year, the novelty, though not the enthusiasm, will have worn off somewhat, and the winemaker will take time to rack his wine. The racking process has been explained under the making of red wines (see also pages 67–71) but it will not hurt to repeat here that the first racking of white wine should take place about the middle or toward the end of November. The second racking should come before the middle of February in the South and during the first week in March in the North. The time for the next racking, the third, is in June, though it is permissible to omit this racking. Anyway, the final racking should be given the wine in October, after which it is ready for the bottle.

The method just described will fit the manufacture of white wine from all white wine grapes, except that not all juices require the addition of sugar. This is always ascertainable by using the saccharometer.

If, however, the maker of white wine wishes to get more for his money, he may vary the procedure given and add equal parts of water before turning the wine into the cask. This should not be tried with the juice of any of the very choice grapes mentioned above, for much more will be lost in quality than can be gained in quantity. But if access is had only to grapes of a lesser quality, such as Niagara, dilution may be practiced. Also, it may be employed, if desired, with the juice of the Catawba. Before diluting any white grape juice, read the section of this chapter entitled *The Place of Dilution in Winemaking*.

If the Niagara is used, mix equal parts of juice and water and dissolve in this mixture 18 ounces of sugar to each gallon. This is an estimate for those who do not use a saccharometer. But if this instrument is employed to test the sugar content of the mixture of juice and water, the exact requirements can be found by consulting Tables I and II. Finally, tannin must be added, as previously described, except that here the proper proportion is one and one-half grams for each five gallons of wine. After water-sealing, let it ferment and stand until fine. This wine may be bottled after the June racking.

White Wine from Dark Grapes. If the home winemaker cannot find suitable grapes for making white wine, he can use dark grapes. It is not only possible to make a light-colored wine from red wine grapes, but this is a common practice in many wine areas. There are two principal steps in this process which have not been described before. The first is the haste required to get the juice away from the dark skins, to press them as quickly as possible, to avoid the dark pigment from the skins finding its way into the juice. Here is where a large press has a decided advantage, though fast work with a small press will also give good results. The pressing is carried out exactly as previously described, except that the third and fourth pressings had best be avoided because of the danger of dark pigment getting into the wine. (Juice from these pressings, however, can be turned into any batch of red wine which is being made or about to be made.)

After the juice has been extracted, it is treated in

exactly the same way as the juice from white grapes, as is explained in the section on the manufacture of white wine from light grapes.

The next step depends upon whether any coloring matter has found its way into the juice intended for white wine. This is treated in the next section.

Decoloring Wine. It sometimes happens that in spite of all precautions some of the dark pigment from the skins does get into the juice. When this occurs, it is usually desirable to decolor the wine before it is bottled. It is the looks of the wine, not its taste, that will be affected by decoloring, for this is not necessary to the flavor. If, however, a white wine is what is wanted, decoloring is necessary to the wine's appearance.

Decoloring should not be attempted until after the secondary fermentation has completely subsided. If at that time the wine still shows traces of color, the following method of removing it may be safely employed. At the time of the second racking in March add some purified animal charcoal to the wine in the proportion of five grams to every five gallons. The charcoal is first stirred into a little wine drawn from the cask and then is thoroughly mixed with the whole. Animal charcoal is made from bone and has the property of absorbing coloring matter. It can be bought in powdered form at the drugstore. Other charcoal may not be substituted for it.

Purified animal charcoal may also be used to great advantage in reducing the "foxiness" of flavor of any wine, red or white. If this "foxiness" is regarded with disfavor by the winemaker, he may help his wine to fit his taste by using the same dosage as required for decoloring, five grams per five gallons of wine.

Racking. During his early attempts at winemaking the beginner will be in something of a hurry to put his wine into bottles, where he can get at it properly. With this in mind, it was earlier hinted that the wine could be bottled when it had cleared up after the secondary fermentation. But this is not recommended. All wine should be racked. Racking is the process of transferring wine from one container to another in such a way as to separate it from the dregs or lees which it has thrown down.

There are pros and cons as to the value of racking. Some insist that the wine should spend its life on its lees, that the latter impart beneficial qualities to the wine and give it character. Others argue with equal vehemence that in the settled dregs there are bad yeasts, as well as good, and that the evil these may do can be avoided only by separating the wine from them. Without going into the details of the argument, it is sufficient to say that so far as this book is concerned, the pros have by far the best of it, and for that reason it urges all readers to rack their wines, that is, to draw the wine off its lees and put it in clean containers. This should be done at least twice, and preferably three, or even four times.

If the beginner can be patient and wait a few months, he will find that racking will help him in several ways. It will aid him in getting rid of dregs and yeasts which are likely to disturb his new wine with the approach of warm weather; racked wine, having lost its sediment, may be handled without fear of its becoming cloudy while it is being bottled; repeated transferring of wine to clean containers is one of the best ways of clarifying wine without resort to artificial means; and, finally, racking is in itself a sort of purifying process in which the wine rids itself of impurities that might possibly cause "sickness" at a later date. In addition to all these benefits, it can further be stated here that wine is improved by several rackings.

The racking of wine is an exceedingly simple proce-dure and consists merely of drawing the wine out of one container and putting it in another. One condition is that the new container be perfectly clean. Another is that is should be filled as nearly full as possible. If the wine is to remain in the cask for a year or more before it is bottled, it is essential that the cask be filled to the bung, and be kept filled, replacing at regular intervals that which has been lost by shrinkage. But if bottling is planned for a month or two after manufacture or within a short time after the first racking, say by January or February at the latest, it is not so necessary to avoid a small air space. Once again the advantage of retaining a surplus can be seen.

This brings up the problem of how to have a surplus of wine on hand. Provision for this must be made early. If a 50-gallon cask is being used, the winemaker should plan to start with a surplus of juice, say with 60 gallons. While the main body of the wine is undergoing fermentation in the large cask, the smaller portion, that is, the "extra" gallons, should be allowed to ferment in a smaller receptacle, in a 10-gallon cask or a carboy. Each time an addition is made to the large cask from this surplus, the latter may be transferred to still smaller containers, in order to avoid overcontract with the air. An excellent way to keep the surplus wine after the secondary fermentation, and to keep it in handy form for using and without much opportunity for loss or waste, is to store it in gallon jugs. These may be opened one or two at a time as is necessary for replenishing the wine lost from the large cask in the racking process or because of shrinkage due to evaporation through the wood.

The time for the first racking is from two weeks to two months after the secondary fermentation has stopped. If the wine is put to ferment in early October in small casks or carboys of 10-gallon size, the secondary fermentation will die down fairly early. As soon as it comes clear, which may be within two or three weeks after the last bubble of gas has passed through water, it may be racked into a fresh container. On the other hand, if the quantity of wine set to ferment is about 50 gallons, it should remain in the cask for about two months after the end of secondary fermentation. At any rate, it should be racked by late November or early December.

The second racking should take place during the first week of March in the North and about the middle of February in the South. The reason for this is that with the approach of warm weather another fermentation may take place, and almost surely will if there is any sugar at all remaining in the wine. Before this occurs, it is desirable to remove any sediment already thrown down.

A third racking is performed by some winemakers to get rid of any lees that may have fallen to the bottom of the cask as a result of this new fermentation. Other people omit this racking. The defense that can be made for this is simply that these secondary lees are not so likely to harbor bad yeasts as were those thrown down by the earlier fermentation. Still, if the spring fermentation is active, it is good policy to rack the wine in June. This racking has the virtue of leaving the winemaker on the safe side.

The fourth, and usually the last, racking for wine made from native American grapes should come in October. If the wine has been properly treated from the beginning, if it has enough alcohol and has not been overexposed to the air, it is now going to be brilliantly fine and in a healthy state. Now is the time to bottle. There are winemakers who leave their wine in the cask for from one to two years more; but this is a practice which offers little advantage to wine made from American grapes. These wines mature early, as compared with most French wines, and in two years' time they begin to be at their best for drinking. The second year should be spent in the bottle. As a matter of fact, the wine can be drunk at the end of the first year, but it improves with some age. At the end of two years it is good; it is better at three years of age, and ordinarily still better at four. For most wines made from Eastern grapes, there is not much to be gained from holding these wines for a much longer time. Likewise, most California wines mature early by comparison with the wines from the same grapes made in France. A *vinifera* wine from the Far West is likely to be at its best in four years' time, and seven or eight years is a safe outside limit.

The beginner will not, almost certainly, wish to wait several years before bottling. Therefore, let him make a sufficiently large quantity, say 100 gallons. If he wants to, then, he may bottle and drink up to half of it any time after the first racking and still have a good supply left over to undergo the other rackings and mature properly. The ability to wait is acquired as one grows older and more experienced in the practice of wine manufacture. Let patience be molded by judgment. One of the worst mistakes commonly made by the beginner is that he is content to manufacture at first too small a quantity of wine—he does not know how little 10 gallons of wine can be. A good minimum for a beginner is 35 gallons; a better one is 50 gallons. Later the head of an average family will find that 100 gallons will not be too much if wine is to become a regular part of the daily diet: 100 gallons of finished wine is only 500 fifth-size bottles. This is somewhat better than one bottle per day during the year, but it is not *two* bottles per day, that is, it is not a bottle for lunch and another for dinner or supper.

Sweet Wines. Most Americans seem to think of wine as a sweet drink, and it is true that by far the major portion of wine sold in the United States today is sweet wine. This is due chiefly to the fact that because America is a "hard-liquor" country it has had little experience with wine, which began to be a serious national industry only in the second half of the nineteenth century. By the time the country's viniculturists had established themselves as manufacturers of first-rate wines, they had but a short time to flourish before the tragedy of Prohibition fell like a blight across the land, killing the wine industry and turning the nation back to strong and dangerous beverages, bought at back doors or in dark alleys, and drunk in peephole speakeasies or in one's own home with the shades drawn and always at the risk of going blind or of being seriously poisoned. When this incredible era came to an end, the nation had forgotten what good wine was. Repeal came in a period of economic tensions. Drinking habits were remade. The stronger drinks, whiskey and cocktails, were necessary now to help one's nerves through the day. Any wine made at home was always sweet and elaborated according to an outsized formula handed down from the dark years when it was illegal and when homemade wine had to compete with gin that never saw a juniper berry. The recipe invariably called for several pounds of sugar per gallon of grape juice. The taste for sweet wine was helped along also by the fact that in the national mind there smoldered a recollection of such well-known type names as Port, Tokay, Muscatel, and Sherry—British influence perhaps, but an influence that has not helped to make us drinkers of dry wines.

With very few exceptions, the world's great wines are dry, and experience with table wine almost invariably pushes one in the direction of dry wine.

Sweet wines have their place, however. They make the best dessert wines, or are finely suited to serving in the afternoon with sweet cookies or cakes, especially the fortified wines.

Most of the recipes in the back of this book that do not call for grapes will produce sweet wines, and some of them are very fine indeed, such as, for example, Fig

Wine number 3. Many of these wines are of ancient history and distinction and were made and drunk while our country was in its earliest infancy. One might say that they are wines of pedigree.

But sweet wine can be made from grapes, too, though it is true that most native American varieties do not lend themselves very well to its manufacture. However, what makes a wine sweet is the amount of unfermented sugar in it.

In California there is no problem in finding grapes adaptable to the manufacture of sweet wine. Among the varieties available there are the several Muscats, especially the so-called Muscat of Alexandria. These grapes have a juice that often runs as high at 35 or 36 percent in sugar. Other suitable grapes, though somewhat less sweet, are Grenache, Maccabeo, Malvasia, and Mission.

In the East the matter of grapes for sweet wines is more of a problem, for there is no native grape that runs anywhere near 36 percent in sugar content. In fact, very few indeed have as much as 28 percent. It is therefore necessary to resort to a practice frowned upon by many and tolerated by all, that of adding enough sugar to assure sweetness in the finished product. The best that can be done is to choose the choicest grapes available and treat them so that they will yield a sweet wine.

Good red grapes for this purpose are Clevener, Eumelan, Ives, and Triumph in the North, and Cynthiana, Herbemont, Lenoir, and Norton in the South. Another resort is to use one or several of the finer white grapes, Catawba, Delaware, Diana, Diamond, Dutchess, Iona, and give color by mixing in, or fermenting with, the juice of any good red grape or grapes.

As for the grape from which to make a sweet white wine, any of the white varieties just named is good. Sweet Catawba was an American stand-by in the nineteenth century and is still manufactured in some areas.

Other grapes suitable for sweet white wines are Berckmans, Eden, and Golden Muscat. These in the North. In the South Gold Coin and Headlight are excellent for the purpose.

The making of sweet red wines begins with the grapes on the vine. They should be decided on beforehand and watched carefully. The proper moment for picking is when the stems have turned brown and are beginning to shrivel. At this time the sugar concentration is greatest. After they have been picked, it is a good idea to let them stand for not more than two days in a warm bright place, unless the berries show signs of excessive cracking or splitting. The grapes are now run through a crusher and into the fermenting vat. A small quantity of fresh juice must be caught at this time, and, after straining, tested with the saccharometer. The additional sugar may be stirred in at the time the crushed fruit is put to ferment in the vat. Or the saccharometer reading may be recorded and the sugar added at the time the wine is turned into the cask for its secondary fermentation. The addition of sugar at this time has the advantage of forcing a renewed and violent activity of the yeasts, with a resultant "boiling over" through the bunghole and the discharge of many insolubles that have remained in the wine and would otherwise settle to the bottom. Some winemakers prefer to "feed" the sugar to the wine at different stages of its secondary fermentation.

A sweet wine is one that contains from 3 to 10 percent of unfermented sugar. To make sure that his product will be sweet, the winemaker should allow for an initial sugar content of at least 30 percent. If a heavier and sweeter wine is desired, the sugar may be raised to 36 percent. To calculate exactly the amount of sugar to be added to a given juice in order to achieve these percentages, consult the table on page 58 after the must has been tested with the saccharometer.

The procedure for the manufacture of sweet white

wines is almost the same as that just described for the making of sweet red wines, except in one or two important details. As in the case of the white dry wines, the juice is not fermented on the skins, but is put directly into the cask after pressing. All necessary sugar must, however, be added first. And for the reason that the juice is not being fermented on its skins, it will be deficient in tannin unless this is supplied. The proper amount to add is one gram for each five gallons of wine. It is best to add the tannin to sweet wines after the "boiling over" so often referred to has subsided, that is, just before water-sealing.

An important step in the making of sweet wines, red or white, is more frequent racking. The first racking should take place two or three weeks after the fermenting wine has become wholly quiet in the cask. The others should follow at intervals of two months during the first year, except that the wine must not be disturbed during its spring fermentation. If it has been given a racking early in March, the next one need not come before the second week in May, by which time it should have quieted down again. If it is still restless, wait until the first week in June.

Sweet wines are sluggish in their maturation, as compared with dry wines. Therefore it is necessary to give them more time in the casks, that is, wait longer before bottling. This means that sweet wine ought to spend at least a second year in the cask (or carboy) and during this year it should be racked at least three times, or even four.

Most of the world's sweet wine is fortified wine, that is, it has had its alcoholic strength raised to 18 or 21 percent by the addition of brandy. This is a very desirable practice, since sweet wines are dessert wines and are drunk in small quantities. The home wine-maker should, however, be cautioned that this is a very expensive practice if followed with large amounts of wine, because he cannot have recourse to the untaxed brandy used by the commercial manufacturer, but must buy brandy on which the government tax has already been paid. If it is decided to fortify a home-made sweet wine, its alcoholic content should be raised to 18 or 20 percent. The amount of brandy to be added can be estimated by knowing the alcoholic strength of the wine from natural fermentation—this is remembered from the sugar reading and from keeping in mind that two percent of sugar normally yields one percent of alcohol. A sweet wine remaining two years in the cask may be expected to develop about 12 percent of alcohol. This is just an ounce and a fraction less than one quart of alcohol for every two gallons of wine. It takes a little more than one-half gallon (actually 0.6 of a gallon) of 100-proof brandy (brandy containing 50 percent alcohol) to fortify up to required strength every two gallons of sweet wine with an alcoholic concentration of only 12 percent. If the domestic winemaker is willing to invest in 100-proof brandies, he can make very good sweet wines from grapes, wines that, because of the added alcohol, will have much better keeping qualities than if they were not fortified. (The method of determining the amount of brandy to be added in fortifying wine is explained in detail in Chapter 11.)

The Yeast Starter. It is important that the winemaker should know how to prepare a yeast starter. The value of beginning fermentation with yeast cannot be denied. This is especially true if any of the conditions is adverse —say, too low a temperature, too high a temperature, doubts about the quality of the grape juice, and so on. The air is full of yeast and other organisms, all of which try to get at the grape juice and the sugar in it. The first to arrive and take hold is the one that wins. Later on an organism known as *Mycoderma aceti,* which has been lying in wait all along, will attack the wine and by deoxidation transform the alcohol into acetic acid; that is, it will change the wine into vinegar. The grape itself is covered with yeasts, some good and, perhaps, some bad. It happens that the bad yeasts in the air and those on the grape thrive under certain conditions; the good yeasts in their turn work best under conditions which are more favorable to them than to their enemies. For example, certain yeasts are vigorous at high temperatures, 80 degrees Fahrenheit or above, and at these temperatures can prevent wine yeast from working properly. Others, like the vinegar germ, can destroy alcohol at a temperature that is either too high or too low, especially if the wine is weak or gets off to a poor start. On the other hand, the good yeasts, the wine yeasts, of the family *Saccharomyces,* live and work best at more moderate temperatures, preferably between 65 and 75 degrees Fahrenheit, although a fluctuation of 20 degrees, from 60 to 80, does not affect them adversely. For this reason many home winemakers who have worked under favorable conditions have never thought of using a yeast starter and do not see its value. But most experienced winemakers working with good juice would never think of setting a batch of must to ferment without a good starter. Neither do commercial wineries ever take the risk of having bad yeasts and other organisms get into their wine; they always begin fermentation with a good yeast starter. For the home winemaker the use of a starter is advisable if the conditions under which he works are in any way adverse or even doubtful. But especially should he use one if he plans to ferment the juice of a superior grape. Always! A good yeast starter will assure good fermentation and, consequently, good wine. It defeats the bad organisms right at the very start of the process.

The initial fermentation—that which takes place in the vat—should be immediate and as vigorous as possible. The best way to make certain of this is to begin it with a starter prepared with good yeast.

There are several ways to make a starter. The simplest is to press out a quantity of juice from sound, ripe grapes a day or so before beginning the wine. Put it in a bottle or flask and plug the mouth loosely with cotton. Set in a fairly warm (not hot) place, such as on the sill of a window through which the sun is shining. In two or three days—sometimes even in one day —it should be fermenting vigorously. As soon as the grapes are pressed, the starter must go into the vat with the rest of the juice. Within a very few hours the whole thing will be in a "boil."

A still better method is to pasteurize the pressed juice by heating it in a double boiler for fifteen minutes at a temperature of 140 degrees Fahrenheit. When thoroughly cool, but not cold, add one quarter of a cake of baker's yeast—or its equivalent in active dry (granulated) yeast—per pint of juice. Again place in a glass bottle or flask, plug the mouth loosely with cotton, and allow to stand in a warm spot until fermentation is vigorous.

Since the amount of natural sugar in the juice is not very great, care should be taken to see that yeasts do not eat it all up and die before the starter can be used. Sugar must be added, if necessary, to keep the yeasts active, for they must be working when put into the fermenting vat.

Although the methods just described are used by many, they are heartily scorned by the more experienced winemaker, especially by one working with juice extracted from grapes of quality. And rightly so. In fact, the following should be axiomatic with the winemaker, whether a beginner or an old hand: *Never ferment the juice of superior grapes with anything but a good wine yeast.* The method of preparing the starter is the second one described above. To those instructions it is only necessary to add that all receptacles and utensils must be absolutely clean. Scald before using.

In recent years new and vigorous strains of yeast have been developed. It is claimed for these that they will convert up to 36 percent of sugar into 18 percent of alcohol. The home winemaker who is making *false* (non-grape) wines who does not want his product to be overly sweet or who wishes to increase its lasting quality will do well to experiment with these new varieties. They will serve, likewise, to guarantee the dryness of wine made from grapes, especially if a good table wine is desired. The newer yeasts are available from some of the supply houses listed in Appendix III.

Herter's, Inc., and Leslie Edelman, Inc. offer the following wine yeasts:

All-purpose	Madeira
Bernkastel	Mead
Bordeaux	Port
Burgundy	Sauternes
Chablis	Sherry
Champagne	Steinberg
Graves	Tokay
Liebfraumilch	Zeltingen

Semplex of U.S.A. (see Appendix III) also offers some of the above, in small bottles, each adequate for fermenting out 12 gallons of grape juice. These come from the wine-growing districts of Germany: Burgundy, Champagne, Liebfraumilch, Port, Sauternes, Sherry, and Tokay. Semplex sells also two general-purpose wine yeasts. One, Liofermenti comes from the Chianti region of Italy. It is a strong, hungry yeast that can be used in making red wines. It comes in dry form, and one small jar will serve for 6 gallons of wine.

The same firm's Respora is another general-purpose yeast, this time in tablet form. Each tablet will ferment into wine one gallon of juice.

Semplex also stocks a French wine yeast, Montrachet, that is used by many commercial wineries and that has the advantage that it can be added directly to the must without the need of preparing a starter.

It is an active dry yeast in granulated form kept in sealed envelopes under nitrogen gas to retain its life.

A third firm selling wine yeasts, also imported, is Budde & Westermann, of Montclair, New Jersey. (See Appendix III.)

The all-purpose yeasts are what their name indicates. Among the others, the Bordeaux and Burgundy should be used for red wines. Most of those with German names should be used with white juice to give the wine a Rhinelike or Mosel (Moselle) quality. The Chablis ought to be added only to a juice not too heavy in acids. The Madeira, Port, Sauternes, and Tokay yeasts will serve in making sweet dessert wines. Mead is honey wine and mead yeast should not be allowed to spoil a good grape juice (but see recipes for honey wine). Sherry, if very dry, is an excellent substitute for cocktails before dinner; if sweet, it is a dessert wine or one to be sipped at afternoon teas. Hence, the user of Sherry yeasts ought to know his objective before preparing his starter. In any case, instructions come with the yeasts listed above—and their prices are reasonable.

Yeast Nutrients. It sometimes happens that yeasts in a must become quiescent. If the saccharometer shows any remaining sugar, renewed activity may be stimulated by adding a yeast nutrient. Another advantage of the nutrient is that it can help the fermentation through to the maximum alcoholic content a yeast can tolerate. For either or both of these reasons, the nutrient may be added at the time the starter is put into the must. (These facts should be remembered in the making of fortified wines described in Chapter 11.) Good wine usually needs two to three years to ferment out to dryness. Starting with 22 percent of sugar, the beginner, using a good yeast, might get his 11 percent of alcohol in one year. With 24 percent of sugar, he ought to allow two years, and with 26, three. But many circumstances can change these estimates, and since a nutrient strengthens yeast activity, it will often produce more alcohol in less time. (The alcoholic content of a *dry* wine can always be read with a vinometer. See Appendix III.)

5

fining the wine

THE CLARIFICATION of wine by removing from it all impurities is known as *fining*. All wine should be absolutely clear, or *fine,* before it is bottled. Otherwise it will deposit a sediment in the bottle which is likely to stir up later when the wine is served. Futhermore, wine should appeal to the eye as well as to the palate. No cloudy, semi-opaque beverage can hope to have the charm of a brilliantly clear and sparkling wine as it is held in the glass or studied in the bottle.

Ordinarily a wine of good body and alcoholic strength will clear itself if allowed to stand. But it sometimes happens, for reasons not yet thoroughly understood, that a wine apparently good in other respects refuses to clear up properly. This is more often the case with white wines than with red. At any rate, whenever this happens in wine of either color, clarification can be satisfactorily carried out by artificial means.

The best time for fining wines is a matter of some debate. There are those who advocate putting the fining substance in the wine at the time that it is first turned into the cask or carboy. This will do all right if the wine is to be bottled early, say, in the fall of the year in which it is made, just after the first racking. But if it is to be kept for a year before bottling, as it should be, the most appropriate time for fining, the present writer believes, is either after the spring racking in early March, or just after the third racking in June, preferably the latter. (See in this chapter the section *Early and Late Fining*.)

Fining Red Wines. Though red wines usually fine well by themselves, it is occasionally necessary to help them along. When this is the case, they may be clarified artificially by using pure leaf gelatin, egg-white, or milk.

Pure leaf gelatin (powdered kitchen gelatin is an acceptable substitute) is obtainable at any drugstore. It should be used in the proportion of 6 grams for every 10 gallons of wine to be fined. The druggist will be glad to measure it out in grams. (If it has to be bought in ounces, it is good to know that there are 30 grams to the ounce.) Dissolve the necessary amount of gelatin in a small portion of water, or wine; just the amount necessary to cover it. When it is dissolved, add a quart of wine and beat well. Now pour the wine containing the gelatin into the cask or carboy holding the bulk of the wine and stir for at least ten minutes. Bung up and let stand until the wine drawn off through the spigot is clear and brilliant, or until the wine in the carboy will stand the candle test.

This is a test every user of the carboy should know. It is easy to administer and is one of the best ways for telling when the wine in a large glass container is perfectly fine. First wipe the dirt or dust off the carboy. Light a candle and set it on one side of the carboy, about halfway up the side and within two or three inches of the glass itself. Then look at the candle from the other side. If the wine is wholly fine, the candle flame will show through the wine sharply and distinctly, without the slightest distortion. If the candle flame is not sharply outlined and clearly defined, or if it appears dull or is distorted in any way whatever, the wine is not yet ready for bottling.

Another easy and effective way to fine red wines is to use egg-white. For each 10 gallons of wine use the white of one egg, a pinch of salt, and a quart of wine. Whip until the egg-white and wine are thoroughly blended; then pour into the wine, stir the whole for a good ten minutes, and bung up tightly. When the wine comes fine, it may be racked and bottled.

A hundred years ago the fining of wine was often accomplished by using milk, and even today milk is the fining agent of an occasional farmer who is not satisfied to drink or serve the murky liquid so often proffered as testimony of rural hospitality. While not to be recommended for white wine, milk may be used very effectively by the amateur in clarifying his red wines. To fine after the fermentation has stopped, mix well two cupfuls of milk and a quart of wine, and then stir this mixture into the contents of the cask or carboy. Agitate well for about ten minutes, after which the container may be sealed up. This wine should come clear in ten days or two weeks. The proportions given are for the fining of ten gallons.

Fining White Wines. The fining of white wines is somewhat—but not much—more difficult. Russian isinglass, or fish glue, was the fining material commonly used in the past by professionals. It is still good if it can be got, and nowadays it seems that the place to look for it is the hardware store. If used, it should be obtained in powdered form, and prepared exactly the same as for fining with gelatin.

And since leaf gelatin will be easier to get, and will do just as well, the manner of preparing this will be described. Have the druggist measure out pure leaf gelatin in the proportion of six grams for every ten gallons of wine to be fined. Dissolve the gelatin in a little water, or wine, then add a quart of wine and agitate well for a few minutes. Now turn this fining mixture into the large container. Stir for at least ten minutes, bung up, and let stand.

The fining of white wines may be performed after the spring racking or after the third, which comes in June. In either case the wine should be clear in about two weeks' time. Consequently, it can be expected to be fine enough for bottling after the fourth and final racking in October.

The white of egg is also used by some for the fining even of white wines. To fine ten gallons of white wine with egg-white, beat well the white of one egg in one quart of wine and pour into the cask or carboy. After stirring for ten minutes, bung up and let stand.

If isinglass or gelatin is used for white wines, there is an important precaution that must be taken. Tannin is essential to the proper maturing of wine, whether it be red or white; and since a fining process carried on with these agents will remove from white wine practically all of its tannin, more must be added. Therefore, when the fining agent is prepared, the additional tannin should be got ready also. Draw a quart of wine and stir into it 5 grams of dry tannic acid for every ten gallons of wine to be fined. When this has been thoroughly mixed, pour it into the receptacle which holds the fining agent and stir the new mixture for another minute or so. Now add this compound of gelatin (or egg-white), wine, and tannin to the cask or carboy and give the whole its requisite ten-minute stirring before bunging up. (It must not be forgotten that each time the cask or carboy is sealed or bunged up, the junctures have to be covered with wax or paraffin.)

An alternative to the fining methods just described for white wines is to fine early, that is, to add the clarifying agent at the time the wine is first set aside to ferment in the cask or carboy. From here on the treatment of the wine will be the same as has previously been described, with the regular rackings coming at their proper intervals. If the fining substance is added early, it means that the finished wine is going to be short in tannin unless the loss is made good. In supplying lost tannin a little less may be used, that is, instead of 5 grams per 10 gallons of wine, use only 4 grams for that amount. Dissolve it in a quart of wine, mix well, and stir into the cask or carboy for ten minutes. Bung up and let stand. Late tannin is best added just after spring fermentation.

Early and Late Fining. If the domestic winemaker is at all concerned over whether to fine early or late, it should be said to him that the question is not wholly academic. Late fining has as least one good point in its favor, namely, that of allowing the wine to clear up naturally and by itself. A good red wine will almost always do so; a good white wine may do so. It can always be given a chance, for it is never too late to fine —any time after the spring racking, or even after the third racking in June, is propitious for clearing wine by artificial means.

On the other hand, there is a strong argument for early fining. Every time the fining solution is added to a cask of wine, this must be filled to the bunghole, and unless an extra supply has been allowed for at the beginning of the manufacturing process, the winemaker is going to run short. There is always some shrinkage or loss due to racking and evaporation (if the cask is used), a loss which is not appreciable, but which will be felt if extra wine is needed at a critical moment. It is always possible to use lukewarm water to make up for this shrinkage if only very small quantities are needed. But in working with 50 gallons of wine or more, it is advisable to prepare for contingencies by starting off with a few gallons extra, as was earlier suggested (see page 69). The value of having extra wine when fining late is this: if the container of wine to which a fining agent is being added is not full to the top, the wine often will not come clear, the air pocket, for some reason, interfering with the precipitation of the particles in suspension. Therefore after the fining substance has been stirred in, the cask or carboy must be filled to the very top. For each of the three succeeding days, the wine container should be checked to see that the wine remains right at the top. If not, more must be added. After the fourth refilling, or the fourth day of checking, bung up tightly, seal, and let stand.

In addition to methods of fining already described, wine may also be cleared by chilling, provided of course that cloudiness is not due to colloidal suspension, a state that exists when certain semi-solid or albuminous substances remain suspended and refuse to settle. But when this state prevails, something is usually wrong with the wine. In cold weather, or at least when the nights are quite chilly, transfer the cask and its contents from the warmer place where it has been set to ferment, or from its storage, to a cold place, either indoors or outside, and let it stand for a while. Often, with a good red wine in healthy condition, overnight will do the trick, though not infrequently it is necessary to leave it for two or even three days. Unless the temperatures are dangerously low, no harm will be done to the wine by remaining even a week in the cold.

A last word on fining should emphasize what was said on the first page of this chapter, that wines of good alcoholic and acidic strength usually fine themselves. White wines, good in other respects, sometimes need help. If the beginner has been careful in making his wine, he is not likely to have to bother with fining it. Except in the case of false wines—those not made from grapes. Many of these are indeed sluggish about coming clear. It is they rather than the grape wines that are often in need of fining. The methods and materials described above will apply. Certain false wines—those made from apricots, peaches, mangos, muskmelons, and from certain flowers—for some reason often do not clear up well. Filtering helps them and a word should be said about this process.

Filtering is done with filter bags, filter paper, or prepared asbestos. The bags really do not do much more than strain out the coarser residues. Filter paper and asbestos are better for a stubborn wine. The paper is made especially for clearing wine; so is the asbestos, which comes in pulp form. To use the latter, place a quantity in the bottom of a large funnel and pour the wine on it. This should come clear as it seeps through. Asbestos can be purchased in varying amounts from different suppliers (see Appendix III). Four ounces are sufficient for many gallons of wine.

6

bottling and storing

THE TIME has come at last to put the wine in the bottle, to lay it down in the bin. Perhaps it has been decided to do this after the first racking, or maybe impatience has been tempered by judgment and experience and the wine has remained for a whole year in the cask with its second, third, and fourth rackings administered at proper intervals. Whatever the case, whether bottled in the fall of the year of manufacture or after spending a full twelve months in the cask, the procedure for bottling is the same.

On the other hand, the amateur, especially if he is making wine for the first time and in small quantities, may have "sampled" his product so frequently that none remains. In this event, he has had his pleasure, and what follows will be of no interest to him until another year and another batch come along.

There are two principal reasons for storing wine in bottles of one-quart, one-fifth, or one-pint size rather than in larger containers. One is convenience and the other, even more important, is that few wines that are any good can be satisfactorily kept after the cork is drawn and contact with the air allowed. This is especially true of table wines, which should be consumed on the day they are opened. A good table wine has long since had its last beneficial contact with the air and now regards this as its enemy. It is true that small quantities remaining in bottles can be put in the refrigerator for later consumption, provided they are kept very cold. But wine thus treated is never so good as that drunk within two or three hours of its opening. The beginner should not be led to doubt this by the bulky displays of wine in gallon and two-gallon jugs which glare out at the passerby from the garish neonlighted windows of drugstores and the cheaper wine shops. Really good wine is not in these containers. The home winemaker should treat his product as if it were the best and put it in the proper receptacle. And the chances are more than good that if he has followed the instructions given earlier and has allowed his wine enough age before bottling, he will have a better wine than he is likely to buy over most counters.

What has been said about table wines does not apply to the same degree to sweet, or dessert, wines. Nearly all fortified wines (those that have brandy added) can stand several contacts with the air, while some, like the great Sherries from Spain, can live exposed to the air indefinitely and without any deterioration in quality. On the other hand, a sweet wine like Sauternes (in France all Sauternes are sweet), good wine that it is, behaves like its unfortified brothers and deteriorates if kept long after the cork is drawn.

If the daily wine requirement is quite small, a good practice is to put wines meant for the table in bottles of one-pint size. The quart size is really pretty large. The fifth size is about right, even for small families, and if wine is taken with the noon and evening meals, it will not be found too big.

It should be added here that many unfortified sweet wines made from fruits other than grapes have pretty good keeping qualities even after the cork is drawn, and seldom offer any problem. This is true of most of the wines made from the recipes given later in this book.

In the bottling of wines there are certain established traditions or conventions that are commonly observed. The principal one is that red wine is usually put in dark bottles and white wine in clear or transparent green bottles. Some people think that light hurts a red wine. Whether it does or not, putting it in dark bottles while the white wine is placed in light bottles, makes them both easily distinguishable at a glance and at a distance. The beginner must decide for himself the kind and size of bottles he wishes to use. He should set for himself one requirement, however. The bottles ought to be round and of uniform size—they will store much better. Bottles of irregular sizes and shapes are difficult to accommodate in the storage bin, especially if a large number of bottles is being laid down. If, for the purpose of satisfying a perfectly legitimate whim, it is desired to put wine into fancy bottles, let the number of these not be too great and they can occupy a separate section of the storage bin.

Certain types of bottles are hardly permissible— large ginger ale and soda bottles and the smaller soft drink bottles. It is best to use wine bottles, for the reasons given in Chapter 2 in the section entitled *Bottles*.

For the average person there is always the problem of where to get wine bottles. If there is no wine-supply house in the vicinity, there are a few things one can do. One can scour the roadsides, hunting for bottles which have been regretfully expelled from passing automobiles. Another is to visit the village refuse heap, where bottles collect by the thousands. A third is to beg used bottles from wine-drinking friends. There is no reason why bottles so obtained are not as good as any, provided of course that they are spotlessly clean before any wine is put in them.

The best and surest way to secure bottles is to buy

them. This will assure containers of uniform size and shape, of desired color, and usually of good quality, and which are ready for use with a simple rinsing out in scalding water. Bottles may often be bought in bar-supply houses, found in almost every city or large town where bars operate openly. If no such house is within easy access, bottles may be ordered from any of the many manufacturers of bottles listed in Appendix III. They may not cost more than five to ten cents apiece in quantity lots; but this is a day of changing prices and bottle costs may go either up or down. Also, the cost will vary according to the quality, size, shape, and number purchased. Yet the investment is a good one, for once made, it will not be necessary to buy bottles again for many years, unless the annual output of home-made wine is augmented.

Bottling the Wine. The actual bottling of the wine is a simple matter. But all bottles must be scrupulously clean before any wine is put in them, for good wine is so pure and delicate a thing that it is easily contamined by contact with foreign substances. Perhaps nothing so readily picks up alien odors and flavors as good wine—its goodness resides in great part in its purity. With bad wine there is no problem, for it shouldn't be bottled anyway. Therefore all bottles must be washed, even new ones and those that have been stored clean. Second-hand bottles must be carefully washed with hot water and soap, using a bottle brush to scour the interior. If there is on the inside any stubborn adherence of foreign matter which the brush will not remove, try putting in a handful of BB shot, some gravel, or coarse sand. Then shake vigorously backwards and forwards, sideways, and up and down. If this does not work, discard the bottle. After the washing, bottles must be thoroughly rinsed, first under the faucet, to remove the soap, and then with scalding water. As a last precaution (especially if the wine is from a superior grape) rinse them once more with a solution of potassium metabisulphite. Let dry and use. (Use the potassium solution even for bottles that have been stored clean.)

Once the bottles are scrupulously clean, it remains only to fill them and cork them. There are few tasks more pleasant than putting home-made wine in bottles. This is when the amateur winemaker, whether he be experienced or only a beginner, realizes that all his efforts and attentions have come to fruition, that the great miracle has been performed, and by him. So, he sits willingly and for hours in delightful solitude, the air filled with vinous aromas and the enticing odors of intangible esters, watching the most beautiful liquid in the world run into clean and sparkling bottles. Perhaps the simplicity of the process lends it charm. It is only necessary to hold the bottle under the spigot until it is filled up into the bottom part of the neck, to within an inch of where the lower end of the cork will be. A small air cushion between the wine and the stopper should always be kept. Otherwise, the cork will be forced out of the bottle.

There is one thing/that will aid in bottling and that is a small funnel. This should be of glass, plastic, or enamel, and must, of course, be washed and scalded before using.

Corking and Sealing. After the bottle is filled, it should be corked. Many winemakers prefer to use screw caps. And these are all right. They are handy, easy to put on and take off, and are available from suppliers of winemaker's aids. They are perhaps the ideal stopper for most of the cheaper commercial wines which are so frequently filtered during their manufacture that the microscopic particles in them which help them to mature and achieve quality are removed. This frequent filtering is a sure guarantee that the wine will never reach greatness, so there is no advantage in using corks instead of caps. Wine in the bottle continues to undergo some very important changes. It is here that it developes its bouquet, that its free acids combine with the esters of the alcohol to give it character, that its body achieves smoothness, that it acquires that great intangible known as "roundness."

All this is helped by using corks instead of caps, for the contact with the cork is good for the wine.

However, this is no great matter for the domestic winemaker. Screw caps have the great advantage of convenience and of being less trouble to put on. But if it is planned to use them, it is necessary to keep it in mind when buying the bottles in order to be sure of getting the kind that will take caps. The one important step in the preparation of the caps is to make sure that they are clean—scald them before using.

If corks are to be used, their preparation requires a little more attention. They must first be boiled, for about five minutes. If the water takes on color, pour it off, add some more, and boil again. The corks must be inserted in the bottle while they are still wet from the boiling.

The insertion of the corks is not so easy as putting on screw caps. If the ordinary cork, purchasable at drugstores and hardware stores, is used, it is inserted with the fingers and pushed down with the hand or thumb until the top of the cork is even with, or better yet, just below, the rim of the bottle neck. But "ordinary" corks are not recommended.

Regular wine corks should be boiled as just explained. It is not easy to insert them with the fingers, so corking machines are recommended. One especially easy to use and economical in cost is the wooden plunger type, a simple hand-operated instrument, available from the firms listed in Appendix III under "Bottle Corking Machines."

After the bottles have been corked, let them stand for two or three days to permit the top of the cork to dry out. At the end of this time examine all corks to make sure that they fit tightly and, if necessary, to press down further any which happen to stand above the rim of the bottle neck. After this inspection it is a good idea to lay all bottles on their sides for another three or four days (or even a week). This is in preparation for the next step, which is described in the following paragraph. At the end of this time, they should be examined again to make sure that there is no seepage of wine through or around the cork. If any moist corks are discovered, they must be extracted and the bottles recorked. All bottles containing dry corks are ready for sealing.

Wine may be kept satisfactorily for years without sealing. But if the corks and the bottle end are sealed against moisture and mold, the wine within the bottles has one more guarantee of safety. A good compound for this purpose can be made by melting together one part of beeswax and two parts of paraffin. (Beeswax is sold at all drugstores, and paraffin can be found either at drugstores or at hardware stores.) While the mixture is still warm, but not so hot as to break the glass, dip the cork end of the bottle into it to the depth of an inch or an inch and a half. No bottle containing a moist or leaky cork should be sealed.

Another excellent material for covering the cork end of the bottle is sealing wax, available from Milan Laboratory (see Appendix III). The fact that is comes in different colors offers the winemaker the opportunity of sealing his red wine with red wax and his white wine with yellow wax, if he chooses. The advantage of sealing corked bottles is that both the sealing wax and the compound of paraffin and beeswax are completely air tight and waterproof, and will prevent mold and moisture from affecting the cork and possibly damaging the wine. Both will do this effectively if applied when melted, but the cork top must be absolutely dry before it is dipped in the sealing material. Otherwise mold may form on the cork, and this sometimes penetrates through and spoils the entire contents of the bottle.

Labeling. Before wine is stored away, it should be labeled. The convenience of having labels on bottles can hardly be appreciated until one has found after two or three years that he has forgotten the year of his wine, or even of what fruit it was made.

Ordinary gummed labels, obtainable at bookstores and five-and-ten-cent stores, will do for indicating the name of the fruit and the year of its manufacture. This information should be written on the label in black waterproof drawing ink. If the cellar or storage room is damp, the labels may come off after a while, for they are backed only by mucilage. A good way to prevent this is to brush each label with transparent and quick-drying shellac. Another, and cheaper, way is to cover them with a thin layer of melted paraffin, applied with a brush. The paraffin has the advantage of being much easier to remove later when the bottles are cleaned for re-use.

Good labels give a professional touch to a bottle. The amateur may be encouraged by the labels illustrated in the center insert of this book to copy them or to invent his own. Other "fancy" labels for the home winemaker can be purchased from Milan Laboratory or from Semplex of U.S.A. (See Appendix III under "Labels.")

A final suggestion which is not far removed from labeling is the keeping of a record book or cellar book. A memorandum book of any desired size can be bought at the bookstore or at the five-and-ten-cent store. In this book should be recorded all the information given on the label, as well as all other information relating to the manufacture of a particular batch of wine: type of grape used, time and place of purchase, price, amount of juice extracted per bushel of grapes, date of pressing, vigor of fermentation, amount of water added (if any), dates of racking, date of fining (if any), amount of tannin added (if any), length of time in cask, date of bottling, number of bottles filled, and any other information which may be of interest to the maker. All this will be of great value as the beginner acquires experience; it will help him to learn, to avoid past errors or to profit by this or that judicious step taken, perhaps, with some hesitation. As the years pass, and they will, the book becomes a priceless and impressive record of achievement, as well as guide to future improvement.

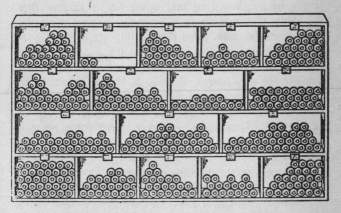

FIGURE 15. WINE BIN FOR BASEMENT CELLAR

Height	5 feet
Width	10 feet
Depth	15 inches
Number of compartments	17
Height of compartments	Approx. 1 foot 3 inches
Width of compartments	Top & bottom rows, approx. 2 feet
	Second row, approx. 2 feet 6 inches
	Third row, approx. 3 feet 4 inches
Thickness of lumber	Sides, 2 inches
	Shelves, 1 inch
Total capacity of bin	More than 650 fifth-size bottles

Storing. After the wine has been bottled, exulted over, and proudly contemplated in its new containers, it should not be left standing, but should be stored away. A cool place is desirable. The ideal storage room would be a subterranean cavern with a constant temperature of about fifty degrees Fahrenheit and un-affected by the changes above ground. Some of the wineries of the Lake Erie region in and near Sandusky have natural limestone caves for storing bottled wine while it matures. But such ideal conditions are not necessary. The fruit room of the average basement or cellar will make an excellent storage room for wine. Every bottle should be laid down on its side so that the wine will remain in permanent contact with the bottom of the cork. This is very important for it pre-vents shrinkage of the cork and subsequent probable spoiling of the wine. *Beware of wine which has stood upright for any length of time.* It is not necessary to keep the bottles in a rack; they may be placed on a shelf, or even on the ground, and stacked on top of each other. They must, however, have some sort of side support so the bottles in the bottom row will not roll out from under the weight of the rows on top.

Here is where it is advantageous to have a storage bin. There are other advantages too—different types of wine can be kept apart, older wines and younger wines can have their own compartments, the bottles are much easier to inspect from time to time for leakage or other possible damage, and above all the wine is more easily accessible. Figures 15 and 16 illustrate simple and inexpensive storage bins which can be easily built by anyone. Over each compartment, or section, a tag or piece of cardboard may be tacked on which are in-dicated the number of bottles in that compartment, as well as the year, the kind of wine, or any other in-formation desired.

The apartment dweller who does not have access to basement or cellar space can build himself an excellent

FIGURE 16. WINE BIN FOR BASEMENT CELLAR
OR FRUIT ROOM

Height	6 feet
Width	5 feet
Depth	15 inches
Number of compartments	24
Height of compartments	Approx. 1 foot
Width of compartments	Approx. 1 foot 3 inches
Thickness of lumber	Sides, 2 inches
	Shelves, 1 inch
Total capacity of bin	More than 400 fifth-size bottles

storage bin in the lower part of a clothes closet. Two suggestions for such a closet bin are given in Figures 17 and 18. An important precaution to be taken is not to build the bin in a closet containing a radiator or heater. Neither should the closet be too near the heating apparatus in the room where it is located, rather on the opposite side. It is best to use the closet of the coolest room in the apartment and to keep the door shut as much as possible. If none is what might be called "ideal" from the standpoint of temperature, use any closet whose lower part can be spared.

In laying down the wine in the bin there is one *minor* detail to which it is worthwhile to call attention. It is advisable to put a thin strip of wood or of other material under the shoulders of the bottles in the bottom row, so as to give a slight tilt or slant to the whole pile. This strip must be thin, about one quarter of an inch thick. This procedure is especially recommended for red wines and for any wine which has been bottled early, that is, within a year's time from the crushing of the grapes. Red wines derive their color and heavier body from minute particles which will always tend to settle to the bottom of the container. The light slant given to the bottles in storage will cause any sediment to fall beyond the neck and into the belly of the bottle, thus permitting easy decanting (pouring the wine off its dregs) later when the wine is served. It is of the greatest importance that the elevation of the bottle shoulder be not so great as to keep the wine from remaining in constant contact with the stopper. If there is any difficulty in tilting the bottles as just described,

Height, floor to top of bin	4 feet
Depth	15 inches
Height of compartments	Top row, approx. 1 foot 6 inches
	Second & third rows, approx. 1 foot

Number of compartments and capacity of bin will depend upon size of closet and amount of space available

Thickness of lumber	1 inch

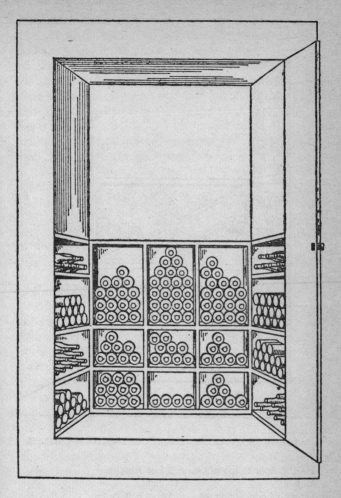

FIGURE 17. CLOSET WINE BIN
FOR APARTMENT DWELLER

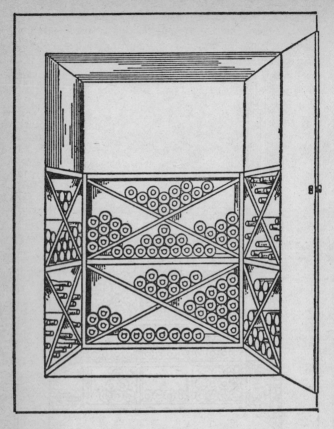

FIGURE 18. CLOSET WINE BIN FOR APARTMENT DWELLER

Height, floor to top of bin   3 feet 3 inches
Depth   15 inches
Height of compartments   1 foot 6 inches
Capacity of bin will depend upon amount of space available
Thickness of lumber   1 inch

it is infinitely better and safer just to leave them lying flat on their sides. Anyway, the above step is recommended only for wines that are going to lie in storage for a long time, several years. Wines that have been well made and properly racked, and which will be drunk by the end of two years, are not going to throw down much sediment.

7

sparkling wines

ALTHOUGH MOST Americans call any sparkling wine champagne, this term is defined by law in France to mean a wine made by a special process from the juice of certain grapes, and within a legally specified area of the country, part of what was formerly the province of Champagne. When produced outside of this district, even though the same grapes and the same methods be used, sparkling wines are called by other names. They are known geenrally as *vins mousseux* (sparkling wines). If he is a stickler for correct terminology, the amateur may keep this distinction. But since the word champagne has overtones possessed by no other wine name, it may be a special pleasure for him to make and serve an effervescent wine and call it "champagne." And he has the right to do so in this country, at least, where the term has acquired an elasticity it never knew abroad.

The rage for champagne which has developed in recent years may encourage the domestic winemaker to try his hand at making some. To manufacture champagne properly is an operation full of complications, hazardous as to result, and calling for much extra equipment. Regarding this last point, for example, it is necessary to have special laboratory testing apparatus, special bottles, special corks, special machines for inserting them, and special racks for holding the bottles after they have been filled. Even with all the obligatory equipment, the process is so beset with difficulties and so full of uncertainty and disappointment that the making of the real thing would more wisely be left to the commercial producer, whose product the home wine-maker can hardly hope to equal anyway.

But it often happens that the amateur, having had some success with still wines, will insist upon trying his hand at sparkling wines. Therefore, this book includes several recipes for making wines that sparkle. Among them are Apple Wines Nos. 3 and 4, Balm Wine, Cherry Wine No. 1, Cider Wine No. 5, Gooseberry Wine No. 7, and Grape Wines Nos. 16, 17, and 18.

Almost as old as the history of our country is a sparkling drink made in the following manner. A 50-gallon barrel is filled with fresh apple cider and in it are dissolved 40 pounds of sugar. From this a good bucketful, or even a little more, is drawn off to allow for an air cushion which will withstand the pressure of the carbonic acid gas thrown off during fermentation and prevent explosion of the container. The barrel is then bunged up tightly and set in a cool place in the cellar, where it is allowed to remain until the following spring, when it should be ready for drinking. It should be drawn off through the spigot, but only in the amount that will run freely. The bung should not be tampered with.

This is not champagne, it is not wine; but it will sparkle. And many "old timers" have been heard to speak reverently of this drink in hoarse and hollow voices.

Perhaps the domestic winemaker will wish to pass this up, since it is only cider, and not real hard cider at that. If so, let him wait until spring or early summer and use gooseberries (proportions and details will be found in the recipe section). When the scum has finished boiling off through the bunghole, enough must be drawn off to form an air cushion in the container. This is then bunged up tightly and left alone in a cool place until January. This very nice drink goes under the name of "British champagne."

Any wine can be made to sparkle if at the time of bottling a cube of sugar or a tablespoonful of sugar syrup is added when the bottle is corked. However, there are certain provisions which must be observed. The wine must be dry enough (with not more than 11 percent alcohol) so that it can ferment in the bottle after the sugar is added. It should be bottled before the cask fermentation is complete so that some yeast cells remain in the wine. The best time is after the first racking and before the second. Also, it is important that it be carefully and properly fined before going into the bottle and before it receives the sugar or sugar syrup; otherwise it will throw down so much sediment that it will be cloudy when opened. If a sparkling sweet wine is desired, more sugar (three cubes or three tablespoonfuls of sugar syrup) must be added at the time of bottling so that all the sweetness will not be used up in the fermenting. Also, it is a good idea to put in the bottle at the same time a little yeast starter.

If the sparkling wine is to be made from grapes, only certain varieties of native grapes should be used. For sparkling red wines the following are good varieties: Clinton, Eumelan, Isabella, and Ives. The juice of any or all of these will do. But it is always best to blend any one, or any mixture of them, with the juice of the Clinton, which is heavy in acid and improves a lot with aging. For the making of sparkling white wines, the Catawba should be considered the base. Delaware is also good, but is better if mixed with Catawba. Both of these are well endowed with acids. To offset their acidity, it is a good idea to blend the juice of these two grapes with that of any of the following, or with a mixture of their juices: Iona, Diana, Diamond, Elvira, Dutchess.

The blending of wines in making sparkling wine from grapes is a very important step. It is necessary to have a good acid base in the wine, and a laboratory would be necessary to determine just how much acid is in a given juice. But among the grapes given above, Clinton for the red, and Catawba for the white, will provide a good acid base. But one thing the laboratory cannot tell exactly is the precise proportions of each which must be included in the blending. In making sparkling wines, the blending takes place just before bottling. There is no formula for blending and no rules can be given. The winemaker mixes the wine to suit his taste, and then bottles. Only experience and a keen sense of the qualities of different wines, or mixtures of wines, can ever lead to the making of a superior sparkling wine at home.

In selecting grapes for making sparkling wine, only ripe fruit is acceptable. It must be picked over carefully and all culls as well as any green grapes hiding in the bunches thrown away. From here on the juice is treated as for still wines, except that special attention is given to the fining process, for the wine must be fined earlier, after the first racking instead of later. (In fining white wine do not forget to add tannin if the wine is fined with gelatin. See page 85). When the wine runs brilliantly clear after fining, it is ready for blending. As soon as this has been carried out, the wine goes at once into the bottle.

Now comes the step that gives sparkle to the wine. Into each bottle put a small cube of sugar (or a tablespoonful of simple sugar syrup) and a small pinch of yeast (or a tablespoonful of a fully active yeast starter). Cork tightly. If the wine has not yet achieved 12 percent of alcohol, the new action of the yeast on the sugar will produce the carbonic gas needed to make it sparkle.

If the winemaker does not wish to buy champagne bottles (and they are more expensive than the others), he may use any second-hand ones that he or his friends may have lying around, or he may use ordinary wine bottles. This "champagne" will not be so full of gas as the commercial product and consequently not so likely to blow up the bottles if they are kept in a cool place. Ordinary wine bottles would never hold regular champagne.

Since the wine is to continue fermenting in the bottles in order that the wine may sparkle, it is necessary to cork the bottles with the best corks available and to wire these in. When they are inserted, they should not be driven all the way in; a good third should be left above the bottle neck. (Figure 19, *A*.) The exposed part of the cork should now be hammered with a wooden (not iron) mallet or hammer until it is flattened or hammered into a mushroom shape. (Figure 19, *B*.) When the cork has been given its correct shape, it must be wired firmly onto the bottle. Metal disks and wires for attaching (called hoods) may be bought from some houses that supply winemaking aids (see Appendix III), but there is an easy home method of wiring on the corks: Purchase at the hardware store some fine pliable wire; cut four pieces of this about seven or eight inches long and fasten them to the bottle neck, as in *C* of Figure 19, twisting each wire with another so as to form four double strands. Then bring these four strands over the top of the bottle and twist them all together until they begin to cut into the edge of the cork. Clip off any sharp wire ends that protrude and then give them a few taps with the mallet so as to bend them down toward the cork. This tying with four strands of wire makes a secure hold for the corks. Two pieces of wire making only two double strands to cross over the cork might do just as well, provided the wires

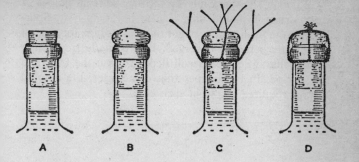

A   B   C   D

FIGURE 19. METHOD OF CORKING CHAMPAGNE BOTTLE

are twisted tight enough to assure that the cork has
no play in the bottle neck. (Figure 19, *D*.)

Wine that is made to sparkle requires cool storage.
It should be laid down in a part of the basement or
cellar where the temperature does not rise above 60
degrees Fahrenheit. If the temperature is around 75
degrees, the wine will not be damaged as long as the
bottles hold; but bottle breakage at this temperature is
likely to be very considerable. If regular champagne
bottles are used, loss from breakage will be much less,
if any, but ordinary wine bottles are not strong enough
to resist much internal pressure. However, if the wine
is made as described, and the bottles stored in a cool
place, there ought not to be great loss. Yet there is
always the danger of having the bottles explode while
they are being handled. In order to avoid the dangers
of flying glass, it is advisable to place around the bottle
a piece of blanket or other heavy cloth when handling.
When it is served later, the pressure of the gas is, of
course, reduced by chilling in an ice bucket or in the
refrigerator, but it is wise to follow the regular practice
of handling the chilled bottle with a large napkin folded
around it so that the warmth of the hand will not cause
the gas to expand and explode.

Whether the sparkling drink be made from grapes or from fruit, it should have age to be at its best. Sparkling wine from grapes ought to lie in storage for at least two years before it is served. If it is made from other fruits, the age it needs will depend upon the fruit and the recipe. In the recipes that come later, the amount of age required is told in each case.

8

fruit and other wines

WINES MADE from fruits other than grapes are known as false wines. In fact, there is great objection on the part of purists to calling any drink wine which has not been made from the juice of grapes. It is true that the dictionary defines wine in this way, as the "fermented juice of grapes," but it also adds that in a broader sense wine is the fermented juice of any fruit or plant used as a beverage. There is no need to quibble over the term, for fruit wines have a long and distinguished tradition in the United States and in England, and a long, if not so distinguished (because of malpractice) tradition in Germany and France, where it has often been attempted to pass them off as grape wines, especially in the export trade. Yet these two countries make sizable quantities of apple wine for home consumption. Spain and Spanish America produce a sparkling apple wine known as *sidra,* the Spanish term for cider. At one time raisin wine was widely made in France—when a disease swept the country's vineyards and there was a shortage of grapes. But this clinches nothing; it only shows that some fruit wines exist and have existed. What does clinch the argument in favor of such wines is that they are good, they are healthful, and they can be made where grapes are not available, for there is no place in either the United States or Canada or England, or, in fact, the Western world, where one cannot find some fruit, flower, vegetable, grain, or tree sap which is convertible into wine.

In England wine has for centuries been made in the home from the various fruits found in the garden and orchard, or in the countryside, such as apples, blackberries, coltsfoot blossoms, cowslip blossoms, currants, cherries, damsons, elderberries, elder blossoms, figs, gooseberries, raisins, and peaches. When the colonists came to America, they brought with them a fondness for these home-made wines and continued to manufacture them, handing down the recipes from generation to generation. New wines were added to the old, until today there is hardly a fruit or flower which somewhere is not turned into wine each year. Certain wines among these, such as dandelion wine, are almost a national institution. Likewise grains and vegetables have found their way into the fermenting vat to be bottled later as wine.

Many of these so-called false wines have their own characteristic qualities, qualities which have won for them a clientele and a demand, with the result that today many of them are made commercially and are found on the shelves of every well-supplied wine store. Among these wines bearing commercial labels are apple, apricot, blackberry, cherry, currant, damson, quince, and peach, to mention only a few. Others are made regionally where special fruits are grown in abundance.

The general procedure for the manufacture of fruit and vegetable wines is about the same as for grape wine. Most of the instructions for these wines which are found in cookbooks, old government brochures or reports, and in other literature, call for the manufacture of the wine in tubs, fruit jars, jugs, and other makeshift containers. The use of a fermenting vat (barrel or plastic trash can) and a cask (or carboy) is much simpler and gives less trouble, while good results are more certain. For this reason all the recipes for fruit and other wines given in this book rely upon these articles, and any variation from the earlier described procedure for making grape wine is described in sufficient detail.

Normally the fruit should be picked when ripe and all culls, decayed, green, or inferior fruit, discarded. Sometimes the fruit should be green or overripe. If this is the case, the proper instructions are given with each individual recipe. Also, any special attention required by a particular fruit or vegetable is explained. Otherwise, the making of the wine calls for the same proper care and cleanliness which is necessary in the manufacture of wine from grapes.

There is one general observation that ought to be made here, namely that most fruits, berries, and vegetables are heavy in acid content. Consequently, they all require the addition of rather substantial amounts of sugar, with the result that most of the wines made from them are sweet. But they are very good wines, usually marked by a characteristic flavor and bouquet.

Most of the non-grape wines need a certain amount of aging, some more and some less than wine made from grapes. For example, a wine made from pie cherries in the spring will be very palatable within a few months of bottling. But by the end of two years it acquires the smooth, full-bodied roundness of a wine of merit. Another fruit wine that matures beautifully, but more quickly, is black fig wine. It is a delicious dessert or tea-time wine, ready for drinking a month after it is put in the bottle. There are others. Let the home winemaker not hesitate to use whatever fruit he has at hand. If he practices care and cleanliness in the process, and follows the directions, his wine will almost certainly be good. It is true that with years and with experience he is going to learn to like some kinds better than others. But the individual must discover what his tastes and preferences are, and once these are known, he need never be without the wine of his choice.

The domestic winemaker will find it convenient to keep a supply of these fruit and vegetable wines in his bins, even if he specializes in grape wine. The sweeter ones make excellent dessert or tea-time wines, or are good for serving after the meal, or with or following the coffee. In hot weather they are nice chilled and drunk either by themselves or mixed with soda, and made into refreshing tall drinks. They will delight both the eye and the palate and find for themselves a thousand opportunities to help out in making the life of the home happier and fuller. And above all, they have the great virtue of being easily made at any time and anywhere, for there is no place in all the land where some or several of these wines may not be made.

A Word of Caution. Good wine can be made from most flowers. Nevertheless, there are certain blossoms that ought, perhaps, to be avoided—those whose pollens are toxic and from which a poisonous honey is made, such as mountain laurel, rhododendron, azalea, Carolina jessamine (jasmine), and others. It is not that the honey will kill immediately, but in large concentrations the pollen going into it can do so, and in lesser ones it can cause illness. Wine made from these flowers retains the pollens (although they do undergo a chemical change) and could possibly produce a reaction in persons with certain sensitivities. By the same token, vegetables with toxic concentrations, such as sunburned potatoes, ought either to be avoided or have the sunburned parts, which show up as green blotches, cut away. More information on this subject can be obtained from *Toxicants Occurring Naturally in Foods,* a report of the National Research Council of the National Academy of Sciences, published April 20, 1967. (The National Research Council's address is 2101 Constitution Avenue, N.W., Washington, D.C. 20037.)

9

diseases of wines and their treatment

WINES, like human beings, have their frailties and are subject to disease. This is true of both real and false wines. A beverage which on one day is the pride of its maker may on the next be cloudy, ropy, sour, or afflicted in still other ways. When this happens the creator becomes the doctor and tries to cure the patient (who, by the way, is very sick). If there is no response to treatment, only one thing remains to be done—destroy the wine and try to save the container.

The first step in dealing with diseases of wine is to employ every means to prevent them, a step which involves measures beginning when the grapes are picked and whose brief recapitulation is in place here. The grapes should be ripe and thoroughly sound. All culls should be removed. It is imperative that mildewed berries be carefully picked out and thrown away, for they often produce a special kind of sickness. The next important requirement is the thorough cleanliness of all apparatus, especially the containers used at different stages of the winemaking process, the fermenting vat, the cask, and the bottles. Thirdly, and this will cover up a multitude of other sins, every effort must be made to bring the alcoholic content of the wine up to a minimum of 11 percent. Wines with little alcohol, 8 percent or less, are infinitely more subject to disease than are those with the healthy percentage of eleven. Hence the amateur will do well to invest in a saccharometer (described in Chapter 2) and learn to use it. The instrument costs little and will provide wine with the nearest thing possible to insurance against sickness.

Acetic Fermentation. This is the most dread of all wine diseases to both amateur and professional. It is caused by an organism known as *Mycoderma aceti,* which lives in the air and which acts upon the alcohol in the wine to convert it into acetic acid, a pungent, colorless substance which is the chief ingredient of vinegar.

There is no really effective method for treating acetic fermentation. Wine that has once been "caught" by the acetic germ can never be absolutely whole again. Hence its real treatment is its prevention. Acetic acidity is usually due to insufficient alcoholic strength and to overcontact with the air, in which the acetic germ is constantly present. The first step in the battle against this peril is taken when the grape juice is being prepared for fermentation, and it is to see that the juice has enough sugar to produce the necessary 11 percent of alcohol. The next is to keep the temperature high enough during fermentation to permit this to be vigorous, for a slow fermentation often invites acetic acidity. On the other hand, the temperature must not be too high, never above 80 degrees Fahrenheit, for there are other germs which thrive best at a high temperature. As previously said, it should be kept more or less constant at between 60 and 75 degrees. During the secondary fermentation only a small air pocket may be left at the top of the cask. This will become a cushion of carbonic acid gas and, if the cask is properly sealed, will prevent entrance of air and its dangerous contact with wine. During racking and bottling, never allow the wine to remain for too long a time in contact with the air. Brief exposure of a few minutes, however, will not only not harm a healthy wine, but will even help to rid it of excess sugar by introducing new yeasts which may induce renewed fermentation after the various rackings.

If in spite of all the wine becomes acetic, there are certain expedients which may be employed, but their efficacy depends upon the degree of acidity and at best can only be considered temporary. If the wine, while in the process of fermentation, or just after, develops a barely recognizable acetic taste, throw into the container a small lump of unslaked lime (one and one-half square inch for every 10 gallons). An old-fashioned method was to throw into slightly sour wine a handful of unpolished marble chips (obtainable at marble or monument works). The efficacy of these is questionable, however, for they can give very little alkali to the wine. A third, and perhaps more effective, treatment is to use potassium bitartrate (do not confuse with potassium tartrate) in the proportion of 16 grams to every 10 gallons of wine. Dissolve first in a small quantity of wine and then stir into the batch which is being corrected. Within a week's time the wine may be corrected. This treatment may be repeated several times, if necessary, but if after the fourth or fifth dosage with potassium bitartrate there is no very marked improvement, the wine is too firmly caught by the vinegar germ and its loss will have to be accepted. (Potassium bitartrate is available at some drugstores only.)

Another method of treating slightly acetic wine is to rack it into a strongly sulfurated cask (see next chapter); fine with egg-white as per instructions already given in Chapter 5, and bottle as soon as it comes clear. Or, mix the sour wine with good, strong, new wine. A final treatment, but no cure, is to stir into a slightly acetic wine a good quantity of fresh lees from a new wine and bottle when clear.

Remember that none of the methods described is more than an expedient, and a temporary one at that. There is no cure for acetic acidity, even when it is only slight. Wine treated in any of these ways has very poor keeping qualities and should, therefore, be drunk as soon as possible. If a wine seems to be "cured," plan to have the batch of it drunk within six months' time, or even earlier.

Should the wine become too strongly acetic to be saved, there are but two possibilities—throw it away, or let it turn to vinegar. The second course is better, for wine vinegar is very good.

At any rate, the cask in which the wine has gone acetic is no longer of any use in making wines, though it may serve for making more vinegar.

Caskiness. Often a cask which is not thoroughly clean or which has not been used in a long time will impart a peculiar flavor, a "casky" flavor, to the wine. This is caused by the presence of an essential oil, and may sometimes be combated as follows: put in the keg of wine a small amount of olive oil, not more than ½ cupful to each 10 gallons, and agitate vigorously for some time. The olive oil unites with the essential oil and brings it to the surface, where it may be removed, or better yet, where the wine may be racked off from under it.

Another way to avoid "caskiness" is to use carboys, especially to be recommended if wine is made in small quantities. However, a cask that is kept thoroughly clean and is stored in a dry place during its periods of non-use will not develop "caskiness."

Cloudiness. Wine low in alcohol is often disturbed by albuminous matter which refuses to settle and remains suspended. This condition is called "cloudiness" and differs from the colloidal suspension previously referred to in that it cannot be cleared up by fining

alone. The treatment of wine for cloudiness is expensive
and the winemaker must decide for himself whether
any particular batch of wine is worth the expense and
the possibility of failure. After the cloudy wine is
racked into a freshly sulfurated cask, its alcoholic
content is raised by the addition of brandy, usually in
the ratio of 2 quarts to every 5 gallons. An individual
wine may call for more; there is no way of being
certain. After the brandy is thoroughly mixed in, the
whole should be fined. (See Chapter 5.) Some experienced home winemakers recommend the addition of
10 grains of tartaric acid to each 10 gallons of wine at
the end of a week after fining.

Flatness. Like cloudiness, which it often accompanies,
flatness is due to insufficient alcohol. To correct, use
the foregoing treatment for cloudiness. There are other
methods which are used in an effort to cure flatness.
One of them is to add new strong wine of the same
kind. The author's opinion is that this, rather than a
cure, is an efficient way to spoil good new wine. Or,
use one to two pounds of honey per 25 gallons of wine,
working it in well and allowing it to ferment anew.
Two pounds of chopped raisins and two quarts of
brandy may be substituted for the honey. Let stand for
from two weeks to a month. If the wine remains flat
but is sweet, add a cake of yeast and set in a warm
place. The new fermentation will convert some of the
sugar into alcohol. At any rate, the treated wine should
be drunk as soon as possible.

Flowers of Wine. This is a ferment which, if left
alone, will reduce the wine to carbonic acid gas and
water through oxidation of the alcohol. It is recognized
as small whitish particles, or "flowers," on the surface
of the wine. Unless attended to, these multiply rapidly
until the whole surface is covered by a thick bacterial
film. The cure for this disease is to get rid of the

flowers. This is done by the addition of the same kind of wine through a pipe or tube whose discharging end is placed well below the surface and held there until the cask is filled and all the scum has been forced out through the bunghole. Since these flowers develop only in the presence of air, it is important to see that the wine, once rid of the plague, should have no surface contact at all with air. Keep the cask or other container tightly bunged up or sealed.

Greenness. This is a defect which often develops in wine made from underripe fruit. The harsh and unpleasant taste is due to an excess of malic and tartaric acids. The condition may be partly overcome by neutralizing these acids through the addition of potassium tartrate (available in all drugstores) in the ratio of ½ ounce per 10 gallons of wine. This is for "average" greenness. The amount of potassium tartrate may have to be varied according to the judgment of the maker.

Mold. Sometimes overexposure to the air or storing in too warm a temperature causes the wine to develop a mold. Like most other diseases of wine, it is most likely to occur when there is a deficiency of alcohol. To treat, rack into a newly sulfurated cask and let stand awhile. The addition of a quart of brandy for every five gallons will help to strengthen the wine and improve its quality. Wine treated for mold does not have good keeping powers and should be consumed as soon as possible.

Scud. This is a mold that often attacks white wines which are alcoholically weak, and sometimes red wines deficient in the same respect. It is easily recognizable as tiny particles of matter which dart or scurry hither and yon at the slightest movement of the bottle. Wines afflicted with scud are uncurable and had better be poured down the drain pipe at the earliest moment.

Sourness. Sometimes wines have a harsh sourness that is not recognizable as acetic. An attempt can be made to correct this by stirring 10 grams of purified animal charcoal into every 10 gallons of wine. Let stand for three or four days and then rack into a fresh container. Another method is to put a few ounces (four or five) of leek seed into a cloth bag and suspend this in the wine for a week or ten days. If it is not corrected by this time, give it up as hopeless and drink the wine as it is or throw it away.

Ropiness or Viscidity. This is caused by a lack of astringent matter, notably tannic acid. To correct it in red wines add 3 ounces of bruised berries of the mountain ash (available at some drugstores) to every 10 gallons of wine. The same treatment may be given white wines but the addition of dry tannic acid is better—2 grams for every 10 gallons of wine. Dissolve the tannin in a cup or so of wine and stir in well. If berries of the mountain ash are used, the wine ought to be racked into a fresh container after three or four days. When tannin is added, wait a week or longer before racking.

10

care of the cask and carboy

ONE OF the most important practices in winemaking is that of cleanliness, cleanliness at all times. If the loss of a batch of wine from acetic fermentation or other disease is disappointing, the discovery of a taint in wine which would otherwise be excellent is only less aggravating. There are few things that more readily pick up foreign flavors than wine. It is sensitive in so many ways that the most careful attention must be given to every step of its manufacture. No single part of the apparatus can so easily impart a bad taste to wine as the cask. This demands the most scrupulous cleanliness. It is easy to ruin a cask. Yet its proper keeping is so simple a matter that there is no reason for the cask's being unfit to receive a new batch of wine at any time.

Type of Cask. This has been discussed to some extent in Chapter 2, but it will not hurt to repeat here that white oak makes the best casks for wine. Some winemakers prefer charred casks, which may be had for very little more than the others. The author does not, for the following reasons: it is more difficult to clean the irregular charred interior; bits of charred wood continually break off and plug the spigot or remain in the wine, and finally charred casks make no noticeable improvement in the finished wine.

For other reasons Coca-Cola and vanilla casks are undesirable, both of them because they impart a foreign flavor to the wine. In Coca-Cola casks this flavor is likely to stay for several years, even with yearly use. Vanilla casks sometimes clear up after a year or two. The Coca-Cola cask, furthermore, is of inferior wood and the loss of wine from evaporation is unduly high. Another reason for condemning both types of cask is that they are too small to be profitable in wine manufacture.

To Sulfurate a Cask. The first thing to do is to make a surfur wick or candle. (Or see under "Sulphur Strips," Appendix III.) Melt a quantity of sulfur over a slow fire. Do it outdoors, if possible, because of the extremely pungent fumes, and do not heat it too much, or the sulfur will burn. Now draw through the melted sulfur a strip of paper or cloth one inch wide and twelve or fifteen inches long, leaving four or five inches uncoated. The melted sulfur dries immediately in the air, crystallizing on the paper or cloth. Draw the strip through the liquid once or twice more, in order to get a good thick wick. It is ready for use immediately. Ignite and quickly insert in the cask. Drive the bung upon the uncoated end of the wick and leave it suspended while burning. Let stand for a day or so. The fumes of the burning sulfur sterilize the cask.

Usually, if the cask is a small one, it is best not to bung up tightly until the sulfur fumes have filled the interior of the cask, because small casks may not contain enough oxygen for the wick to burn long enough if they are stopped up too soon. On the other hand, a 50-gallon barrel does have enough oxygen for the burning wick to fill its interior with enough fumes to do the job of thorough sterilization.

As the sulfur burns in the cask, it falls to the lower side where it crystallizes again. Some winemakers claim they like to have their wines, especially the whites, stand on sulfur, and therefore leave these drippings in the cask. Others inveigh against this practice. It would not be fair to say to the amateur that he may do as he pleases, for it is a dangerous business to leave sulfur drippings in a cask of fermenting wine. During fermentation the yeasts may react upon them to produce hydrogen sulfide, the compound that gives rotten eggs their obnoxious odor. To protect the wine from this smell and its accompanying taste, it is necessary to prevent the sulfur drippings from falling into the cask and lodging on the lower side. Get a small tin cup about two inches high and one and one-half inch in diameter, just small enough to go through the bunghole of the cask. Or such a cup may be made by trimming it from any long round tin box that is not too wide, or from any of the several round boxes or containers with metal (tin) ends in which biscuit and other prepared small baked goods are sold in all chain groceries and supermarkets. In the sides of the cup make two small holes and through these run strings or fine wires. These should be long enough to permit the cup to be suspended below the burning wick. The strings, like the wick, rise through the bunghole and are held in place by driving in the bung. (See Figure 20.)

If in spite of all, the melted sulfur drips onto the interior of the cask, the winemaker who does not want to risk losing his wine (and it is a big risk) must open the cask by knocking off the end hoops and removing the head. The crystallized sulfur is chipped off with a chisel or a screwdriver or knocked off with a hammer. The head is then replaced and the cask is ready for use or for storage.

Wine casks that have been used should be sulfurated

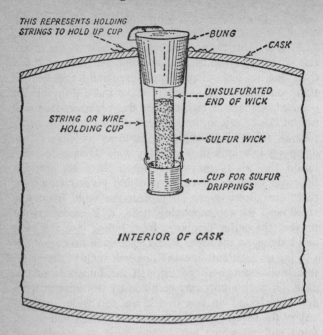

FIGURE 20. METHOD OF CATCHING DRIPPINGS
FROM SULFUR WICK

just as soon as they are dry, *as soon as possible,* to avoid having the cask ruined. If they have been out of use for a long time, they must be sulfurated before using again. Sulfuration serves as a sterilization process in both cases, killing molds and fungi that attach themselves to the wood of the cask and grow under circumstances propitious to each.

Cleaning the Cask. If the cask is brand new, fill it with cold water and let stand for a day.

A cask which has just been emptied of wine should be given several rinsings of cold water immediately. When the rinsing water runs clear, it is a good idea to empty a half pound of baking soda into the cask and then pour in a gallon or two, depending on the size of the cask, of boiling water. Bung up tightly and shake or roll back and forth vigorously. The pressure of the steam may blow out the bung when the cask is agitated. To correct this, bore a gimlet hole in the center, or use a large cork with a hole bored through it. Rinse out again and the cask will be sweet.

Now it must be allowed to dry thoroughly and then subjected to sulfuration at once. This is the best way to protect a cask from being attacked by molds while it is stored away. After sulfuration it should be opened to let the fumes out and then stored in a place which is dry. Do not store the cask in a damp place. It is better to put it in the attic than in the basement, for basements and cellars are likely to be humid unless a furnace or heater is going.

Never allow a cask to stand for any length of time with water in it. Water will putrify after a while, and this can foul a cask beyond recovery.

To clean a moldy cask, remove the head and fill with water into which several ounces of slaked lime have been stirred (two or three pounds if it is a 50-gallon barrel). Let stand for several days, then pour out the water and replace the head. Refill now with boiling water in which a good quantity of salt has been dissolved (five to ten pounds for the 50-gallon size). After two or three hours, empty again and rinse out with clear, cold water. Drain and after several days, when it is completely dry, sulfurate and bung up.

Another way is to burn out the inside of the cask with straw and then fill with strong lime-water. On the following day, empty and rinse out well with fresh cold water. Later sulfurate and bung up.

If the mustiness of a cask is only slight, it may be remedied by burning sulfur in the cask and driving in the bung while the sulfur is still burning, thus retaining the fumes. After a couple of days, remove the bung, rinse the cask in cold water. It is ready for use again. If it is to be stored, remove the stopper to let the fumes escape, bung up again, and store away in a dry place.

To Sweeten a Sour Cask. Put a few ounces of un- slaked lime into the cask and fill it with water. (For a 50-gallon barrel use a pound or more of unslaked lime.) Agitate thoroughly by rolling and shaking, and let stand for a few days. Rinse out, and then use the soda and boiling water treatment already described.

If the sourness is due to acetic acid, there is no way to save the cask for winemaking. Do not try it, for wine made in it will certainly be lost. It will do as a vinegar barrel, however.

Preparing a Stored Cask for Use. A cask that is to be used after having been stored for some time should always be tested for cleanliness and tightness. If the staves have shrunk or if leaks appear anywhere, the condition may easily be corrected by filling with water and allowing to stand for a few hours, or for a few days if necessary.

A cask that has been stored for any length of time must always be sulfurated before using again.

If there is the slightest sign of mustiness or sourness after storage, the treatments already described must be given. In any case, it is always advisable to rinse the inside of the cask with soda and boiling water, following this with a good douching of clear cold water.

A still better treatment, if there is any doubt as to the effectiveness of the baking soda method, is to fill the cask at least half full of water and drop into this a stick of caustic soda. Plug up and roll the cask around so that the contents may reach again and again every inch of the inside. This treatment will take care of any fungi or molds which have accumulated during storage. Afterwards, of course, the cask must be rinsed well with cold water.

Cleaning a Carboy. All the foregoing attentions required by the cask are cited by the devotees of the carboy as arguments in support of using large glass bottles instead of barrels of any size. And, indeed, the carboy, if not too large, is much easier to keep clean than a cask. Normally there is nothing to do after the wine has been drawn off but to rinse it out and store it away. However, it often happens that the wine deposits layers of tartaric acid (cream of tartar) on the bottom, on the sides, or just below the bottom of the neck. Because of the size of the bottle and because tartaric acid crystals are very hard, especially if neglected for a year or two, it is almost useless to try removing these deposits with a bottle brush of any kind. There are, however, other recourses already known in most homes. Drop a pound of BB shot carefully into the carboy and agitate vigorously against the stain or deposit. The lead shot are heavy, and that is their advantage. But they are also round, and that is their disadvantage. If they don't work, try several handfuls of fine gravel or coarse sand. If this doesn't clean the carboy, there isn't much that can be done except to continue to use it, stains and all. Since it is natural tartaric acid obtained from good grape juice, it will not hurt a new wine. But if the deposit is not liked by the winemaker, the best thing is not to allow it to form, that is, it should be prevented by cleaning the carboys with BB shot, with gravel, or with sand after every use.

Sulphiting. The interiors of casks and carboys which have just been emptied of their wine may be sterilized by sulphiting. However, this must not be taken as a substitution for killing fungi that have developed in a cask as a result of being stored in a damp place. (See pages 124–28.)

It is a good idea to sulphite before using any cask or carboy (and even bottles), no matter how well they have been stored. Especially is this a safe step if the amateur is working with the juice of superior grapes.

Sulphiting can be performed with potassium meta-bisulphite or sodium metabisulphite. To prepare a large quantity of sterilizing liquid, dissolve one pound of either of the above in 1 to 1½ gallons of water. This is the stock solution. To use, mix one part of the stock solution with nine parts of water (1 pint with 9 pints) and thoroughly rinse the inside of a cask or carboy with the diluted solution. When not in use, keep the stock solution plainly labeled and tightly stoppered.

Sodium metabisulphite for killing yeasts in wine, sometimes called Camden Tablets, can be purchased from accessory suppliers. (See Appendix III.) A bottle of 20 tablets should be enough for two to three gallons of rinsing solution.

11

blending and fortifying

THE BLENDING of wines is an art of august antiquity and great modern respectability. The purposes of blending are to raise the alcoholic content of a weak wine, to produce certain types of wine (e.g., Sherry, Sauternes), to increase the acid body of a wine deficient in this respect, to soften a wine that is harsh to the palate, to improve an old wine with new, thus giving it freshness and fruitiness, and to produce uniformity in an established type of wine. All these are the ends of commercial blending; some of them may be practiced by the home winemaker.

Blending. Blending is really an advanced stage of the winemaker's craft and can hardly be carried out properly by anyone who does not have long experience and training. In addition to a knowledge of the purposes of blending, the maker of wines must have a keen sense of smell and of taste. The beginner will find himself handicapped in all these respects, for his little experience will scarcely permit him to know what to do. Furthermore, he will have no laboratory in which to analyze his wines, to determine whether they are short in a given acid, or have too much of another. About the only attitude he can adopt is the very good one that blending is performed for the purpose of bettering wine. Within the limits of this general objective there are certain specific objectives he can try to work for: A weak wine can be made stronger (and healthier) by mixing it with one of high alcoholic content; a harsh new wine can be smoothed off by adding to it an old and well matured vintage; the color of a wine may be heightened by blending; acidity, if it is recognized by him, can be increased or decreased through mixing with another wine of appropriate contrasting qualities, and the vinosity of subnormal wines can be improved. These are limited objectives, to be sure; but more limited still are the blending skills of the beginner.

There are no hard-and-fast rules which can be passed on to the neophyte. There is one basic thing he should know, however, namely that wines to be blended should complement each other. Furthermore, that his tongue must be his guide if he is blending to improve the taste of the wine; if it is the bouquet he wishes to better, then his nose must tell him what and how much to do; and, finally, if the blending is performed to correct the color of a wine, it is his eye upon which he must rely.

Normally, blending should be carried out with wines of about the same age, except when it is desired to reduce the harshness of a young wine. In this case the proper thing to do is to add a fully aged wine from the same or a similar grape. Also, a wine that has overaged can be made more drinkable and fresh by adding to it a strong young wine of the same sort. Ordinarily, the blending of different and complementary wines should be performed after the first racking. (Sparkling wines, as has already been said, are blended just before they are bottled.) After the first racking the wine is not at the most palatable stage, although it *is* in a condition where it can be examined for color, acidity, alcoholic content, and rawness. But the future slow maturation in the cask, and later in the bottle, is required to do what cannot be done by mere mixing. If this were not so, blending could best be done after the wine was all made and bottled, or even when serving.

It is easy to see from what has just been said why experience is so necessary, for the blender ought, at the moment of blending, to have a pretty good notion of what each of the individual wines would be like if allowed to mature alone. It is this knowledge that comes from experience, and it is this knowledge that permits him to have a sensible understanding of what he is doing at the moment of blending and while the wines are still young.

To avoid the risk of accident with large quantities, blending should first be undertaken with small carefully measured portions. A measuring glass of the kitchen variety may be used for this and the mixing done in a bottle or other small container.

Finally, a red wine should not be blended with a white wine, a sweet wine must not be mixed with a dry wine, and above all, a sound one must never be added to one that is afflicted with acetic acidity. This would not improve the one wine and would certainly spoil the other. The mixing of a sound wine with one only slightly acetic, as described in Chapter 9, is not blending—this mixture must not be set aside for further maturing, but must be drunk as soon as possible.

After reading what has been said about blending, the home winemaker who is just beginning to work with grapes may well think that it is best to ferment one juice straight through into wine and not try to blend. This book would say yes to that, for blending wine is not for beginners and for only a few experienced winemakers.

Fortifying. The fortification of wine simply means the raising of the alcoholic content of naturally fermented wines to a percentage sufficiently high to stop fermentation and to prevent its occurring again. Most wines are fortified up to a minimum of 18 percent and a usual maximum of 26 percent of alcohol. For the commercial manufacturer of wine there exists a fortifying brandy of very high alcoholic strength and which is used in the process of fortification under the supervision of government agents who, for taxation purposes, keep a record of every step of the process.

The domestic winemaker does not have access to regular fortifying brandy. If he wishes to fortify any of his wine, he must use a brandy on which the tax has already been paid. Consequently this makes the fortification of large amounts of wine an expensive business. Most fortified wines are sweet or dessert wines, not table wines. The home winemaker should, therefore, never think of fortifying his dry or table wines, for this will waste good brandy and not improve wine which might otherwise be very good. Let him save his brandy for fortifying his sweet wines, especially those made from fruits, flowers, and vegetables. However, there is no reason at all why he should not make a fortified sweet wine from grapes, and any of those which produce good table wines will also produce good sweet wines. America has no native grape which will produce either a Sauternes, a Sherry, a Port, a Tokay, a Madeira, or a Muscatel. But the Eastern white grapes, such as Berckmans, Catawba, Delaware, Diana, Iona, Diamond, and Dutchess, can be turned into light dessert wines of good quality.

In commercial fortification it is customary to stop the fermentation of the must by adding the fortifying brandy when the alcoholic content has reached 6 or 7 percent. The domestic winemaker may imitate the commercial manufacturer in this if he wishes. The first step is to take a careful saccharometer reading of the sugar in the must and record it. The fermenting wine must now be carefully watched and daily saccharometer readings should be taken. When the alcoholic content has reached 6 or 7 percent, the fermentation may be checked and the wine fortified by the addition of brandy in sufficient quantity (explained below).

Another way, in working with native grapes, is to raise the sugar content to 30 or 36 percent, depending on the degree of sweetness desired, and allow the juice to ferment until it stops, at which time it should have 10 to 11 percent of alcohol. (But see page 262 under *Yeast Nutrients*.) Now treat the wine as explained in earlier chapters, but do not fortify until after the spring racking.

In the author's opinion it is best to save fortification for the fruit and vegetable wines. They will make very nice dessert wines when fortified, and their keeping qualities will be improved, for there will be much less danger of their being spoiled by repeated opening of the bottle or by being kept in a decanter.

In the section on recipes it is often suggested that brandy, or even whiskey, be added to a wine. This is not for purposes of fortification, but to improve the flavor and quality of the wine for which it is recommended.

If it is planned from the beginning to make a fortified wine, a record of the sugar concentration of the must should be kept. After fermentation has stopped, a second reading with the saccharometer will indicate the amount of sugar remaining, as well as the alcoholic strength of the wine (for two percent of sugar makes one percent of alcohol by volume). If the fruit or vegetable wines can be brought up to 10 percent alcohol by natural fermentation, it will be less expensive to fortify them up to 19 percent, which is a good goal for the home winemaker to aim at.

The amount of brandy to be added will depend upon three things, the alcoholic concentration of the wine, the amount of alcohol in the brandy, and the percent of alcohol desired in the finished product. In the following calculations it will be assumed that wine to be fortified has 10 percent of alcohol, that the brandy to be used is 100 proof, that is, that it has 50 percent of alcohol, and that it is desired to fortify the wine up to 19 percent alcohol.

There is a convenient formula which may be used by the domestic winemaker. The diagram of it given above is known as the Pearson Square. This is explained in Bulletin 651 published by the College of Agriculture of the University of California and entitled *Commercial Production of Dessert Wines,* by M. A. Joslyn and M. A. Amerine (September, 1941). It is reproduced in Figure 21.

The use of the formula diagramed here consists of five successive steps:

    1. Place in the upper left-hand corner of a rectangle the alcoholic strength of the brandy to be used in fortification. It has been assumed to be 50 percent.

    2. In the lower left-hand corner place the alcoholic

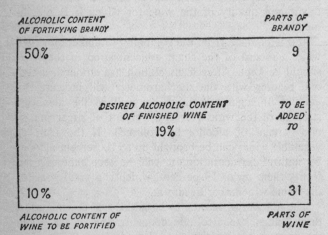

FIGURE 21. THE PEARSON SQUARE

strength of the wine which is to be fortified. It has been assumed to be 10 percent.

3. In the center of the rectangle place the desired alcoholic strength of the finished product. It has been assumed that this is to be 19 percent.

4. Now subtract the center figure from the figure in the upper left-hand corner, and place the remainder in the lower right-hand corner ($50 - 19 = 31$).

5. Subtract the figure in the lower left-hand corner from the figure in the center of the rectangle and place the remainder in the upper right-hand corner ($19 - 10 = 9$).

This last figure (9) is the number of parts of the specified brandy required to fortify 31 parts of wine of the indicated alcoholic strength up to 19 percent of alcohol. Or, more clearly: 9 gallons of brandy containing 50 percent of alcohol will fortify 31 gallons of 10-percent wine up to an alcoholic strength of 19 percent. After the brandy is added, the total amount will be 40 gallons of fortified wine with an alcoholic content of 19 percent.

In order to determine the amount of 50-percent brandy needed to fortify any given quantity of 10-percent wine up to an alcoholic strength of 19 percent, simply divide the total amount of wine to be fortified by the number in the lower right-hand corner of the rectangle (31) and multiply by the number in the upper right-hand corner (9). For example, suppose the winemaker wishes to fortify to indicated strength 10 gallons of sweet wine which has an alcoholic content of 10 percent by natural fermentation. First, divide 10 by 31 ($= 0.322$), then multiply the quotient by 9—($0.322 \times 9 = 2.898$). The result will be the number of gallons required; in this case, 2.898 gallons, or for operating purposes 2.9 gallons of brandy.

When the fortifying brandy is added, it should be well stirred in, for at least five minutes. The container, whether cask, carboy, or wine bottle, should be sealed up. However, if the fortified wine is put in a cask, it should be examined after a few days, for often there is shrinkage, not due to the loss of wine, but to the fact that the addition of brandy usually generates heat and expands the wine in its container. If the wine is to be left in the cask for aging, this should be filled to the bunghole again from a supply retained at the time of adding the brandy. In most cases it is likely that domestic fortification will take place shortly before bottling, in which event it is not necessary to try to retain a surplus. The wine in its new state needs age, how much it is not possible to say, for it will vary from wine to wine. But usually it will be from six months to a year at least. The maker can tell when the wine is ready for serving by opening a bottle from time to time. Age is necessary to produce a proper blending of the brandy with the wine to which it was added, for only time can make the mixture into a new wine.

12

serving wine

THERE ARE no secrets, no mysteries, in the judging of wine. The two tests to which all wine should be put are very simple. First, it should be pleasantly flavored, agreeable in taste, and perfectly clear. Second, it should provide the drinker with a gentle stimulation, it should agree with him, and should leave his head clear and without any unpleasant aftereffects.

Wines should be drunk under proper conditions in order to be appreciated. One of the most important of these conditions is the temperature at which wine is taken. The qualities of red wines are best brought out at one temperature, and those of white wines at another, while sparkling wines demand still a third. The various wines of the Continent—Claret, Chablis, Sauternes, Sherry, Champagne—require service at different degrees of warmth or coolness. The beginner need only know a simple scale.

Red Wines. Serve at or near room temperature; 65 to 70 degrees Fahrenheit is ideal; 80 degrees is the top limit. Normal cellar temperature will do unless the cellar is quite cool. If red wine is drunk chilled, one will not know why it is red.

Good red wine is best after it has stood open from a half hour to an hour before being served.

White Wines. White table wines are best when served at a temperature of from 45 to 50 degrees. They may be cooled in the refrigerator.

White dessert, or sweet, wines that have been fortified are better if not chilled. Most of them are good at 60 degrees.

Sparkling Wines. Serve cold, just above freezing, at 34 to 35 degrees. If they are dry, put on ice or in the refrigerator (near the freezing unit) an hour before serving; if sweet, they should be chilled for from two to three hours. Do not shake the bottle when putting in the cooler, and always wrap a napkin around the neck when handling or serving so that the warmth of the hand will not cause the carbonic acid gas inside the bottle to expand.

Wineglasses. Since good wine is a delight to the eye, as well as to the palate, it should always be served in plain, crystal-clear glasses. Wineglasses should never be tinted, for colored glasses deprive the wine of its true and natural beauty. Wine also shows off better if it is drunk from uncut glass, except a Port or Port type or a brown dessert wine, both of which will look well in cut glass (brown type: Black Fig wine).

For most of the wines in this book a three- or four-ounce glass will do. These can be found at many wine stores, at wine- and bar-supply houses, at most large department stores, at the mail-order houses, and at the five-and-ten-cent stores.

Sparkling wines show off best in tall champagne glasses, next best in the hollow-stem glass, and thirdly

1. DIFFERENT BOTTLES FOR DIFFERENT WINES. FROM LEFT TO RIGHT: RHINE WINE, CHAMPAGNE, BURGUNDY, CLARET, AND TWO WHITE WINE.

1. *Wine bottles*
2. *Basket press*
3. *Carboy or demijohn*
4. *Large crock*
5. *Saccharometer in jar*
6. *Cast-iron fruit press*
7. *Making measurements*
8. *Bottling the wine*
9. *Home-made water-seal*
10. *Wineglasses*

2. OPPOSITE. A SMALL BASKET PRESS IS EXCELLENT FOR CRUSHING GRAPES. IT IS AVAILABLE AT SOME HARDWARE AND FARMERS' SUPPLY STORES.

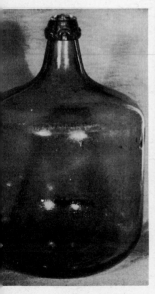

3. IT IS A GOOD IDEA TO HAVE SOME CARBOYS OR DEMIJOHNS AROUND. THEY ARE CONVENIENT FOR MAKING SMALL QUANTITIES OF WINE.

4. A LARGE CROCK OR STONE JAR MAKES AN EXCELLENT FERMENTING VAT. IT IS EASY TO KEEP CLEAN AND DOES NOT SHRINK WITH NON-USE.

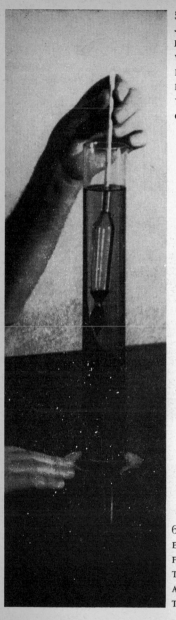

5. PLACE THE HYDROMETER JAR ON A LEVEL TABLE AND INSERT THE SACCHAROMETER. WHEN THIS HAS BECOME PERFECTLY STILL, TAKE THE READING AT THE SURFACE OF THE JUICE AND NOT AT TOP OF THE MENISCUS.

6. OPPOSITE. THOUGH MORE EXPENSIVE, THIS CAST-IRON FRUIT PRESS, WITH ITS TWO-TO-ONE GEAR RATIO, WILL DO A MORE EFFICIENT JOB THAN THE LITTLE BASKET PRESS.

7. ABOVE. ALL MEASUREMENTS SHOULD BE CAREFULLY MADE.
8. OPPOSITE, TOP. THERE ARE FEW TASKS MORE PLEASANT
THAN BOTTLING WINE. A GOOD WHITE OAK CASK IS THE BEST
CONTAINER FOR WINE DURING ITS SECONDARY FERMENTATION.
9. BELOW. A HOME-MADE WATER-SEAL GUARANTEES PROTEC-
TION FROM THE AIR.

10. WINE LOOKS AND TASTES
BETTER IN ITS APPROPRIATE
GLASS. FROM LEFT TO RIGHT:
TWO CHAMPAGNE GLASSES,
TWO FOR CLARET OR WHITE
WINES, THREE SHERRY
GLASSES, AND TWO CORDIAL
GLASSES WHICH ARE GOOD FOR
SERVING HEAVY SWEET WINES
WITH OR AFTER THE COFFEE.

Suggestions for Making Labels

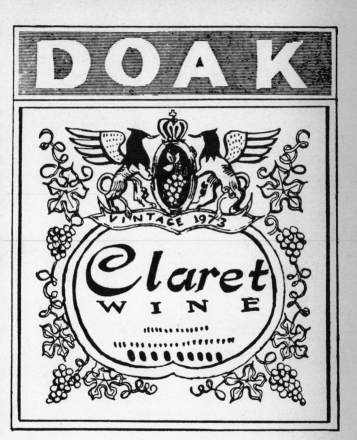

BLACK ★ STAR

TOMATO WINE

Superior Quality 1973

Product of Joseph E. Doak

JONES 1973 WINE

A product by Jim Jones & son
Vintners of the very best wines

FINE WINE

Smith's
Choice

PRODUCED BY
STEVEN S. SMITH & SONS

BLACK FIG

VERY
SPECIAL

PLUS

ULTRA

BOTTLED
1973

Joseph E. Doak

Smith's Wine Cellar Presents

WINE

produced and bottled, U.S.

CHATEAU DOAK

1973

PREMIER GRAND CRU CLASSÉ

Produced & Bottled at the Chateau

VINTAGE ❦ OF 1973

ISLE OF DREAMS
Dandelion Wine

Bottled by Jos. E. Doak, Keokuk, Iowa

one of the very finest domestic wines

JONES SPECIAL

produced and bottled by Jim Jones

VINTAGE 1973

Joseph E. Doak

GOOSEBERRY

Champagne

19 73

in the champagne saucer. A good substitute while waiting for tall champagne glasses is the tall, clear Pilsner glass.

Wine and Food. The combinations of wine and food are a complicated, if fascinating, ritual. It is enough here to indicate a few simple, but sound, rules for the serving of wine at the table.

Serve dry wines before sweet wines.

Serve white wines before red wines.

Serve a dry white wine with soups, fish, and other sea food, and with chicken.

Serve a dry red wine with red meat, such as beef and lamb, and with turkey and duck, wild fowl and game.

Serve either a dry red or dry white wine with pork or with veal. Pork, however, is not a good meat for wine. On the other hand, ham takes it very well, white or red, and preferably a dry sparkling wine.

Serve no wine with the salad, for the vinegar in the dressing is a most deadly enemy of everything good in wine.

With sweet desserts serve a sweet wine. Most fruits go well with wine and prefer to have it poured over them in generous quantities. Fruit in dry red wine, sweetened with plenty of sugar, is a treat of the first order. Fruit in white wine is not bad either, and most sweet wines help fruit to become an even better dessert than it is in its own right. Ices and cold cream desserts are best without wine. Sweet pastries go well with wines that are quite sweet. And any sweet fortified wine, sipped with the coffee, helps to end the meal with a grand flourish.

Opening the Bottle. Before wine can be served, it must be got out of its bottle. The opening of a wine bottle is not the same as the opening of a bottle of catsup—it is an important act, if not ceremony. If the cork end of the bottle has been sealed with wax or paraffin, this must first be broken. The bottle mouth is then wiped with a napkin to remove any particles of wax that may have remained on the cork.

The next step is drawing the cork. For this extremely important function the ordinary corkscrew of bent wire which comes in combination with can openers and other kitchen utensils will not serve. The diameter of its spiral is too great and the shape of its threads is wrong. The result is that it often destroys the cork

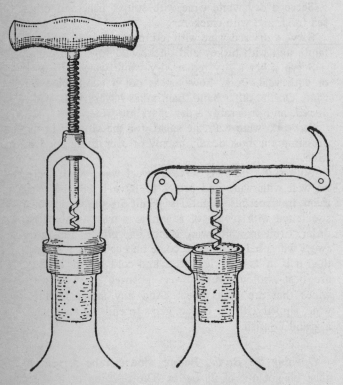

FIGURE 22. CORKSCREWS. LEFT: T-TYPE.
RIGHT: JACKKNIFE TYPE

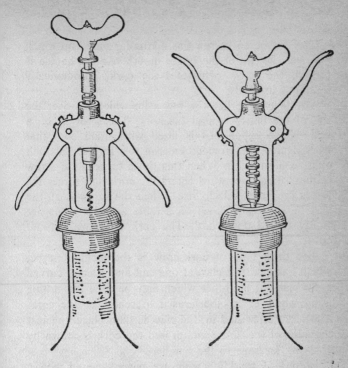

FIGURE 23. LEVER-TYPE CORKSCREW.
LEFT: INSERTING IN CORK.
RIGHT: FULLY INSERTED

without removing it, so that sometimes, if the wine is to be had at all, it is necessary to push what is left of the cork down into the bottle.

There are on the market three excellent types of corkscrews which have a narrower and flattened spiral, and which make the extraction of the cork a simple matter (see Figures 22 and 23). These vary in cost according to where they are bought, but they are usually available at from seventy-five cents to two dollars. Many hardware and department stores carry them.

They can always be had at wine- and bar-supply stores in any city.

The T-type corkscrew has a circular metal lip which fits over the rim of the bottle mouth. As the handle is turned, the screw penetrates the cork, automatically pulling it upwards.

The lever-type likewise has a lip which fits over the rim of the bottle around the cork. The screw is on a bolt whose upper part is fitted with small cogs that work against the crotched ends of two levers. This bolt ends in a wing tip. When this tip is turned, the screw in its motion downward enters the cork and forces the levers on either side to rise. When the screw is all the way in, the bottle is set on a table and the levers are gently forced downward. The cork is drawn without effort.

The third kind of corkscrew is the jackknife-type, which has a sort of claw at one end and a small curved knife blade at the other which may be used for cutting away whatever has been used to seal over the cork. The screw is twisted in; the claw is then placed against the edge of the bottle mouth and the cork is drawn by applying leverage to the handle.

Bottles of sparkling wine are never opened with a corkscrew. To open, remove the chilled bottle from the refrigerator or from its ice-bucket, wrap the body of the bottle with a folded napkin so the heat of the hand will not cause the gas in the wine to expand. Now cut or untwist and remove the wires tied over the cork. Then, *holding the bottle at an angle of forty-five degrees,* take hold of the mushroom-like cork head and twist it gently. If it is stubborn, give it a few pushes from two or three sides with the thumb to start it. Twist once more and keep twisting gently until the cork comes quietly out of the bottle. Don't straighten the bottle immediately, but hold it at the forty-five degree angle for two or three seconds. It is this angle and the gentleness of handling that prevent the wine from foaming out of the bottle and going to waste.

Pouring the Wine. When the cork of any wine bottle has been drawn, the bottle mouth is wiped again, and the wine is poured. The host politely serves himself a few drops first, as a token of his willingness to receive any bits of cork that may be in the bottle neck. Then he serves around the table from his right, ladies first, and always pouring from the guest's right. After the guests have been served, he may now give himself the rest of his share. It is customary in serving table wines to fill the glasses one-half or two-thirds full. This permits the wine's bouquet to be enjoyed better. In serving sparkling wines the glasses may be filled to within a fraction of an inch of the top.

SOME WAYS TO SERVE WINE

Mulled Wine

1 bottle dry red wine	10 cloves
¼ cup sugar	lemon peel
1 stick cinnamon	slice of orange

Put wine in a pan with sugar and spices. Stir until sugar is dissolved. Add piece of lemon peel size of thumbnail and bring just to a boil. Remove quickly and pour in preheated cups, in each of which a slice of orange has been placed. Stir with a spoon and touch with a lighted match. Serve.

This can also be made with dry white wine or with sweet wine.

Wine and Soda

½ tall glass wine	ice cubes
(red or white)	club soda

Mix together and serve. May be sweetened if desired.

Wine Collins (or Lemonade)

½ tall glass wine   ice cubes
  (red or white)   club soda
juice ½ lemon

Sweeten to taste with sugar and stir well. Serve.

Wine Cooler

2 oz. wine (red or white)   club soda
1 slice orange   ice cubes
twist lemon peel

Put wine in glass with orange. Give lemon peel a twist and drop it in. Add 2 lumps of ice, pour in soda, stir and serve. Serves one.

Wine Daisy

⅓ tall glass fortified   1 tsp. grenadine
  white wine   cracked ice
1 jigger orange juice   club soda
2 jiggers lemon juice

Fill glass half full of cracked ice, put in the ingredients and serve. Enough for one person.

Wine Float

red wine   mint
lemonade

Hold a spoon just under the surface in a tall glass of ice-cold lemonade and pour in enough red wine to color the top of the lemonade for an inch or so in depth. Dress with mint spray and serve.

Wine Frappé

1 cup white wine   2 tbs. lemon juice
  (fortified)   sugar to taste
1 cup orange juice   ice

Mix all together and stir until sugar is dissolved.
Serve in tall glasses filled with cracked ice.

Wine Flip

1 glass wine (fortified, red or white)
1 egg

1 tsp. sugar
nutmeg

Beat egg slightly and add sugar. Put in shaker with
glass of wine and shake. Sprinkle with nutmeg and
serve.

Wine Cobbler

Sweeten to taste any dry wine and serve in a glass
filled with cracked ice. Decorate with fruits: orange,
pineapple, maraschino cherries, strawberries, or any
fruit in season.

This can be made, also, with any sweet wine.

Cherry Cup

2 bottles cherry wine
½ cup cherry brandy
1 qt. club soda
8 maraschino cherries

2 oranges, sliced
2 lemons, sliced
sugar to taste

Pour wine, brandy, and soda in a punch bowl containing a large piece of ice. Add sugar and fruit, and stir
until sugar is dissolved. Will serve a dozen.

Ginger Punch

1 bottle ginger wine
2 bottles ginger ale
1 cup brandy (or rum)
1 oz. lemon juice

2 oz. maraschino
2 slices pineapple
4 slices orange
sugar

Pour wine and ginger ale into a punch bowl containing large piece of ice. Add brandy, maraschino and
fruit. Sweeten to taste and serve. Will serve about
twelve people.

Gooseberry Punch

2 bottles sparkling
    gooseberry wine
1 bottle club soda
4 oz. brandy

2 oz. maraschino
1 lb. sugar
ice

Mix in a punch bowl. Sweeten to taste with sugar, and add any fruits in season. Will serve about twelve.

Sparkling Wine Cocktail

1 cube sugar
dash Angostura bitters

twist lemon peel
sparkling wine

Douse the cube of sugar with bitters. Drop in a twist of lemon peel, fill to top with sparkling wine and serve.

Onion Soup

3 medium onions
1 cup dry wine
    (red or white)

1 tbs. flour
1 qt. bouillon
Parmesan cheese

Chop onions fine and brown in a pan under a little water to keep them from burning. When they are a nice brown, add flour and stir gently until this is brown. Pour in the bouillon and add the wine. Bring all to boiling point, then simmer gently 15 to 20 minutes. Serve in individual casseroles or soup dishes. Top each dish with croutons or two-inch squares of toast. Cover all with grated Parmesan cheese.

Black Bean Soup

Excellent black bean soup is available in cans at any market. When preparing for the home, improve the soup by adding ¼ cup of dry wine to each can of soup. It is better if the wine is fortified.

Baked Fish in White Wine

1 lb. fish (filets or slices)	green peppers
1 medium onion	2 tbs. butter
¾ cup dry wine	1 tbs. Worcestershire sauce
(red or white)	salt and pepper to taste
tomatoes	

Salt and pepper fish and put in pan. Slice onion and cover fish with slices. Pour wine over fish and onions and let stand for 30 minutes. Remove fish and onions and put in baking pan containing melted butter. Place on top of fish 4 or 5 slices of tomato and the same number of slices of green pepper. Bake until done, basting frequently with the wine in which fish was soaked.

Kidneys in Wine

6 lamb or 4 veal kidneys	1 bay leaf
2 tbs. butter	1 tsp. flour
pepper and salt to taste	½ cup dry white wine

Drop kidneys in boiling water. Take out immediately and remove skins, then soak for 30 minutes in cold salt water. Drain, dry, and slice, removing tubes and tissues. Melt butter in iron skillet and, when hot, add sliced kidneys. Salt and pepper to taste and sprinkle with flour. Drop in a bay leaf and cook over a hot fire for 5 minutes, stirring continually. Now pour in wine and cook until sauce or gravy has thickened.

Beef Stew with Wine

½ cup red wine (dry)	½ cup oil (or lard)
1 lb. beef	2 tbs. flour
1 cup chopped onions	garlic to taste
1 cup tomato sauce	salt and pepper to taste
bay leaf, thyme, cloves,	
marjoram	

Cut beef in small squares and brown in oil in iron

skillet. Add onions and amount of garlic desired. Sprinkle in flour while stirring. When brown, add tomato sauce, salt and pepper, and the wine. Place herbs in a little cloth bag and let them hang in the stew while it cooks. When done, serve with red dry wine as the beverage.

Baked Ham with Wine

1 ham (10 to 12 pounds)	15 or 16 apricot halves,
½ cup brown sugar	stemmed
2 tsp. dry mustard	cloves
	wine

Prepare a ham for baking, or select one ready for the oven, remove the rind and rub surface with a mixture of brown sugar and mustard. Cover top of ham with the apricot halves held in place by long-stemmed cloves (use as many as necessary). Bake uncovered at 400° F., basting frequently with wine (red or white).

Veal Wine Casserole

2 lbs. veal	½ cup white wine (dry)
½ tsp. sugar	rind ¼ lemon (grated)
¼ cup chopped onion	salt and pepper to taste
1½ tbs. butter	⅓ cup unskimmed milk
1 qt. boiling water	1½ tbs. flour

Cut veal into pieces suitable for serving. Melt sugar in a pan and add onion, stirring until this is coated and brown. Now put in the veal, moving it about for a couple of minutes, then add boiling water and grated lemon rind. Bring to a good boil, cover and let simmer until nearly done. Add salt and pepper. Have butter and flour creamed together and ready to add at this time. Stir for a few minutes, then add wine and milk. Stir briefly once more, cover and simmer for another half hour before serving.

Liver and Onions with Wine

1 lb. liver	cooking oil or fat
½ cup red wine	salt and pepper to taste
4 medium onions, sliced	flour

Slice liver, place in a dish and pour the wine over it. Put in refrigerator and let stand for an hour or two, turning slices now and then so wine will reach all sides equally. Half an hour before serving, brown the onions in some fat in a skillet. Remove from skillet and keep warm. Add more fat to skillet. Drain and dry liver. Salt and pepper to taste and dredge in flour. Cook in skillet. Serve with the fried onions.

Wine Sauce

½ cup butter	1 tsp. grated orange and
⅓ cup fortified wine	lemon peel

Put ingredients together in a pan and heat. Just before boiling point is reached, remove from flame. Serve hot.

Dandelion Custard

Make a soft sweet custard, flavored to taste with dandelion wine. Serve cold with fresh fruits or jellies, with a small glass of sweet dandelion wine on the side.

Fruit in Wine

Slice several fruits together (bananas, grapes, peaches, apricots, pineapple, etc.). Place them in individual sauce dishes and cover with 1 or 2 heaping tsp. of sugar. Pour on dry wine, red or white, until the fruit is nearly submerged. (Sweet wines can be used, but dry wines give the dessert a fillip.)

Blackberries in Wine

Put fresh blackberries in individual sauce dishes,

sprinkle with sugar, then drown them with blackberry wine. Since blackberry wine is usually sweet, not so much sugar is needed as in the previous recipe.

Cherries in Wine

Pit 1 qt. of ripe sweet cherries. Place in a saucepan and cover with red wine (grape or cherry). Sweeten to taste, but do not overdo this. Add 1 tbs. red currant jelly, 8 or 10 cloves and a stick of cinnamon. Boil ever so gently for ten or fifteen minutes and remove from flame. Pour juice and strain in order to clear of spices. Place cherries in another dish. Return juice to pan and simmer for another 15 or 20 minutes. Remove from fire and pour over cherries. Let cool and then put in refrigerator. Serve chilled (very cold) with whipped cream into which some cherry brandy has been stirred. These are delicious alone or with ice cream.

Strawberry Ginger

Wash and stem berries and cut in two. Sprinkle rather heavily with sugar and put in refrigerator to cool slightly. Serve in individual sauce dishes with 3 or 4 tbs. of ginger wine poured over the berries.

Home Winemaker's Café Diable

6 sugar tablets	¼ cup black fig wine
1 spiral lemon peel	(fortified)
8 or 10 cloves	¼ cup brandy
1 stick cinnamon	4 cups strong coffee
2 tbs. grated orange peel	

Put sugar, lemons, spices, and grated orange peel in a pre-warmed bowl and add the wine and brandy. While stirring, pour into it coffee, which should be boiling hot and strong. Touch a lighted match to it while stirring and learn why it is called *Café Diable*. This makes eight to ten demitasse servings.

Wine Serving Chart I

Except for dessert and for after-dinner drinking, all wines should be dry unless otherwise indicated. The home winemaker should take this into account when making his wines. By judicious planning and a wise use of the saccharometer he can assure himself a varied supply of dry wines. Number refers to the wine recipes in the section *220 wines*.

Appetizers, olives, salami, smoked salmon, etc.	Cocktail, dry grape or cherry wine, apricot (6), choke-cherry
Oysters, shrimp, lobster, seafood not highly seasoned	Grape (12, or 13 if made dry), cider (2), apricot (5)
Soups, fish	Same as for above
Beef, lamb, turkey, duck, and all game	Cranberry, dry cherry, choke-cherry, or any dry red wine from grapes
Chicken	Grape (12, 15), apple (3), apricot (5)
Pork	No wine
Ham	Apple (3), grape (15), or any light dry red wine
Veal	Cider (2), apricot (5), grape (12, 13)
Salad	No wine
Cheese	Any dry wine, red or white
Desserts: Heavy pastries	Fig (3), blackberry (2, 4), elderberry (3), caraway, date (2), grape (5, 7)
Desserts: Light pastries	Raspberry (3), strawberry (3), peach (2, 3), or any light sweet wine

Desserts: Fruits	Any good wine poured over the fruit in quantity. If wine is dry, add sugar.
Desserts: Ice creams, sherbets, mousses, etc.	No wine
Coffee	Fig (3), caraway, elderberry (3), date (2), grape (5, 7)
After the meal	Mint, mulberry (3), or any flavorful heavy sweet wine

Wine Serving Chart II

If only one wine is served.	Begin serving with the soup or fish if the wine is white. If it is red, begin with the meat.
If two wines are served.	A dry wine always comes before a sweet one. If both are dry, serve the white wine first.
If three wines are served.	Dry white before red before sparkling Dry white before red before sweet white Dry white before red before sweet red
For buffet or cold suppers, or for picnics.	If only one wine is to be served, choose one that corresponds to the main dish. (See Wine Serving Chart I) If more than one wine is served, follow rules given above.

points to remember

THE DETAILS listed below emphasize important observations made earlier in the book, and supply additional bits of information which will be of help to the winemaker.

The proportions of ingredients in the wines described in the following recipes are always given with reference to specified weights or measurements. These may be reduced or increased if lesser or larger quantities of wine are desired.

Most of the following recipes produce sweet wines. Satisfactory dry wines cannot be made from the majority of fruits and vegetables. Where dry wines are indicated, the saccharometer should be used to obtain accurate readings of sugar in the liquid being fermented (see Chapter 4). Test only clear and strained liquids.

The cask or carboy in which the wine is put to ferment should be kept filled to the very top of the opening during the "boiling over" period, and then reduced as described below before it is water-sealed.

To keep a cask or carboy filled as the scum "boils over," add wine from a surplus retained for that purpose. Always make a gallon or two extra of wine. This may be safely kept in 1-gallon jugs and used as needed.

The cask is the container referred to in all the recipes, but the carboy may always be substituted for it.

The bottom of the water-seal must not be allowed to touch the surface of the fermenting liquid. Before sealing, lower the wine in the cask or carboy until its surface is one and one-half or two inches below the bunghole or the bottom of the bottle neck, respectively. The wine thus drawn off may be stored in jugs or small bottles for future use in filling the cask or carboy when the water-seal is removed.

Whenever the wine has to stand in the cask or container for any length of time after all fermentation has stopped, it is advisable to remove the water-seal and bung or cork up tightly. But before doing this, the container must be filled to the opening with some of the surplus wine mentioned above. The reason for removing the water-seal is that the water evaporates, and since its function is to let out gas and keep out air during fermentation, the solid bung or cork is less bother after fermentation has ended.

Hot paraffin or melted candle wax should be spread over all junctures when the wine is water-sealed or bunged up. This guarantees protection from air. Do not forget that air can spoil any wine.

When sugar is added, it must be stirred in thoroughly, that is, it should be stirred for about 10 or 12 minutes. A good method is to withdraw a quantity of wine and dissolve the sugar in this, and then return the whole to the wine and stir briefly. Remember that undissolved sugar will not ferment.

Water which is boiled with sugar or honey demands frequent skimming.

Boiling water for any length of time reduces its amount. Therefore more must be added to make up for that which is lost, otherwise the recipe may fail to produce its quota of finished wine.

Soft water or spring water is always to be preferred to hard water. However, the latter can always be improved by boiling for 30 or 40 minutes. Never use commercial softeners for water that is to be used in making wine.

Fermentation is often best started in fruit and vegetable wines by the addition of yeast. Some of the wines made from berries and apples, as well as a few other fruits, will ferment well without help; others will not ferment without a starter. If yeast is needed, it is so indicated in the recipe.

A liquid once "caught" by yeasts will usually ferment itself out. But sometimes the yeasts become inactive. It is necessary then to start it again by the addition of more yeast or a nutrient.

A good rule of thumb in trying to ferment heavy wines with large quantities of sugar is to allow 1 cake of compressed yeast for every 5 gallons of wine.

To add yeast, lay it on top of the wine or dissolve it in a cupful of wine or warm water and then stir it in. Always use this second method if fermentation is started in a cask with yeast. Never add yeast to hot liquids; always allow them to cool off until they are lukewarm.

Fining is often a very important step in the making of fruit and vegetable wines. Before trying to fine any wine, read Chapter 5, which describes fining in detail. What is said there applies to all the following wines, except that it is necessary to add tannin only when instructed to do so.

Skimmed milk is good for fining red wines. Use 1 cupful of milk for each 5 gallons of wine, stirring it in thoroughly.

Gelatin is better for fining white wines. It should be pure leaf gelatin and should be used in the ratio of 3 grams for every 5 gallons of wine to be fined. It is first dissolved in a quart of wine, or a cup of water, by allowing it to stand overnight. On the following day stir it in thoroughly, that is, for about 10 minutes.

Blossoms used in making wine should always be picked when they are dry. Dew or rain on them deprives them of their essential oils which are an important factor in making wine from them.

Brown sugar wines usually require more aging than those made from white sugar.

Bottling should never take place before the wine has come brilliantly clear. If it is not clear, the wine may have to be fined again.

Sweet wines, unless they are several years old and have all the fermentation they can possibly get, should be stored in a cool place. Otherwise, yeasts remaining in the wine may become active again. Dry wines like a cool place too, but do not need it so much as sweet wines.

The addition of brandy may be considered optional in all the recipes which call for it. It will, however, improve those wines to which it is added.

All measurements in grains and grams, and even in ounces, should be made by the druggist, unless the home is provided with delicate scales.

No two of the following wines are alike, even when made from the same fruit. Each one has its own distinguishing character—more body, more alcohol, more fruitiness, more acid—or it will differ from very similar wines in some other way. Any of them can be made with the assurance that they will be sound and healthful beverages, and some will become favorites, occupying permanent places in the home winemaker's cellar.

Although the term *cask* is used in the following recipes, the reader should understand that he may substitute a carboy or a large glass bottle.

Apple Wine 1

In this and the following recipes for Apple Wine, do not use a juice to which a preservative has been added.

Apples   Yeast
Sugar   Gelatin

Press a quantity of sound ripe apples. Let the juice stand for an hour or so, and then strain through cheesecloth. Now add 2 lbs. of sugar to every gal. and boil. Skim until scum no longer rises to surface, then remove from fire. When lukewarm, pour into cask, start fermentation with yeast, and water-seal after 3 or 4 days. When fermentation has stopped, mix in well a small amount of leaf gelatin (2½ gm. per 5 gals. of wine) dissolved in a portion of the liquid, fill up cask and bung up tightly. Bottle when wine comes brilliantly clear. It may be drunk at any time.

Apple Wine 2

Apples	Brandy
Sugar	Yeast
Cream of tartar	Gelatin

Use the juice from sound, ripe apples. To each gal. add 2 lbs. of sugar and start fermentation in a vat with yeast. Turn into a clean cask after two days. Now stir in ½ oz. cream of tartar for every 5 gals. of wine and water-seal. When fermentation has stopped, add 1 qt. brandy and bung up tightly. Bottle when fine. Serve when desired.

Apple Wine 3 (Sparkling)

Apples	Brandy
Sugar	Yeast

Press enough apples of good quality to give 10 gals. of juice. Let stand for 2 or 3 hours, then strain through cheesecloth. Add 3 lbs. of sugar and 2 qts. of brandy. Start fermentation in a vat with yeast. On the following day put in cask and let stand for 2 weeks. Do not seal, but keep filled to top for a while so that all impurities will work out. At end of this time mix in 1 pt. of skimmed milk, seal and let stand again. The wine will fine shortly and should be bottled at once. Kept until winter before serving, this wine should sparkle well when opened.

Apple and Plum Wine (Sparkling)

Apples	Sugar
Plums	

The apples for this wine should be of good quality, not overripe or decayed, and preferably peeled and cored.

Weigh apples before pressing out juice. Add to the fresh cider the juice of large yellow or reddish plums.

The amount of plums used should be one-fourth by weight of the apples. Dissolve in the liquor 2½ lbs. of sugar for every gal. and ferment in a cask, keeping this filled from a surplus retained for that purpose. Bottle the liquor before fermentation has completely subsided in order to retain some of the carbonic acid gas. This wine will sparkle when served.

Apricot Wine 1

   Apricots   Sugar
   Water

Use only ripe apricots and do not remove pits. For every 12 lbs. of fruit use 2 gals. of water. Boil together until fruit is well cooked, then let simmer. After 15 minutes strain off liquor and add to each gal. 1½ lbs. of sugar. Boil again, skimming until no more scum rises to surface, and pour into the vat. On following day it may be bottled if clear; if not, let stand another day. If there is considerable sediment, siphon off carefully into another receptacle. Add 1 lump of sugar to each bottle and keep in a cool place for 6 months before serving.

Vary the above by removing the stones and cutting the fruit into pieces. From half the stones take out the kernels and return to the mixture to be boiled. Proceed with recipe as given.

This makes a very fruity and almost non-alcoholic beverage.

Apricot Wine 2

   Apricots   Sugar
   Water

Select ripe, but not overripe, fruit. Remove the stones, put in a vat and crush well. The mashed fruit must now be measured. To every 8 lbs. of pulp add 1 qt. of water, stir well, and let stand for 24 hours. Now press out through a cloth bag and dissolve 2 lbs. of sugar in each gal. of juice. Start fermentation with yeast in an open vat. When wine is more or less quiet, skim off and pour into cask. Water-seal and let stand until perfectly fine, when it is ready for bottling.

Apricot Wine 3

Apricots	Sugar
Water	

Prepare a syrup by boiling 4 lbs. of sugar in 4 qts. of water, skimming as necessary. Place in this 8 lbs. of apricots which have been peeled and stoned. Continue boiling until fruit is soft. Remove fruit from liquid, strain this carefully and bottle when cool. This, of course, is non-alcoholic. If left exposed to the air for 3 or 4 days before bottling, it will develop a very slight tang. Or the recipe may be varied as follows: Instead of removing fruit, mash it well and pour the whole into a vat. Start fermentation with yeast. After three days press out liquid and strain. Turn it into a cask to continue fermentation, keeping the container filled to the bunghole. When scum no longer rises through opening, lower slightly and water-seal. This is a good wine and will be ready for bottling in about 3 months' time.

Apricot Wine 4

Dried apricots	Cream of tartar
Raisins	Brandy
Water	Yeast
Sugar	

Run through a meat grinder 8 lbs. of dried apricots and 3 lbs. of seeded raisins. Place in the vat containing 8 gals. of warm water and stir in 15 lbs. of sugar. Add 1 oz. cream of tartar and start fermentation with yeast. When fermentation has subsided, strain off and put in a clean cask. Water-seal and when wine has become absolutely quiet, add 1 qt. of brandy and bung up tightly. It may be bottled as soon as it comes perfectly fine.

Apricot Wine 5

Dried apricots	Sugar
Raisins	Cream of tartar
Water	Yeast

Run through a meat grinder 5 lbs. of dried apricots and 2 lbs. of seeded raisins. Put in the vat and add 10 lbs. of sugar and ½ oz. of cream of tartar. Pour over the whole 6 gals. of water and stir well until all sugar is dissolved and the fruit thoroughly mixed in with the liquid. Start fermentation with yeast and let stand for 7 or 8 days, stirring at least once every day, then strain off and pour in a clean cask. Water-seal and leave for 6 weeks, when it should be racked into a fresh container, filling to the bunghole. Now bung up tightly and allow to stand for another 3 months. If wholly fine at the end of this time it may be bottled. The wine is ready for serving after it has lain for 2 months in the bottle.

To make this wine extra sweet, add 15 lbs. of sugar instead of 10, and add an extra cake of yeast when fermenting.

Apricot Wine 6

Apricots (fresh)	Sugar
Water	

Use 12 lbs. of ripe apricots. Remove the stones and cut the fruit in pieces. Crack open half a dozen pits and put the kernels from these into the prepared fruit. Now add 2 gals. of water and boil until the fruit is well cooked, then let simmer for 15 minutes more. Strain off liquid and add to each gal. 1½ lbs. of sugar. Return to stove and boil again, skimming until scum no longer rises to surface, then pour into a vat. Let stand for a day so that sediment may fall. Siphon off into a clean receptacle and ferment with yeast. When violent activity has subsided, turn into cask and water-seal. As soon as the wine comes brilliantly fine, it is ready for bottling and drinking.

Balm Wine

Balm	Sugar
Water	Yeast

Boil together for 1½ hours 5 gals. of water and 20 lbs. of sugar. Skim frequently and add water at intervals to keep up to original amount. When water has cooled to lukewarmness, pour it over ½ lb. of freshly picked and gently bruised balm tops. Start fermentation with yeast in the vat. After 2 days pour all into a cask and water-seal. The wine should come fine in about 2 months. A lump of sugar placed in each bottle will make the wine sparkle when served 4 months later.

Barley Wine

Follow recipe for Wheat Wine.

Beet Wine 1

Beets	Cream of tartar
Water	Yeast
Sugar	

Clean thoroughly 4 lbs. of beets, being careful not to scrape off the skin. Slice or cube them and boil gently in 1 gal. of water until soft. Pour off liquid carefully and strain. When lukewarm add 3 lbs. of sugar and ¼ oz. of cream of tartar (use 1¼ oz. of cream of tartar for every 5 gals.). Dissolve a cake of yeast in warm water and stir into mixture. When violent working is over, strain off, put in cask, and water-seal. Bottle in March or April.

Micronite filter.
Mild, smooth taste.
For all the right reasons.
Kent.

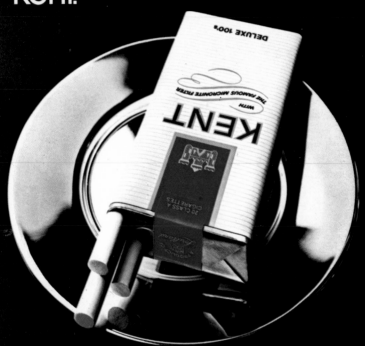

America's quality cigarette.
King Size or Deluxe 100's.

Beet Wine 2

Beets
Water
Sugar

Yeast
Brandy (optional)

Boil 3 lbs. of beets thoroughly cleaned and sliced or cubed in 1 gal. of water for 1½ hours. Drain off liquid and add enough water to restore the original gal. Squeeze the beets for what juice remains in them and pour this into that already obtained. Strain through a fine sieve or muslin bag and boil again for ½ hour. When cool, put into vat and add 3 lbs. of sugar and start fermentation with yeast. Stir daily and when fermentation has stopped put in cask, bung up tightly and let stand for a year. At end of this time, bottle and serve.

One quart of brandy for every 5 gals. may be added at the time of bunging, if desired.

Birch Wine

Birch sap
Sugar
Hops

Cloves
Lemon
Yeast

If birch trees are plentiful in the vicinity, tap a few in the month of March. Use 2½ lbs. of sugar for every gal. of sap and boil together for 10 or 15 minutes. Skim well and remove from fire. To every 4½ or 5 gals. of this prepared liquid add 1 oz. cloves, ½ oz. of hops and the rind of 1 lemon. When lukewarm, start fermentation in vat with yeast. After fermentation has completely subsided, skim, strain, and pour in cask. Before sealing stir in 1 oz. of pure leaf gelatin dissolved in a little of the liquid. At the time of fining add dry tannic acid in the ratio of 2½ gm. for every 5 gals. of wine. Seal and let stand for 2 months before bottling. Serve after 2 more months. This wine will improve with age.

Blackberry Wine 1

Blackberries   Sugar
Water

Mash berries and allow to ferment for three days in a covered vat. Press out juice and put in clean cask. Pour on the pressed remains warm (not boiling) water equal to the amount of juice obtained from the first pressing. Add sugar in the amount of 3 lbs. to each gal. of the mixture. If cask is not full, add water containing 3 lbs. of sugar per gal. to bring the liquor to within an inch or so of bunghole. Water-seal and let stand until late fall, at which time it should be racked off into a fresh cask. Bung up tightly and set aside. Bottle in July. Serve when desired.

In adding water to fill the cask before sealing, it is understood that no considerable amount is to be used, i.e., not more than 1 gal. at the most for a 10-gal. cask. This means that enough berries must be used to fill the cask with the proper mixture of juice and water.

Blackberry Wine 2

Blackberries   Sugar
Water

Mash ripe blackberries in a vat and to each gal. of crushed fruit add 1 qt. of boiling water. Let stand for 24 hours, stirring occasionally. Now strain off juice and add 2 lbs. of sugar to each gal. This can be bottled immediately and allowed to work off in open bottles before driving in corks; but it will be easier in the long run to ferment in a cask and bottle only after the wine has come fine. At any rate it should be ready for serving by dinner time of Thanksgiving Day.

Blackberry Wine 3

Blackberries   Sugar
Water

Mash ripe blackberries and measure them. To every gal. of crushed fruit add 1 qt. of boiling water and let stand for two days. Stir twice daily. On the third day strain off juice and dissolve in it 2 lbs. of sugar for each gal. Pour in cask, water-seal and let stand until winter.

Blackberry Wine 4

Blackberries   Sugar
Water

Over each gal. of ripe berries pour 2 qts. of water and let stand for 3 days. At the end of this time press out juice and to each gal. add 3 lbs. of sugar and put aside for 3 more days. Strain, put in keg, and water-seal. Bottle in December and serve when desired.

Blueberry Wine 1

Blueberries   Sugar
Water

Over 5 gals. of ripe blueberries pour 10 gals. of hot water. Let stand for 3 days, stirring twice daily. Now press out juice and add to each gal. 3 lbs. of sugar. Stir thoroughly to dissolve sugar and then let stand for 3 more days. Strain again, turn into cask and water-seal. Bottle in 6 months.

Blueberry Wine 2

Blueberries   Sugar
Water   Yeast

Over each gal. of ripe berries pour 1 gal. of boiling water and let stand overnight; then press out juice and add sugar in the proportion of 2 to 2½ lbs. per gal. of wine. Return to vat and ferment with yeast. At the end of 5 days strain into cask and water-seal. Bottle in midwinter.

Boysenberry Wine

Boysenberries	Sugar
Water	Yeast

Mash ripe boysenberries in the vat and to each gal. of crushed berries add 1 qt. of boiling water. Allow to stand for 24 hours, stirring occasionally. At the end of this time strain off juice and add 3 lbs. of sugar to each gal. Turn into cask, filling to bunghole. This should ferment naturally. If it does not, start fermentation with yeast. When violent "boiling" has stopped, lower surface of liquid about two inches below bunghole and water-seal. In early November rack off into a fresh cask. Bung up tightly and set aside. This can be drunk by Christmas, but is a little better 6 months later.

Cantaloupe Wine

Use recipe for Muskmelon Wine.

Caraway Wine

Caraway seed	Cream of tartar
Water	Brandy
Sugar	Yeast

Boil for 45 minutes 1 gal. of water containing 3 lbs. of sugar, skimming frequently. Keep water up to original level by adding more. Remove from fire and pour into vat. When lukewarm, lay a cake of yeast on top and stir it in on following day. Five or 6 hours after second stirring, give it another stirring and turn the whole into a cask. Now add 1 oz. of caraway seeds which have been soaked several hours in a cup of brandy (add brandy, as well as seeds). Water-seal and bottle after 4 months if brilliantly clear.

Carnation Wine

Allow 1 pt. of gently pressed blossoms for every gal.

of water and proceed according to recipe for Cowslip Wine 1, using all the other ingredients given there.

Celery Wine

Celery	Lemon
Water	Yeast
Sugar	Brandy (optional)

Cut in fairly small pieces (one inch long) 25 lbs. of celery stalks, place them in the vat and mash thoroughly. Pour upon the crushed stalks 5 gals. of boiling water and stir vigorously until the celery is in shreds, or nearly so. Let the whole cool, then press out the juice and add to each gal. 3 lbs. of sugar. Start fermentation in a crock with yeast. Drop into the fermenting wine the peel of 1 lemon. When the violent stage of fermentation has passed, strain off into a cask, water-seal. When the wine is completely quiet, bung up tightly and set aside for 9 months before bottling. If it is desired, 1 qt. of brandy may be added to each 5 gals. as soon as fermentation has stopped.

Cherry Wine 1

Unless otherwise stated, this and the following cherry recipes are adapted especially to the sour or pie cherry. Recipes No. 7 and No. 8 call for black cherries, but may be used just as well with any sweet cherry. No. 8 will make a nice heavy wine from wild or chokecherries.

Cherries	Sugar

Use ripe, but not overripe fruit. Stem and crush in the vat without breaking pits. Press out juice through bag or cheesecloth and dissolve in it 2 lbs. of sugar to each gal. Start fermentation in a vat and after 3 or 4 days, turn into a cask and water-seal. It may be bottled after 4 or 5 months and is ready for drinking at any time after bottling.

This wine may be made to sparkle by adding a small lump of sugar to each bottle just before it is corked. If sugar is added, it must be stored in a cool place.

Cherry Wine 2

Cherries   Cream of tartar
Water   Brandy (optional)
Brown sugar

Measure the cherries and mash them in the vat, taking care not to break the pits. To every gal. of measured fruit add 1 gal. of water and let ferment. When active working seems to have come to an end, press out liquor and put in it 3 lbs. of brown sugar for each gal., and 1 oz. of cream of tartar to every 5 gals. Stir well and turn into cask. Now remove from the pressed remains some of the pits (10 or 12 pits for each gal. of liquor), crush them and after the heavy scum has stopped rising through bunghole, drop them in the wine and water-seal. Bottle after it has stood for 4 months.

Brandy may be added, if desired, in the ratio of 1 qt. to every 5 gals., at the moment of sealing.

Cherry Wine 3

Cherries   Yeast
Sugar

Mash ripe, but not overripe fruit, being careful not to break the stones. After it has stood in the vat for 24 hours, press juice and to every 3 gals. add 8 lbs. of sugar. Start fermentation with yeast. Stir daily, and when nearly quiet, skim off top, strain juice and turn into cask. Water-seal and bottle after 5 months.

A nutty flavor may be imparted to the wine by adding a handful of crushed pits just before sealing in the cask.

Cherry Wine 4

Cherries   Sugar
Currants

Crush together 15 lbs. of cherries which are not quite ripe and 2 lbs. of currants. Let stand overnight. Press out and strain juice and put all into cask with 1 lb. of sugar for every gal. of liquor. Break a handful of stones and drop them in the wine. When fermentation has stopped completely, drive the bung in tightly and let stand 2 months before bottling.

Cherry Wine 5

Cherries   Sugar

Mash *black* cherries in the vat without breaking pits and let stand for 24 hours. Press out juice and strain. Now add 2 lbs. of sugar to each gal. and stir until dissolved. Start fermentation in the vat and after 3 or 4 days transfer to cask. If no scum "boils" through the bunghole, water-seal and bottle after 6 months. It may be drunk at any time.

Cherry Wine 6

Cherries   Sugar
Water   Cream of tartar

Crush without breaking stones 4 gals. of *black* cherries and pour over them 5½ gals. of warm water. Stir well and add 15 lbs. of sugar and 1 oz. of cream of tartar. Stir once more to assure that sugar is thoroughly dissolved. Now break a handful of pits and throw into the mixture. Ferment in a vat for 4 or 5 days, then turn into cask and water-seal. Bottle after 6 months. Because of the cream of tartar it should have another 2 months of aging before drinking.

Chokecherry Wine 1

Chokecherries	Sugar
Water	Yeast

Crush 8 gals. of ripe chokecherries by running them through a fruit crusher (not hopper type) or through a sausage grinder, using only the coarsest blade. The fruit should be crushed, but not the seeds. However, if a few do get broken, so much the better; if not, break a handful or two and throw them in with the fruit. Place all in the fermenting vat and pour over them 10 gals. of warm water. Now mix in well 25 lbs. of sugar. Ferment with five cakes of yeast. Stir daily for 10 days. Strain into a cask (or carboy) and water-seal. This wine often works vigorously for 2 or 3 months. To assure that the sugar is used up, remove water-seal about every 3 weeks and stir with a clean stick. Bottle when absolutely fine. It can be drunk at once, but is better after standing in the bottle for a year.

This wine needs little praise. If properly made and given a little time, it is one of the best, if not the very best, of the fruit wines not made from the grape. It has good alcoholic strength, good body, beautiful color, and is dry enough to be used as a table wine.

Chokecherry Wine 2

To make a sweet chokecherry wine, use the recipe above, but add from 5 to 7 more pounds of sugar. Treat as for number 1.

Cider or Malic Wine 1

Apple cider	Cloves
Honey	Mace
Cream of tartar	Rum
Cinnamon	

It is *important* that the cider used in this wine be

made from thoroughly sound apples which are ripe but not overripe, and that it contain *no preservative*.

To every gal. of fresh cider add 1 lb. of honey and ¼ oz. cream of tartar. Fermentation may be allowed to take place in an open vat or in a cask, and while it is in process, keep suspended in the liquor a cloth bag containing 1 oz. each of cinnamon, cloves, and mace. When the wine has stopped fermenting, remove spices and add ¾ gal. of rum for every 5 gals. of wine, seal in cask and let stand. Bottle after 6 months. Drink any time.

Cider Wine 2

Apple cider	Brandy
Sugar	Alum

Use fresh cider made from good-quality apples. Expose a quantity to the air for 10 or 12 hours. To every 3 gals. of cider add 1 qt. of brandy, 1 lb. of sugar, and 1 oz. of powdered alum. (A few slices of red beets may be thrown in to give color, if desired.) Stir well and let ferment in cask, keeping this filled from day to day. When wine becomes quiet, water-seal. In March it will be ready for bottling and serving.

Cider Wine 3

Cider	Sugar

To 15 gals. of the very best apple cider add 40 lbs. of sugar. As soon as this is thoroughly dissolved, turn into a cask, but do not fill—about 2 gallons of space should be left. Place in a cool part of the cellar for 48 hours, then bung up, leaving a small gimlet hole open in the bung. When through fermenting, the wine must be sealed in by plugging up the hole tightly. Let stand for a year. This wine does not need to be racked at any time, and may be served from the cask without bottling.

Cider Wine 4

Cider   Sugar

Fill a cask ¾ full of the best apple cider, and put in it 2 lbs. of sugar for each gal. of liquor, stirring until this is thoroughly dissolved. Water-seal, or bung up, as above, after 48 hours. Treat as in case of the previous wine.

Cider Wine 5

Cider   Cloves
Brown sugar   Ginger root
Bitter almonds

Dissolve in 30 gals. of the best quality cider 28 lbs. of sugar and let ferment in a cask. When this process has ended, rack off into a clean cask and add ⅛ oz. bitter almonds, 8 or 9 cloves, and 1 or 2 pieces (depending on size) of bruised ginger root. Bung up tightly and put aside in a cool cellar until perfectly fine.

A lump of sugar placed in each bottle at the time of bottling will make a nice sparkling wine in about 3 months' time.

Clary Wine

Clary blossoms   Yeast
Water   Brandy
Sugar

To every qt. of clary blossoms and tops allow 1 gal. of water in which 3 lbs. of sugar have been boiled for 15 minutes. Pour this liquid over the blossoms only after it has cooled to lukewarmness. Ferment in a vat with yeast, stirring daily for a week. Then turn into a cask, add ½ cup brandy per gal. of wine, and water-seal. It may be bottled after 4 months, but 6 months more are needed for the wine to be at its best for drinking.

Clover Blossom Wine

Clover blossoms	Yeast
Water	Lemon
Sugar	

Over 3 qts. of clover blossoms, which are not packed, pour 1 gal. of boiling water. Let steep for 3 days and then strain off liquid. To the same blossoms add the peel of 1 lemon and 3 more gals. of water and boil together for 15 minutes. Strain off again and add to the liquid already obtained. Now stir in 4 lbs. of sugar for each gal. of wine and start fermentation with yeast. Put into vat or cask and let stand in contact with the air for 3 weeks, then water-seal and keep for a month or so before bottling.

Coltsfoot Wine 1

Coltsfoot blossoms	Orange
Water	Lemon
Sugar	Yeast

Pick and stem 1 gal. of coltsfoot blossoms and place them in a vat. Now pour over them 4 gals. of boiling water and let stand until cold—overnight is even better. Now strain off liquor, put in it 3 lbs. of sugar to every gal. and boil, skimming frequently. When no more scum rises to the top, return to vat and add the peeling of 1 California orange and 1 lemon for each gal. When the mixture is lukewarm, start fermentation with yeast. After 5 days skim and pour into a fresh cask. Now add the juice of 1 orange and 1 lemon. Water-seal, and bottle after about 3 months.

Coltsfoot Wine 2

Coltsfoot blossoms	Oranges
Water	Lemons
Sugar	Yeast
Raisins	Brandy (optional)

Spread freshly picked coltsfoot blossoms in the sun for 2 days. Now measure the blossoms gently packed and for every gal. allow ½ lb. of seeded raisins which have been run through a meat chopper, and the thin parings and strained juice of 2 oranges and 2 lemons. Put all these ingredients in the vat. Now boil water and and sugar together for 30 minutes, alowing 2 gals. of water and 6 lbs. of sugar for each gently pressed gal. of blossoms. Skim well and pour over contents of the vat. Start fermentation with yeast, cover vat, and let stand for 6 days, stirring occasionally. At the end of this time strain off into fresh cask, add 1 pt. of brandy per gal. of pressed blossoms, if desired, and water-seal. The wine will be ready for bottling in 6 months.

Comfrey Wine

Comfrey roots	Sugar
Water	Yeast

In early spring dig up 20 or 25 comfrey roots and prepare by washing, peeling, and cutting into fairly small pieces. Boil these in 5 gals. of water until tender, skimming when necessary. Strain liquor into vat and add 15 lbs. of sugar. When lukewarm, start fermentation with yeast. Stir once daily for a week, then turn into cask and water-seal. Bottle at end of 6 months if perfectly fine.

Cowslip Wine 1

Cowslip blossoms	Orange
Water	Brandy
Sugar	Yeast
Lemons	

Boil 3 lbs. of sugar for 20 minutes in a gal. of water. Have prepared in a vat the rind of 2 lemons and 1 orange, and the juice of 1 lemon and 1 orange, and pour the boiling syrup over them. When this is luke-

warm, strain off liquor and pour it over 1 gal. of cowslip blossoms which have been picked free of all stems.
Ferment with yeast. After 4 or 5 days skim and turn
into cask. Add 1 qt. of good brandy and water-seal.
Bottle and serve after 2 months.

Cowslip Wine 2

Cowslip blossoms	Lemons
Water	Oranges
Brown sugar	Yeast
Hops	Leaf gelatin

Boil together for ½ hour 2½ gals. of water, 7 lbs.
of brown sugar, and 2 oz. of hops. Pour the boiling
mixture upon the rinds of 4 lemons and 4 oranges.
Start fermentation in the vat with yeast, and after 4
days add 1 qt. of fresh cowslip blossoms free of all
stalks. Stir until the flowers have sunk into the liquid.
When violent fermentation has ceased, pour into a cask
without removing the blossoms. Now dissolve a little
pure leaf gelatin (3 grams for every 5 gals. of wine)
in a cup of the wine and mix it well with the contents
of the cask. Water-seal and leave in the cask for at
least 6 months. It is then ready to bottle, although 4
or 5 months more in the cask will improve it.

Cowslip Wine 3

Cowslip blossoms	Lemons
Honey	Sweetbriar
Water	Yeast

Boil together for 45 minutes 9 lbs. of honey and 5
gals. of water, skimming when necessary and adding
enough boiling water to restore original amount. Now
put into a vat ½ bu. of fresh cowslip blossoms, 2
lemons (sliced) and 2 or 3 sprigs of sweetbriar, and
pour the boiling water over all. When lukewarm, start
fermentation with a cake of yeast. Stir once a day for

5 days, then strain and turn into a cask and water-seal. It should be wholly fine and ready for bottling in 6 months.

Cranberry Wine

Cranberries   Sugar
Water

For every gal. of uncrushed fruit allow 1 gal. of water. Mash ripe berries to a pulp and put into a vat. Pour water on them, stir well, and let stand for 2 days. At the end of this time press out liquor and strain through cloth. Now mash the same amount of berries as before and pour upon them the liquid already obtained. Mix together well and allow to steep for 2 days. Press off and strain the juice again. In every gal. dissolve 1½ lbs. of sugar and boil for 5 minutes, then turn into keg, filling to the top. When scum no longer rises through bunghole, water-seal. As soon as it comes fine, it is ready to bottle. Age will improve cranberry wine.

Currant Wine 1

Red currants   Sugar
Water

Use only ripe fruit. Press out juice and add water in the ratio of 2 gals. to every 3 gals. of juice. For each gal. of the mixture use 3 lbs. of sugar. Stir well and pour into cask. When violent stage of fermentation has passed, water-seal and put aside until some time in October. It may now be racked into a fresh cask or allowed to remain on lees. This currant wine is ready to be served by Christmas time, but it can be improved by leaving it in the cask for as much as 2 years.

Currant Wine 2

Red currants	Sugar
Red raspberries	Cream of tartar
Water	Beets

Stem 4 gals. of red currants and 2 pts. of red raspberries and mash together into a vat. Press out juice, return the pressed husks to the vat and pour over them 5½ gals. of water. Let stand for 12 hours with frequent stirrings. Press out liquor and add to the juice already obtained. Put in this mixture 10 lbs. of sugar, 1½ oz. of cream of tartar, and 1 lb. of good red beets (for color). Fermentation should take place in a cask, and when it is through, rack off the wine into a clean container, water-seal and allow to stand for 2 months. At end of this time it should be racked once again into a clean cask, which should be filled to the bunghole. Bung up tightly and put away until spring. If it suits the taste, it may be bottled and served now, but more age will improve it.

Currant Wine 3

Red currants	Sugar
Water	

Strip from their stems 4 gals. of currants and place in vat. Now boil for 15 minutes 2½ gals. of water which contain 5 lbs. of sugar. Skim off the surface and pour on the fruit in the vat, where all should stand for 2 days with occasional stirrings. Strain through cloth bag into cask, and when scum no longer rises through opening, water-seal. When perfectly fine, it is ready to bottle, but will be much better at the end of a year.

Currant Wine 4

Red currants	Sugar
Water	

Stem and crush 1 bu. of red currants and pour over them 8 gals. of water. Stir well, until skins and pulp are separated. Now press out the liquid and dissolve in it 35 lbs. of sugar. Put in cask and fill to bunghole. When the violent stage of the fermentation has ceased, water-seal, and allow to stand until December. If perfectly fine, it may be bottled; if not, rack into a fresh cask and let stand 3 months more.

Currant Wine 5

Red currants   Sugar
Water

In a 5-gallon cask put 4 gals. of currant juice, 15 lbs. of sugar, and enough water to fill. Let stand until scum no longer rises through bunghole, then water-seal. Remove to cooler place and allow it to stand for 6 months more. If its clarity and taste are suitable, bottle it; if not, leave it in the cask.

Currant Wine 6

White currants   Cream of tartar
Water   Brandy (optional)
Sugar

Strip from their stems 20 lbs. of *white* currants and mash in a vat. Pour upon them 2 gals. of water and stir well, until the pulp and skins are well separated. After they have stood for 2 or 3 days, strain off juice by pressing through a cloth bag. Add to the liquid obtained 13 lbs. of sugar, and stir until all is dissolved. Now add 5 gals. more of water and stir again. Turn into a cask and mix in 1 oz. of cream of tartar dissolved in a little of the wine. As soon as active fermentation has stopped, water-seal and let stand for 4 or 5 months, at the end of which time rack off into a fresh cask. After 6 months more, the wine will be ready for bottling.

A pint of brandy may be added, if desired, a month after cask has been sealed.

This recipe makes a fairly dry wine. To make it sweeter, add 20 lbs. of sugar.

Currant Wine 7

White currants	Cream of tartar
Gooseberries	Bitter almonds
Water	Brandy
Sugar	

Mash together in the vat 4½ gals. of *white* currants and ½ gal. of gooseberries (not red). Let stand for 2 days and strain off juice through cloth. Add to the liquor obtained 12½ lbs. of sugar, 1 oz. of bitter almonds, ½ oz. of cream of tartar, stir well and turn into keg. After one week has elapsed, water-seal. When fermentation has stopped, remove seal, stir in 2 qts. of brandy, re-seal and let stand for 7 months before bottling.

Some prefer to boil the juice of the currants for a few minutes in order to soften a harshness of flavor imparted by the husks. If juice is boiled, start fermentation with yeast.

Currant Wine 8

Currants	Sugar
Water	Egg-whites
Honey	Cream of tartar

Boil together 15 gals. of water and 8 lbs. of honey. When lukewarm, strain and add the juice of 8 lbs. of *red* or *white* currants and ferment in a warm place for three days. Now dissolve in the wine 1 lb. of sugar for each gal. Beat thoroughly into the whites of 2 eggs 1 oz. of cream of tartar. Stir this into the liquor and turn into cask. Let stand under water-seal until perfectly fine, at which time it may be bottled.

Currant Wine 9

Black currants	Cream of tartar
Water	Yeast
Sugar	Brandy

Mash rather lightly a gal. of *black* currants and boil them in a gal. of water for 10 minutes. Press out the juice well and add boiling water to make up for any loss. Into this liquor stir 2½ lbs. of sugar and 1 oz. of cream of tartar. Cool to about 85 degrees and ferment with yeast. Turn into a cask and keep this filled. When fermentation has stopped completely, add 3 qts. of brandy and let stand for 8 months before bottling.

Currant Wine 10

Black currants	Sugar
Strawberries	Cream of tartar
Water	Brandy

Mash together in the vat 6 gals. of *black* currants and 3 gals. of strawberries and allow them to stand for 2 days. Press out juice through cloth bag and add 25 lbs. of sugar, 4 oz. of cream of tartar, and 10 gals. of water. When sugar has been thoroughly dissolved, put in a cask, and water-seal after 4 days. When fermentation has ceased, add 2 qts. of brandy, re-seal, and put aside for 8 months before bottling.

Currant Wine 11

Currants	Sugar
Water	Cream of tartar

Use equal parts of *red, white,* and *black* currants from which the stems have been removed. Crush 4 gals. of them and press out all the juice. Pour over the pressed husks 5½ gals. of water, stir well, and let stand for a day. Now press out this liquor and add to the juice already extracted. Dissolve in the mixture 11 lbs. of sugar and 1½ oz. of cream of tartar. When violent fermentation dies down, water-seal. Bottle after 3 months.

If white currants are difficult to obtain, use red and black in equal proportions, but allow 3 more months before bottling.

Daisy Wine

Daisies	Sugar
Water	

Over each gal. of daisy heads firmy, but not tightly packed, pour 1 gal. of water and let stand for two days. Strain off the liquid, squeezing the blossoms lightly to make them give up their flavor and juice. Now dissolve 3 lbs. of sugar in each gal. of liquid and let ferment in an open vat, or in a cask, for 2 weeks. If fermentation takes place in the vat, strain the liquor before putting in cask. If it is fermented in a cask, rack into a fresh one at the end of this time. Bung up tightly if the wine is wholly quiet. Let stand until it comes thoroughly clear. Bottle and serve when desired.

Damson Wine 1

Damsons	Cream of tartar
Water	Yeast
Sugar	

Mash well 4 gals. of damson plums in the vat. Break open the kernels of two or three handfuls of fruit and throw into the vat. Pour on the whole 5½ gals. of water and mix well by stirring for at least 10 minutes. Press out and strain liquid and let stand for a day. Now add 15 lbs. of sugar, 3 oz. of cream of tartar, and start fermentation with yeast. Turn into cask and when scum no longer rises, water-seal and let stand 4 months before bottling.

Damson Wine 2

Damsons
Water

Brown sugar
Yeast

Pour 1 gal. of boiling water over 8 lbs. of damson plums and allow to stand for 3 or 4 days. At end of this time press and strain off liquor, in each gal. of which should be dissolved 3 lbs. of good-quality brown sugar. Put in cask and ferment with yeast. When violent stage is over, water-seal and let stand for 4 months before bottling.

Damson Wine 3

Damsons
Water

Brown sugar
Yeast

Place 8 lbs. of damson plums into a vat and pour 1 gal. of boiling water upon them. After 2 days press out juice and pour it in a cask, adding 2½ lbs. of brown sugar of good quality. Ferment with yeast, and water-seal when wine quiets down a bit. After 4 months in the cask the wine is ready to be bottled. Put a lump of sugar in each bottle. The wine will be ready for serving in a month or two.

Damson Wine 4

Damsons
Water
Brown sugar

Cloves
Cream of tartar

Bruise 4 gals. of ripe, but not overripe, damson plums in a vat and pour 6 gals. of water on them. Stir well and dissolve in the liquid 15 lbs. of good brown sugar. Let ferment in the open for about 5 days; then press out juice and strain. Now add to this ⅛ oz. of whole cloves which have been bruised and 2 oz. of cream of tartar. Turn into cask, water-seal, and allow to stand 4 months before bottling.

Damson Wine 5

Damsons	Sugar
Bullace	Yeast
Water	Brandy

Mash together in the vat 20 lbs. of damson plums and 4 lbs. of bullace and pour over them 3 gals. of boiling water. Cover and leave a week, stirring twice daily. At end of this time draw off liquor, pressing the fruit to get all, and strain into cask. Add sugar in the proportion of 2½ lbs. per gal., and start fermentation with yeast. Water-seal after 4 days and let the whole stand until through working. Now remove seal, add 1 qt. of brandy, stir it in and bung up. Bottle in 8 months.

Dandelion Wine 1

Dandelion blossoms	Oranges
Water	Lemons
Sugar	

Use only fresh blossoms from which all stems have been removed, otherwise the wine will be bitter. To every gal. of flowers, well packed but not crushed, add 8 sliced oranges and 4 sliced lemons, and pour over the whole 1 gal. of boiling water. Let stand for 24 to 36 hours and strain off liquor. Allow 2 lbs. of sugar for each gal. and put in cask to ferment, keeping filled to bunghole until scum no longer rises. Lower an inch or so, water-seal and let stand until all fermentation has stopped. Bottle when perfectly fine.

Dandelion Wine 2

Dandelion blossoms	Oranges
Water	Lemon
Sugar	Yeast

Pour a gal. of boiling water over a gal. of firmly pressed, but not bruised, dandelion blossoms from which the stems have been carefully picked. Allow to stand for 3 days and then add the juice and rinds of 1 lemon, 3 oranges and 4 lbs. of sugar. Start fermentation with yeast. At the end of 10 days strain into a cask under water-seal, being sure not to leave any sugar in the vat. When the wine comes clear, it may be bottled.

Dandelion Wine 3

Dandelion blossoms	Brandy
Water	Yeast
Sugar	

Over every gal. of lightly packed dandelion blossoms pour 1 gal. of boiling water. Let steep for 5 full minutes, then strain off, pressing flowers well to get all their juice and flavor. Stir in 4 lbs. of sugar and ½ cup of brandy per gal. of liquid. Start fermentation in an open vat with yeast. In a week's time, skim off surface, pour into clean cask and water-seal. As soon as the wine has come fine, it may be bottled.

Date Wine 1

Dried dates	Sugar
Raisins	Cream of tartar
Water	Brandy

Run through meat chopper 8 lbs. of dried dates from which the stones have been removed and place them in the vat with 4 lbs. of chopped raisins. Now pour upon dates and raisins 8 gals. of warm water in which 8 lbs. of sugar and 2 oz. of cream of tartar have been dissolved. Ferment in an open vat, stirring daily. When working has subsided, strain off and turn into cask. Mix in 1 qt. of brandy, water-seal, and let stand until perfectly fine. Bottle at any time.

Date Wine 2

Dried dates	Cream of tartar
Raisins	Brandy
Water	Yeast
Sugar	

Run through the meat-chopper 10 lbs. of dried dates and 2 lbs. of raisins, and pour over them 9 gals. of warm water. Now stir into the liquor 15 lbs. of sugar and 2 oz. of cream of tartar. Start fermentation with a cake of yeast in an open vat. Stir once or twice daily. When active fermentation has stopped, strain into cask, add 1 quart of brandy, and water-seal. Bottle when perfectly fine.

Dewberry Wine 1

Dewberries	Sugar
Water	Yeast

Mash thoroughly in the vat 1 gal. of ripe dewberries and pour over them 1 gal. of cold water. Let stand for 24 hours, stirring several times during this period. Press out and strain, and add 2½ lbs. of sugar to each gal. of liquid. Pour into a cask, start fermentation with yeast. When violent stage has passed, turn into cask, water-seal and let stand. Bottle after 4 months.

Dewberry Wine 2

Dewberries	Sugar
Water	Yeast

To every gal. of ripe dewberries which have been thoroughly crushed, add 1 qt. of boiling water. Let stand for 2 days, stirring twice each day. On the third day strain off juice and dissolve in it 2 lbs. of sugar for each gal. of liquid. Start fermentation in a vat with yeast and when violent stage has passed water-seal in a cask and let stand for the entire winter. Bottle in the spring.

Dewberry Wine 3

Dewberries   Sugar
Water   Yeast

Mash ripe dewberries in the vat and pour over each
gal. of crushed berries 1 qt. of boiling water. Let stand
for 24 hours, stirring occasionally. Strain off juice and
to each gallon of liquid add 2 lbs. of sugar. Ferment
for a few days in a vat with yeast, and then turn into
cask under water-seal to finish. When it is perfectly
fine, it may be bottled. This is usually drinkable by
Thanksgiving time.

Elderberry Wine 1

Elderberries   Ginger root
Damsons   Hops
Water   Allspice
Sugar   Cinnamon

Gather elderberries on a dry day and to every gal.
of berries add 1 qt. of ripe damsons (or purple plums).
Boil in ½ gal. of water until fruit is soft and skins are
broken. Stir while cooking to aid in breaking skins and
pulp. Press and strain off liquid. Now boil 25 lbs. of
sugar in 11 or 12 gals. (the amount needed to give 10
gals. of finished wine) of this liquid for 30 minutes.
Skim off and put in the vat. When fermentation has
passed its violent stage, turn into cask and suspend
in the wine a small cloth bag containing ¾ oz. of
bruised ginger root, ½ oz. of allspice, ½ oz. of cinnamon, and 3 oz. of hops. Let stand for 2 weeks, filling
cask every morning. At end of this time remove spice
bag and bung up tightly. The wine is potable and ready
for bottling after 2 months. It is not improved by being
left in cask.

The same recipe may be followed with elderberries
alone, omitting the plums.

Elderberry Wine 2

Elderberries	Cloves
Water	Raisins
Sugar	Yeast
Ginger	Brandy

Over each peck of elderberries pour 3 gals. of water which has been brought just to the boiling point and let stand for 2 days. Now strain off juice, pressing berries to get it all, and dissolve in it sugar in the ratio of 3 lbs. to the gal. Add ½ oz. of powdered ginger, 6 cloves, 1 lb. of raisins, and boil all together gently for 1 hour. As the slow boiling proceeds, skim off the surface from time to time. Let cool, put in cask, and start fermentation with yeast. At end of 2 weeks add brandy (1¼ pts. per 5 gals.) and seal. It is ready for the bottle after 3 months.

Elderberry Wine 3

Elderberries	Cream of tartar
Water	Brandy (optional)
Sugar	Spices

For every gal. of fruit use 1 gal. of water, 4½ lbs. of sugar, and ½ oz. cream of tartar.

Crush fruit in a vat and add water, sugar, and cream of tartar at once. When violent stage of fermentation has passed, turn into keg and water-seal. After all fermentation is over, remove seal and add brandy, if desired, in the proportion of 1 pt. to 5 gals. of wine, and reseal. Do not bottle before 3 months have elapsed.

If a spicy flavor is desired, at time of placing the water-seal, suspend in the liquor in a cloth bag 4 oz. of bruised ginger root (or allspice) and 3 oz. of bitter almonds. Be sure to remove spices when fermentation has stopped.

Elderberry Wine 4

Elderberries	Cloves
Water	Ginger
Sugar	Yeast

On 3 gals. of ripe elderberries pour 2 gals. of boiling water, stir well, and let stand quietly for a day; then press out juice, squeezing the berries to get it all, and add to every gal. 3 lbs. of sugar, ¾ oz. of cloves, and 1 oz. of ginger. Now boil the whole together for 20 minutes, skimming constantly. When lukewarm, put in cask and start fermentation with yeast. In 3 or 4 days water-seal and let stand for 3 to 4 months before bottling.

Elderberry Wine 5

Elderberries	Cream of tartar
Water	Yeast
Sugar	Spices (optional)

Crush berries and press out juice. Place in a fresh cask equal parts of juice and water and dissolve in the mixture 11 lbs. of sugar to every 2 gals. For the same amount of liquid use 1 oz. of cream of tartar. Start fermentation with yeast. During this process 1 oz. allspice, 1 oz. bruised ginger root, ¼ oz. cloves placed in a small cloth bag may be suspended in the wine if desired. After fermentation has stopped completely, remove spices, seal up, and let stand for 3 months. If perfectly fine at the end of this time, it may be bottled.

Elderberry Wine 6

Elderberries	Raisins
Water	Brandy
Brown sugar	Yeast

Bake elderberries for a while in a moderate oven, but do not burn to a crisp or evaporate juice. Remove from oven, press out juice. Now boil 3½ lbs. of sugar in 6 gals. of water for one hour. Skim surface well and set to cool. Turn into a vat and for every gal. of water add 1 qt. of berry juice. Start fermentation with a cake of yeast. At end of 1 week turn into cask and add 1 lb. of chopped seeded raisins for each gal. of liquor and 1 pt. of brandy for every 3 gals. Water-seal and bottle after 3 months.

Chopped seedless raisins may be used instead of seeded raisins.

Elderberry Wine 7

Elderberries	Sugar
Water	

Strip from their stems 5 gals. of ripe elderberries, place in a vat, and pour over them 5 gals. of warm (not boiling) water. Let stand *without* stirring for 10 days, then strain off carefully through sieve, taking care not to crush the berries. To each gal. of liquor add 3 lbs. of sugar well dissolved, and ferment in cask. One month after fermentation has completely subsided, the wine is ready for bottling.

This recipe may be varied by stirring berries twice daily while in vat. This will give a different flavor to the wine, which must now remain at least 3 months in the cask before being put in bottles.

Elderberry Wine 8

White elderberries	Sugar
Raisins	Lemon
Water	Yeast

Boil 1 gal. of *white* elderberries in 1 gal. of water for ¾ of an hour. Press out juice gently, squeezing berries only enough to extract the free liquor. To each gal. add 3 lbs. of sugar and boil again. After 2 or 3 skimmings, remove from fire, pour into vat and when lukewarm start fermentation with yeast. After it has worked for a week, pour into a cask with 3 lbs. of seeded raisins for every 5 gals. of wine. Water-seal and when fermentation has stopped, remove seal and add the juice and rind of one lemon for each 5 gals. of liquor. Bung up tightly and set aside for 3 months before bottling.

Chopped seedless raisins may be used instead of seeded raisins.

Elder Blossom Wine 1

Elder flowers	Eggs
Water	Gelatin
Sugar	

Boil 3 lbs. of sugar in 1 gal. of water for ½ hour, skim and pour over 1 qt. of elder flowers gently packed but not crushed. Let stand in the vat for 3 or 4 days, then strain off liquor and put in cask. For every 5 gals. of wine add 3 gms. of pure leaf gelatin thoroughly dissolved and the well-beaten whites of 3 eggs. Mix in thoroughly, seal cask, and let stand for 6 months. At end of this time draw off and bottle.

Elder Blossom Wine 2

Elder flowers	Sugar
Raisins	Yeast
Water	

Run 6 lbs. of seeded raisins through a meat chopper and boil for ½ hour in 6 gals. of water. Add, while still hot, 12 lbs. of sugar, and when the liquid has cooled to the milk-warm stage, put in a vat and start fermentation with yeast. Stir daily for 5 or 6 days, and then turn into cask. Before water-sealing, suspend in the wine a cloth bag containing ½ lb. of fresh elder flowers. Bottle the wine when it is perfectly fine.

Elder Blossom Wine 3

Elder flowers	Sugar
Water	Yeast

Over every 1½ qts. of elder flowers pour 5 gals. of water in which have been dissolved 20 lbs. of sugar. Add a yeast cake and let stand in the vat for a week, stirring every morning. At end of this time skim well and turn into a cask. Seal and put aside for 6 months. Draw off and bottle.

Fig Wine 1

Dried figs	Cream of tartar
Water	Yeast
Sugar	

Chop well 6 lbs. of dried figs and pour over them 2 gals. of warm water. Add 3 lbs. of sugar and 1 oz. of cream of tartar. Stir well and start fermentation with yeast. Let stand with daily stirrings for 8 or 10 days. Now strain off liquor, run into cask and seal. Wine can be bottled when fine, but it is better for serving after it has aged for 9 or 10 months.

Fig Wine 2

Dried figs	Sugar
Raisins	Cream of tartar
Water	Yeast

Chop 4 lbs. of dried figs and 2 lbs. of seeded raisins and pour over them 2 gals. of warm water. Stir in 3 lbs. of sugar and 1 oz. of cream of tartar. Ferment in a vat with yeast. Stir daily for 10 days, then strain off and put in cask. Seal and bottle after 3 months. Serve after 8 or 9 months.

Fig Wine 3

Black figs	Sugar
Water	Yeast

Run through meat grinder 6 lbs. of *black* figs, sometimes called Smyrna figs. Put into vat and pour over them 18 qts. of warm water containing 12 lbs. of sugar. Ferment with yeast and let stand for 10 days, stirring daily. At end of this time, strain off and turn into a clean cask, water-seal, and let stand for 3 or 4 months before bottling. Improves with a little age.

A handful or two of crushed peach kernels or cherry pits will impart to this wine a delightfully nutty flavor, making the beverage suggest Sherry when drunk.

Fig Wine 4

Fresh figs	Sugar
Water	Yeast

Measure 15 gals. of *fresh* ripe figs and mash them in the vat. Pour over them 5 gals. of water containing 2½ lbs. of sugar. Stir well and start fermentation with yeast. Let stand for 1 week with daily stirrings. Strain off liquor, put in cask and water-seal. Bottle when perfectly fine. The wine should be ready for serving after 2 or 3 months.

Flower Wine

Wine, sometimes very good wine, may be made from almost any sweet blossom and from many that are not sweet, like the dandelion. Not all the possibilities are suggested in this book, but see under carnation, clover, cowslip, daisy, dandelion, elder blossom, primrose, rose, and violet. If there are other flowers in abundance, (not lilies, nor zinnias, nor their kind), they may be used for wine. Use recipe for Cowslip Wine 1, or use any of the other cowslip recipes, varying the proportions of flowers and other ingredients according to instructions. (But see in Chapter 8 the section entitled "A Word of Caution," pages 114–15.)

Fruit Wine 1

Numerous fruits and berries, such as cherries, blackberries, currants, and dozens of others, may be made into wine in the following simple way: Press fruit well, extracting all the juice possible. Put pressed remains into a vat and pour upon them boiling water equal in amount to juice already extracted. Stir well and leave for 2 hours. Press again and add the liquor obtained to the first batch. Now allow sugar in the proportion of 2 to 4 lbs. per gal. of mixture. (The amount of sugar depends upon the fruit and any preference for dry or sweet wine. Here the saccharometer will come in handy.) When sugar is dissolved, turn into cask, and after the first 2 or 3 days of violent working, lower surface slightly and water-seal. When fermentation has completely subsided, allow wine to remain in cask until brilliantly clear before bottling.

This recipe may be varied as follows:

1. Instead of using a single fruit, combine 2 or more.
2. Use 1 part of juice to 2 or 3 parts of water. In such a case the wine will be lighter in body. The diluting thus of sweet juices makes more sugar necessary for proper fermentation. Use the saccharometer.
3. Brown sugar may be substituted for white sugar. Usually more is required and the wine will need more aging.

Fruit Wine 2

Cherries	Water
Raspberries	Sugar
White currants	Brandy (optional)
Black currants	

Mix equal quantities of cherries, raspberries, white currants, and black currants and mash well. For every

4 lbs. of fruit used allow 1 gal. of water, stir together and let stand for 3 or 4 days in an open vat, mixing daily. At end of this time press out juice, measure, and allow 3 lbs. of sugar to each gal. When sugar is well dissolved, return the pressed husks to the liquor, mix well again and allow to stand for 3 more days. Strain off juice once more, pressing well to get it all, turn into cask, and water-seal. When fermentation has ceased, add 1 pt. of brandy, if desired, for every 4 gals. of wine. Now bung up tightly and put aside for 4 or 5 months before bottling.

Ginger Wine 1

Ginger root	Raisins
Water	Yeast
Sugar	Brandy
Lemons	Gelatin

Boil together for 30 minutes 6 gals. of water, 6 oz of bruised ginger root, 14 lbs. of sugar, and the peelings of 6 lemons. When nearly cool, pour it all over 6 lbs. of chopped raisins, and add the juice of all the lemons. Ferment with yeast in an open vat for 2 weeks, stirring every day. At end of this time, strain off and put in cask. Just before sealing, mix in well 3 gms. of pure leaf gelatin, add 1½ pts. brandy. It will be ready in about 3 months' time.

Ginger Wine 2

Ginger root	Lemons
Raisins	Yeast
Water	Gelatin
Sugar	Brandy (optional)

Place 8 lbs. of chopped raisins in the vat. Boil for ½ hour 8 gals. of water containing 8 oz. of bruised ginger root, 19 lbs. of sugar, and the thin parings of 8 lemons. Skim as necessary and when it has cooled to lukewarmness, pour it all upon the raisins in the vat.

Now add the juice of the 8 lemons and start fermentation with a cake of yeast. Stir daily for 2 weeks, then strain and turn into cask. Three cups of brandy may be added at this time, if desired. As this wine is likely to need fining, it is advisable to mix in well 5 gms. of pure leaf gelatin dissolved in some of the liquor before sealing. The wine will be ready for bottling and serving after 3 months' time.

Ginger Wine 3

Ginger root	Yeast
Water	Lemon peel (optional)
Sugar	

To 10 gals. of water just boiled add 20 lbs. of sugar and 10 to 12 oz. of bruised ginger root. Boil together for ½ hour and allow to cool to lukewarmness. Place on top 2 cakes of yeast. Two hours later stir in the yeast and pour the whole into a cask to ferment. After scum no longer rises through bunghole, water-seal and let stand until absolutely fine.

The flavor may be improved for some tastes by adding the pared rinds of half a dozen lemons at the time of water-sealing.

Ginger Wine 4

Ginger root	Raisins
Water	Brandy
Sugar	Yeast
Lemons	

Boil for 1 hour in 9 gals. of water 12 oz. of bruised ginger root, rinds of 9 lemons, and 27 lbs. of sugar. Skim frequently. Finish boiling, pour into a vat and when still lukewarm add 2 lbs. of chopped raisins and the juice of the lemons whose rinds have been used. Mix well and then lay on top of the liquid a cake of yeast. Let stand for 2 weeks, stirring daily. Strain off, put in cask, add 1 pt. of good-quality brandy, seal and let the whole remain for 3 months. It may now be bottled and served.

Gooseberry Wine 1

Gooseberries	Sugar
Water	

Crush well 10 gals. of red-ripe berries and let stand in the vat for 24 hours. Squeeze through cloth bag, pressing as much as the mashed berries and the bag will stand. Return the husks to the vat and pour over them 5 gals. of hot (not boiling) water. Stir well and allow to stand for 12 hours. Now press through bag again and mix the liquid obtained with the original extraction. Add sugar in the amount of 12 lbs. for each 5 gals. of liquid and stir until dissolved. Lay a cake of yeast on top of the liquor and set in a warm place to ferment—the riper the berries, the more warmth will be required. When the violent stage of fermentation has passed, the wine may be skimmed and water-sealed in a cask.

Wine made from *red* gooseberries requires more time to mature than does that made from white berries. It should stand for a least a year before being served, though it will be found that wine from either white or red berries will improve by remaining even longer in the cask.

Gooseberry Wine 2

Gooseberries	Brandy
Water	Sassafras
Sugar	Beets
Cream of tartar	

Use only red-ripe fruit. Mash 6 gals. of gooseberries in the vat and pour upon them 5 gals. of cold water. Add ½ oz. of cream of tartar and 8 lbs. of sugar, stir well and let ferment. When fermentation has subsided, skim and pour in keg. Now put in the liquor ½ lb. of sassafras chips, 1½ qts. of brandy, and, for color, two or three red beets (sliced). Water-seal and set aside for 5 months. At end of this time bottle and let stand for 6 months more.

Gooseberry Wine 3

Gooseberries   Brown sugar
Water

Over 36 lbs. of red-ripe gooseberries crushed in the vat pour 3 gals. of boiling water. After 24 hours strain off through a cloth bag, pressing to get all the juice and flavor. Now dissolve in the wine 12 lbs. of good brown sugar and let stand 24 to 36 hours, stirring occasionally. At end of this time skim and pour in cask, and let ferment for a week with bunghole open. The cask should now be watersealed and after fermentation has completely subsided, put aside for 4 months before bottling. It is ready for serving after another 6 months.

Gooseberry Wine 4

Gooseberries   Raisins
Water   Brandy
Brown sugar

Use only red gooseberries. Mash them in the vat and add 1 gal. of cold water for each gal. of crushed fruit. After it has stood for a day, strain off by squeezing juice through cloth. Now dissolve 3 lbs. of brown sugar in each gal. of liquor and let stand for 2 or 3 days more, when it should be put in a cask with 1 lb. of chopped raisins per gal. of wine. Add 3 pts. of brandy for each 5 gals., water-seal and put aside for 4 months before bottling. It is best for drinking after 6 or 8 months more in the bottle.

Gooseberry Wine 5

Gooseberries
Water

Brown sugar
Gelatin

For this wine use berries that are just turning red. Remove carefully the stem and blossom ends and mash in the vat. Over every gal. of crushed fruit pour 3 qts. of cold water. Stir often and vigorously to assure separation of skins, seeds and pulp. Now press off and strain liquor, and dissolve in it 4 lbs. of brown sugar per gal. Let this ferment for 3 or 4 days and strain once more, this time into a clean cask. Water-seal and when fermentation has stopped, mix in 3 gms. of pure leaf gelatin for every 5 gallons. Bung up tightly and bottle at the end of a year.

Gooseberry Wine 6

Gooseberries
Water

Sugar
Gelatin

Weigh a quantity of full grown but still green berries. Remove stem and blossom ends and mash to a pulp. To every 6 lbs. of berries add 1 gal. of warm water and let stand 24 to 36 hours in a covered vat, stirring frequently. Press out liquid and for every gal. of water previously added allow 3 lbs. of sugar. Let this mixture stand for 2 or 3 days in an open vat kept in a warm place. At end of this time put in a clean cask and when scum no longer rises through bunghole, water-seal. After fermentation has stopped for good, mix in well 3 gms. of pure leaf gelatin for every 5 gals. of wine. Now bung up tightly and set aside until January, when it may be bottled.

Gooseberry Wine 7

Gooseberries
Water

Sugar
Gelatin

This recipe makes wine of the sparkling variety.

Thoroughly mash in the vat 40 lbs. of green gooseberries which have attained their full growth and pour upon them 4 gals. of water. Stir well with the hand, working so as to separate the pulp from the skins as much as possible. Let stand overnight, but not more than 24 hours, and then squeeze out juice. Return husks to the vat and rinse off with a gal. of fresh water. Stir well and squeeze again, adding this liquor to the previous extraction. Now dissolve in the total liquid obtained 30 lbs. of sugar and add enough water to make 11 gals. of wine. Cover vat and allow to stand for a full day, after which time pour the wine into a 10-gallon cask, filling to opening in bung stave. When fermentation has become languid, drive home a wooden bung in the center of which a small gimlet hole has been drilled. In a week or 10 days plug this hole firmly with a peg and let stand until March. Some winemakers prefer to rack this wine in December, but leaving it on its lees adds to the flavor and gives more body. It is ready for bottling by March. If it is not sparkling at this time, add one cube of sugar to each bottle of wine before corking.

Gooseberry wine should be fined. For the above recipe use 6 gms. of pure leaf gelatin dissolved in some of the wine and thoroughly stirred in at the time of bunging. Tie on corks with wire. (See Chapter 7.)

Gooseberry and Currant Wine

Gooseberries	Sugar
Currants	Cream of tartar
Water	

Crush in a vat 1 gal. of grooseberries and 1 gal. of currants and pour over them 3 gals. of water. After the whole has stood for 24 hours, strain off juice through a cloth bag and dissolve in it 4 lbs. of sugar per gal. of liquid. Add 1 oz. of cream of tartar previously dissolved in a little warm water and allow to stand for 5 months before bottling. This can be drunk at any time after it is put in the bottle, but is better if it lies still for 4 or 5 months more.

Grape Wine

Most of the recipes for grape wines that follow are already part of the American tradition. For the most part they produce sweet wines. And some of them are "makeshift" recipes. They probably had their origin in England where the home winemaker was trying to imitate the sweet, heavy Port wine to which the English were so accustomed. These were perpetuated in those sections of America far removed from wine-producing areas and where people had little experience with dry table wines. They have come down by oral transmission and in cookbooks. The winemaker interested in making dry table wines from grapes should turn to Chapter 4, where the matter is treated in detail.

Grape Wine 1

The classic recipe for grape wine is this: Simply press off the juice and let it ferment.

This can be done with any grape, but it is best to test the grape juice with a saccharometer (see pages 54–55) and then add the sugar necessary. (See Table I, page 58).

If the Concord grape is being used and it is not desired to purchase a saccharometer, it should be kept in mind that Concord juice averages from 13 to 14 percent of sugar. Therefore, it is necessary to add to every gal. of straight juice at least 10.2 oz. of sugar. This will see the wine safely through to dryness and about 10 or 11 percent of alcohol. If a sweet wine is desired, add 1 lb. of sugar to each gal. of juice.

Grape Wine 2

Grapes   Sugar
Water

Mash well a quantity of dark grapes and let them stand in a vat for a week or 10 days, stirring twice daily. Press off juice at end of this time and place in a cask. Add an equal amount of water and 20 oz. of sugar per gal. of mixture if the juice is from the Concord grape. If from another variety, test it with the saccharometer before adding sugar. Stir thoroughly and allow to ferment through bunghole for 3 or 4 days before water-sealing. Bottle when fine.

This wine is light and fairly dry. It a sweeter wine is preferred, add 2 lbs. of sugar to each gal. of liquid. Store in a cool place after it is bottled, or the wine may work again.

Grape Wine 3

Grapes   Sugar
Water

Mash grapes thoroughly and place in a vat. Add to them ⅓ their volume of water and 2½ lbs. of sugar per gal. of mixture. Allow to stand from 12 to 24 hours, stirring once or twice during this time. Then press out juice, pour it in a cask and water-seal. Bottle when fine and store in cool place.

If more body is desired, allow the mash to ferment longer in the vat.

To make a dry wine, test with saccharometer before adding sugar.

Grape Wine 4

Grapes   Sugar
Water

Stem 30 lbs. of grapes and put into a vat. Pour over

them 2½ gals. of boiling water. When this has cooled somewhat, stir well or mash by hand until all skins and pulp are separated. Cover vat and leave for 3 days. Now press out juice and add 15 lbs. of sugar, making sure that it is thoroughly dissolved. Let stand for 7 days more. At the end of this time strain off liquor, turn into a cask and water-seal. Bottle when it comes fine.

Grape Wine 5

Grapes   Sugar
Water

Mash a quantity of grapes in the vat and pour over them 1 gal. of water for every 4 lbs. of fruit. Let stand for 4 days, stirring daily, then strain juice through a cloth bag. To every gal. add 3 lbs. of sugar and turn into cask, filling to bunghole. Water-seal after 3 or 4 days and let stand until perfectly fine.

Grape Wine 6

Grapes   Sugar
Water

Over 20 lbs. of grapes in the vat pour 6 qts. of boiling water. When lukewarm, mash thoroughly with hands, separating skins and pulp. Cover vat and allow to stand for 3 days, then squeeze out juice. Dissolve in it 10 lbs. of sugar and turn into cask. Water-seal and leave alone until fine. Bottle.

Grape Wine 7

Grapes   Sugar
Water

Know the size of the cask to be filled and allow 4 lbs. of grapes and 2½ lbs. of sugar for 1 gal. Put grapes into a vat with a handful of stems and crush well. Add ¼ of the entire amount of sugar to be used, stir well and let stand for 10 to 14 days. Be sure to stir at least once a day during this time. Strain off juice, pressing skins dry, and turn into cask. Now add balance of sugar dissolved in warm water and bring contents up to bunghole with additional water. Let stand a few days more and water-seal. Bottle when fine.

Grape Wine 8

Grapes   Sugar
Water

Make grape juice by placing 4 cups of grapes and 4 cups of sugar in a gallon jug or jar (2 cups of grapes and 2 cups of sugar for a 2-qt. jar) and filling with boiling water. Turn upside down immediately. When cool, it may be stored away right side up. (Any time after 6 weeks this is a delightful, palatable beverage.) Next year, when ready to make wine, mash the new grapes and let them ferment in the vat as usual. Press out juice and to every 3 gals. obtained add 4 gals. of the grape juice made the year before, and 9 to 10 lbs. of sugar. Put in cask and water-seal.

If a dry wine is desired, it will be necessary to test with the saccharometer both the fresh grape juice, before it ferments, and the prepared grape juice which is to be added. Consult Table I to see how much sugar is necessary.

Grape Wine 9

Grapes   Sugar
Water

This recipe makes what is known as *piquette* or jerk wine.

Over the pressed remains of red grapes (preferably of the *Vitis vinifera* or California variety) pour boiling water in the proportion of 10 gals. for each 5 or 6 bu. of grapes (not of pressed remains). Stir only once a day for the first three days and then let stand for three more. On the seventh day strain off the liquor and bring the sugar content up to 22 or 24 percent by saccharometer reading. Now turn the whole into a cask and let stand for another 3 or 4 days, stirring well each day. At the end of this time, lower the wine an inch or two from bunghole and water-seal. Bottle when fine.

Grape Wine 10

Wild grapes   Sugar
Water

Gather the grapes only when they are fully ripe. To every bu. add 1½ gals. of warm (not hot) water and mash well, taking care not to crush seeds. Let stand for a week, stirring once a day. Dissolve sugar in the liquor until a fresh hen's egg will float at the surface exposing to the air an area of the shell about the size of a silver quarter of a dollar. Turn into cask and water-seal after it has stopped "boiling" over.

This wine will be ready for early sampling by Christmas time, but ought not to be bottled until March. A year of aging will help to mature this wine.

Grape Wine 11

Grapes   Sugar
Water   Brandy

Pick 2 bu. of wild grapes when they are fully ripe. Strip from stems and mash well without crushing seeds. Transfer to a 25- or 30-gal. cask. Add 25 lbs. of sugar and 5 gals. of grape brandy, and fill with water. Allow cask to lie in sun for several weeks, or if climate does not permit this, put in a warm part of the basement and let stand until April under water-seal. At this time it may be racked off into a fresh cask or bottled. This makes a fortified wine of the Port type.

To fill a 10-gal. cask, use 1 bu. of grapes, 15 lbs. of sugar and 1½ gal. of brandy.

Grape Wine 12

Grapes   Sugar
Water

White wine. When *white* grapes are available, mash a quantity of them and allow them to ferment for from 12 to 24 hours. Press out juice and add 1 gal. of water to every 2 gals. of juice obtained. Dissolve in the mixture 2 lbs. of sugar for each gal. and turn into cask. Water-seal after 3 or 4 days and let stand until perfectly fine.

This *white* wine can be improved by testing the juice with a saccharometer and by not fermenting on the skins. (Read in Chapter 4 the section entitled *Making White Wine.*)

Grape Wine 13

White wine may be made from any grape, red or white, by simply pressing out the juice and allowing it to ferment off the skins. Many white grapes have enough sugar to ferment through to full alcoholic strength, but it is always wise to test with a saccharometer.

An excellent white wine can be made from the Catawba or Delaware grape as follows:

Press out juice and let ferment 3 or 4 days. Then add to every 2 gals. of juice 1 gal. of water in which 2 lbs. of sugar have been dissolved. Turn into cask, water-seal and carry through as with other wines.

More wine can be made by adding equal parts of water to the grape juice. Always test with saccharometer in order to determine amount of sugar to be added. There are not many white grapes whose juice has enough acid to take as much as a gallon of water for every gallon of juice, but this has often been done with Catawba juice, one of the most acid of American white grapes.

Grape Wine 14

White wine from dark grapes. Press grapes without mashing too much or too long and strain juice at once. Test with saccharometer, add any sugar that may be necessary, and set aside to ferment. Before trying to use this recipe, read the section of Chapter 4 entitled *White Wine from Dark Grapes.*

Grape Wine 15

Rhine type—red. Mash well the remains from the above recipe and add water equal to the total amount of the juice already taken off. Let mixture stand for from 24 to 48 hours, then strain off and put in cask. Sugar, 2 lbs. per gal. of water, may be added at the time the water is poured on the mash. If the sugar is added after the liquor is strained off, allow another day or two of fermentation before water-sealing in the cask. Bottle when fine.

Grape Wine 16

Grapes   Sugar
Water

Home-made champagne. Use Catawba grapes. Isabellas or Delawares will do also, as will the juice of any white grape with a high acid content.

Press out and strain juice, and to every 2½ gals. of this add 3 gals. of water and 18 lbs. of sugar. Pour into a cask and allow it to ferment vigorously, keeping cask filled to bunghole. After a week or two, when scum ceases to rise through opening, drive home a bung in the center of which a gimlet hole has been drilled. Plug up this hole, but remove peg on following day. If the fermentation shows itself to be very active, leave peg out for another day, then plug up once more and try it again the next day. When satisfied that fermentation is no longer violent, drive in peg and let stand until perfectly fine, when it should be bottled without delay. Wire on corks and store in a cool place. (For the manner of wiring on corks, see Chapter 7.)

Grape Wine 17

Sparkling wine. A champagne-like wine may be made from green grapes gathered just as the seeds are forming, that is, when the berries are about two-thirds of the way to maturity. Use the recipe for Sparkling Gooseberry Wine 7, substituting green grapes for gooseberries.

Grape Wine 18

| Green Grapes | Sugar |
| Water | Cream of tartar |

Sparkling wine. Mash in the vat 15 lbs. of unripe grapes, picked just as seeds are beginning to form, and pour over them 2½ gals. of water. Cover with a cloth and let stand for 24 hours. Now press out juice and strain, and to the amount obtained add 9 lbs. of sugar and 2 oz. of cream of tartar. Turn into a cask. This may be left open for a few days, but should be bunged up tightly before fermentation has stopped. Use the gimlet hole test described in recipe 16. Keep in cask until March, then bottle.

Grape-Leaf Wine

| Grape leaves | Sugar |
| Water | |

Pick 25 lbs. of young vine leaves and tendrils and pour upon them 4 gals. of boiling water. After they have steeped from 36 to 48 hours, pour the liquor off, pressing the leaves dry. Now rinse these with ½ gal.

of water and press again, adding the second batch of liquor to the first. Dissolve in it 16 or 17 lbs. of sugar; ferment with yeast in a cask with open bung. If process is slow, stir with a stick or stop up cask and roll it back and forth. When fermentation has ceased, bung up tightly and let stand for one year.

Greengage Wine 1

Greengages	Yeast
Water	Cream of tartar
Sugar	

Mash well a quantity of greengages and pour upon them 5 gals. of hot water for every 5 gals. of crushed fruit. Stir several times during day, using hands if necessary to separate pulp from stones. On the following day, press out liquor and strain through cheesecloth. Into this must now be dissolved 15 lbs. of sugar and 2 oz. of cream of tartar. Start fermentation with yeast and as soon as it is well under way, put in cask. When scum no longer rises through opening in bungstave, water-seal. Bottle after 4 months if brilliantly clear.

Greengage Wine 2

Greengages	Brown sugar
Water	Yeast

Over each gal. of mashed fruit pour 1 gal. of boiling water, cover and allow to stand for 3 or 4 days, stirring daily. Now strain off liquor and dissolve in each gal. 3 lbs. of brown sugar. Start fermentation with yeast, turn into cask, and treat as in foregoing recipe.

Hock Wine

Plum juice	Lemon juice
Beet juice	Sugar
Apple cider	Cream of tartar

Mix together 1 gal. of purple plum juice, 1 gal. of

red beet juice, 1 gal. of fresh apple cider, and 12 oz. of lemon juice. Heat the mixture, but do not boil, and pour into a vat. Now dissolve in it 8 lbs. of sugar and 2 oz. of cream of tartar. Put in cask to ferment, filling to top every morning from a supply kept for that purpose. When it has stopped boiling over, water-seal and let stand for 4 or 5 months. At the end of this time it should be perfectly fine and ready for bottling.

Honey Wine 1

Honey	Hops
Water	Yeast

Pour 5 gals. of boiling water upon the same amount of honey, and continue boiling for 15 minutes, skimming frequently. Now add ¼ lb. hops and boil for 10 minutes more. When the liquor has cooled to lukewarmness, set in a warm place and start fermentation with yeast. When violent working has stopped, water-seal and allow to stand for 9 months before bottling.

Honey Wine 2

Honey	Cream of tartar
Apple cider	Cloves
Brandy	Bitter almonds
Rum	Yeast

Dissolve 10 lbs. of honey in 6 gals. of apple cider. Ferment with yeast. Keep in a warm place until all fermentation has stopped, then pour into a cask, add 1 qt. of bandy, 1 qt. of rum, 3 oz. of cream of tartar, 1 tbs. of cloves, ⅛ oz. of bitter almonds, and bung up tightly. After 10 months this wine is ready to be bottled and served.

Honey Wine 3

Honey   Lemons
Water   Hops
Ginger root

Place in a kettle 2 gals. of strained honey, 2 oz. of
bruised ginger root and 2 lemons (sliced), and pour
upon them 10 gals. of warm water. Boil for ½ hour,
keeping surface of liquor skimmed clean. Five minutes after boiling has started add 2 oz. of hops. When
the wine has cooled to lukewarmness, pour in a cask
to ferment. When fermentation has ceased completely,
bung up and let stand. It should be fine and ready to
bottle in a month's time.

Huckleberry Wine 1

Huckleberries   Sugar
Water   Egg white

Over every gal. of crushed fruit pour 1 gal. of water
and let stand in the vat for 24 hours. Stir frequently,
and at end of this time strain off liquor. Dissolve in
each gal. of it 2 lbs. of sugar and turn into clean cask
to ferment. When violent activity has subsided, water-
seal. Some time later, when all fermentation has
stopped, remove seal and mix in the well-beaten whites
of 4 eggs for every 5 gals. of wine. Bung up tightly
and let stand in basement for 3 months. The wine may
now be drawn off and bottled.

Huckleberry Wine 2

Use either of the recipes for Blueberry Wine, substituting same quantities of fruit.

Lemon Wine 1

Lemons   Cream of tartar
Raisins   Yeast
Sugar

For each gal. of water use the juice of 4 lemons, the parings of one, 1 lb. of chopped raisins, and 3½ lbs. of sugar. Boil water and sugar together, skim and pour, while still boiling, over the parings and the juice. Now add the chopped raisins and stir well. When lukewarm, put into a vat and start fermentation with yeast. Stir daily and keep vat covered. When violent activity has subsided, put in cask, adding ¼ oz. of cream of tartar per gal. and water-seal. Bottle after 8 or 9 months.

Lemon Wine 2

Lemons   Brandy
Water   Gelatin
Sugar

Peel and slice 40 lemons, keeping the parings of 25. Place the fruit and rinds in 4½ gals. of cold water. Stir daily and press with hands or stick with each stirring. After 10 days strain off liquor and add 17 lbs. of sugar. Let it work and when fermentation has stopped, add 3 gms. of pure leaf gelatin dissolved in a little of the wine. Now seal and set aside for 6 months. Open and add 1 pt. of brandy, and bung up tightly. After 2 months more in the cask the wine is ready to be bottled and served.

Lemon Wine 3

Lemons   Yeast
Water   Brandy
Sugar

Allow 10 lemons for each gal. of water. Put the parings of 5 in the vat and pour upon them 1 gal. of water which has been boiled for ½ hour with 4 lbs. of sugar. When cool, stir in the strained juice of all the lemons and a cake of yeast which has been dissolved in warm water. Let ferment for 3 or 4 days, stirring each day. At end of this time strain off into cask and water-seal. When fermentation stops, remove seal, add ½ cup of brandy per gal. of wine and re-seal. Bottle in 6 months.

Lime Wine

Limes	Cream of tartar
Water	Brandy
Sugar	Yeast

Squeeze out the juice of 7 or 8 limes and put into a vat with the rind of 1 lime. Add 1 gal. of water which has been boiled for 15 minutes with 4 lbs. of sugar. When liquor has cooled to lukewarmness, start fermentation with yeast. Cover vat and let stand, stirring daily for a week. Strain off, mix in ¼ oz. of cream of tartar and water-seal. Bottle in 7 or 8 months.

Loganberry Wine

Loganberries	Sugar
Water	Yeast

Put a quantity of ripe loganberries into a vat and mash with a potato masher. To 1 gal. of crushed berries add 1 qt. of boiling water and let stand for 24 hours, stirring occasionally. At the end of this time strain off the juice, measure it and in each gal. dissolve 3 lbs. of sugar. Start fermentation in the vat with yeast. When the violent stage has passed, turn into a cask and water-seal. Rack this wine in the fall into a fresh cask—in November. Bung up tightly and set aside for another month or 6 weeks. If it is perfectly fine by this time, it may be bottled and drunk.

Malt Wine

Sweet-wort	Raisins
Tun	Rock candy
Water	Brandy
Sugar	

Sweet-wort is the liquor from malt mash before it is boiled with hops. Tun is new beer, after the whole of the brewing process is finished. Both may be obtained from a brewery.

Boil together 1 gal. of water and 5½ lbs. of sugar for 10 minutes, skim well and put into a vat. Add 1¼ qts. of sweet-wort and the same amount of tun. Stir daily for 4 days, then turn into cask, filling to bunghole and let stand for 3 days more. Water-seal and keep for 2 to 3 months. At the end of this time remove seal and add 3 lbs. of chopped raisins for every 5 gals. and ½ lb. of rock candy (and hard pure sugar candy will do), and 1 pt. of brandy. Seal again and put aside for 6 months more before bottling.

Marigold Wine

Marigold blossoms	Lemons
Water	White wine (optional)
Sugar	Yeast

To each peck of marigold blossoms allow 1 gal. of water, 2 lbs. of sugar, 2 lemons, and, if desired, 1 pt. of good white wine. The water and sugar should be boiled together with frequent skimmings for ½ hour. Pour into a vat and add yeast when lukewarm. Wait until fermentation has started before mixing in the blossoms, at which time the lemons, sliced, should also be added. Let stand for 4 or 5 days, stirring every day. If the wine is used, it should be added at the time of sealing. In 6 months it will be ready to bottle.

Mango Wine

Use recipe for Peach Wine 2.

Mint Wine

Mint leaves	Sugar
Water	Yeast

This wine may be made with the same ingredients in various ways.

Over 1 gal. of freshly picked mint leaves, pressed lightly, but not packed, pour 5 gals. of cold water. Add 15 lbs. of sugar (to make it sweeter use 20 lbs.) and start fermentation with yeast. Let stand in a covered vat, set in a warm place for 10 or 12 days, stirring every day. Strain off, turn into cask and water-seal. It should be fine and ready for bottling at the end of 4 months.

Or, use 2 qts. of leaves and have water boiling. Proceed as above, except that the liquor should be strained and put in cask at the end of 4 days.

Again, boil for 30 minutes 1 qt. of leaves in 5 gals. of water. Strain off at once, add sugar and let ferment in cask.

Molasses Wine

Molasses	Hops
Water	Yeast

Boil together for 15 minutes 1 gal. of cane molasses (blackstrap not preferred), 1 gal. of water and 1 oz. of hops. Skim and remove from fire. When lukewarm, start fermentation with yeast, and turn into a cask on the following day. Water-seal and let stand until perfectly fine before bottling. This wine will age in the bottle and should remain at least 6 months in it before being served.

Mulberry Wine 1

Mulberries	Tannic acid
Apples	Cream of tartar
Sugar	Yeast

Mix together equal quantities by weight of mulberries and good apples (these should be peeled and cored) and run them through a press to extract all the juice. To 1 gal. of this add 1 lb. of sugar and stir until thoroughly dissolved. Now pour into a cask. Tannin, in the form of dry tannic acid, must now be added in the proportion of 2 gms. to every 5 gals. of wine, and the cream of tartar in the proportion of 1¼ oz. to the same amount of liquid. Stir well to insure that ingredients are thoroughly dissolved, and start fermentation with yeast. When the violent stage of fermentation has passed, water-seal. Bottle in March or April.

This wine should be racked into a fresh cask about 2 months after it has been sealed in.

Mulberry Wine 2

Mulberries	Sugar
Water	Cinnamon
White wine	

Pick the berries when they are changing from red to black and squeeze from them all the juice they will give. To each gal. allow the following proportions: 1 gal. of water, 1 oz. of cinnamon and 2 lbs. of powdered sugar candy. Boil these together for 10 minutes, making sure that the sugar is well dissolved, then skim and remove from fire. Strain through cheesecloth and add to the juice. Now add to the mixture 1 pt. of white wine, and put the whole in a cask to ferment. After a week's time, water-seal and put aside until perfectly fine. It may now be bottled at any time.

Mulberry Wine 3

Mulberries	Sugar
Water	

Pick the berries when they are just turning from red to black. Mash the fruit and to each gal. of crushed berries add 1 gal. of water. Stir and let stand for 24 hours. Now strain through a sieve with not too fine a mesh and dissolve 3½ lbs. of sugar in each gal. of liquor. Ferment for a few days in open vat and then turn into a cask. When the most active stage has passed, water-seal and let stand until perfectly fine before bottling.

Muscadine Wine 1

Muscadines   Sugar
Water

Crush a quantity of muscadines in the vat and let stand for a week. Stir daily in such a way as to immerse the husks in the liquor. At the end of this time press out all the juice and put in a cask, and add an equal amount of water. Now mix in 2½ lbs. of sugar for every gal. of wine, making sure that it is well dissolved. Leave cask open for 3 or 4 days, then water-seal. The wine may be bottled when fine or allowed to remain in the cask for a year.

Muscadine Wine 2

The simplest way to make muscadine wine is to press out the juice, place it in a cask, and water-seal after 2 or 3 days. It should be through fermenting in about 5 weeks and may be bottled when fine.

Another way is to mash the fruit and ferment for a week or so on the husks. Then press off juice and put in a cask under water-seal.

Sugar, of course, may be added to the juice in any amount desired.

Muskmelon Wine 1

Muskmelons   Cream of tartar
Water   Yeast
Sugar   Brandy (optional)
Lemon

Use only sound, ripe melons carefully pared of all rind. Mash to a pulp and to every 5 lbs. of melon allow 1 gal. of warm, not boiling, water. Stir well and let stand for 12 or 15 hours—overnight is all right. Then stir well once more and press off juice, straining it into the vat. Dissolve in this 2 to 2½ lbs. of sugar for each gal. of liquid, and ⅛ oz. of cream of tartar. Drop in, too, the parings of 1 lemon and start fermentation with a cake of yeast. Stir daily to make sure that all sugar is kept exposed to the yeasts. At the end of a week, or a little less time, skim off any surface accumulation and pour into a fresh cask. A pt. of brandy for each 5 gals. may now be added if desired. Water-seal and let stand until April, when it may be bottled.

Muskmelon Wine 2

Muskmelons	Yeast
Sugar	Brandy (optional)
Cream of tartar	

Fill a large barrel, whose head has been removed, with the flesh of sound melons carefully pared and cut into pieces an inch or two square. Over every 25 lbs. of melon pour 50 lbs. of white sugar and let stand overnight. On the folowing day stir as well as possible. Repeat the stirring on the following day, then press out juice, strain and return to barrel. Add 1 oz. cream of tartar for each 8 gals. of liquid and start fermentation with yeast. When violent activity has ceased, turn into a fresh cask, water-seal and let stand until spring before bottling. One pt. of brandy for each 5 gals. of wine may be added, if desired, at the time of turning into cask.

Oat Wine

Follow recipes for Wheat Wines, but use rolled oats and strain into cask at the end of 8 days instead of 10 or 12. Rolled oats need not be used if the grain has been carefully freed of its husks, in which case follow the Wheat Wine recipes exactly.

Onion Wine

Onions	Water
Potatoes	Sugar
Raisins	Yeast

Pare and slice ½ lb. of onions, then pare and dice
½ lb. of potatoes. Put both in a vat and add 1 lb. of
chopped raisins. Pour upon these ingredients 1 gal. of
warm (not hot) water in which 2 lbs. of sugar have
been dissolved. Lay a cake of yeast on top of liquid
and allow to stand overnight. On the next morning stir
in vigorously. Repeat stirring every day for 10 days.
This should allow a week's active fermentation in the
open vat. At the end of this time turn into a cask and
water-seal. The wine should come fine in 2 months. It
may be bottled now, but is better for drinking after 2
more months.

Onion wine is temperamental in the results it gives.
One way to help it is to use mild onions; for example,
to insure success, large sweet Bermudas.

Orange Wine 1

Sweet oranges	Yeast
Water	Brandy (optional)
Sugar	

Know the height in your vat to which 10 gals. of
liquid will reach. To make 10 gals. of wine, use a crate
of sweet oranges. Pare 18 of them and pour 2 qts. of
boiling water upon the peelings. Let stand for 24 hours.
Peel the remaining oranges, press out juice and put it
into a vat. Now dissolve in the juice 30 to 35 lbs. of
sugar and add the water in which the parings have
stood. Pour upon the pressed pulp of the oranges
enough water to cover well and let soak for 24 hours.
Press out and add to the liquid already in the vat.
Repeat this last step as often as is necessary until the
10-gal. mark in the vat has been reached, stirring

thoroughly each time a new batch of water is added. Use three cakes of yeast to start fermentation. As this may be slow, keep the liquid in the vat for 2 or 3 weeks before turning into a cask. Leave under water-seal until all fermentation has completely subsided, then refill cask from a surplus retained for that purpose, and bung up tightly. Bottle after a year in the cask. At the time of bunging brandy may be added in the amount of 1 qt. to every 5 gals. of wine.

Orange Wine 2

Sweet oranges   Sugar
Water

Pare 100 sweet oranges and press out the juice. Place the pulp in one vat and the parings in another. Put 35 lbs. of sugar in a 10-gal. cask and add the juice, stirring well to make sure that the sugar is thoroughly dissolved. Now pour 3 qts. of water upon the pulp and an equal amount upon the parings. After 24 hours strain off and add to the contents of the cask. Add more water to pulp and parings and repeat this process each day until the cask is full. Contents of the cask should be stirred daily, and when it is finally full, allow it to stand open for 3 more days before sealing with water-seal. After 9 months the wine is ready for bottling and is potable 3 months after that.

Orange Wine 3

Sweet oranges   Yeast
Water   Lemons (optional)
Sugar

Allow 13 or 14 sweet oranges and 3½ lbs. of sugar to each gal. of water. Boil sugar and water together for 15 or 20 minutes and skim. Let cool and add the juice of the oranges along with ⅓ of the parings cut thin. Stir well and let stand for 24 hours in an open vat.

Now add a cake of yeast dissolved in a cup of warm water and let ferment for 3 or 4 days. Strain into cask and water-seal. Bottle after 9 months. The wine is ready for drinking one year from the date of making.

Before sealing the cask, the flavor of the wine may be enhanced by adding the juice and rind of 3 lemons per gal. of liquor.

Orange Wine 4

Sweet oranges   Sugar
Water

To the juice of 1 doz. sweet oranges add 1 gal. of water and 3 lbs. of sugar. Stir well and let ferment in cask. Fermentation is slow and the mixture should be kept in a fairly warm place for a few weeks. After sealing, it should be put aside for a year before bottling.

Orange Wine 5

Sour oranges   Sugar
Water   Yeast

To 1 gal. of juice pressed from sour oranges add 4 gals. of water and 20 lbs. of sugar. Boil together gently, skimming frequently, and when no more scum rises to the surface, remove from fire and strain through a flannel bag into a cask. Now add 1 qt. of uncooked juice from the same kind of oranges, and let the whole ferment under water-seal in a relatively cool basement. If fermentation seems slow in starting, urge it along with a cake of yeast dissolved in a little warm water. Bottle afer 6 months if perfectly fine.

Orange and Raisin Wine

Oranges   Water
Raisins   Sugar

Select 16 large oranges and pare 6 of them thinly,

dropping the parings in a vat. Run 24 lbs. of good quality muscat raisins through a meat chopper and put these in with the parings. Now add 5 gals. of warm water and let stand for 7 days, stirring daily, then strain off into fresh cask. Now cook together for 15 minutes the juice of all the oranges and 1 lb. of cane sugar. When cool, mix with the contents of the cask, water-seal and let stand for 3 months before bottling. Like all wine in which oranges are a principal ingredient, this improves with age.

Parsnip Wine 1

Parsnips	Cream of tartar
Water	Yeast
Sugar	

Thoroughly clean 3 lbs. of parsnips, slice them thin and boil in 1 gal. of water for 1½ hours. Drain off the liquid without bruising the parsnips and add enough boiling water to restore the original quantity. Allow 3 lbs. of sugar and ¼ oz. of cream of tartar per gal. of liquor and stir well. When nearly cold turn into cask and start fermentation with yeast. Keep in a warm place and stir daily for 12 to 14 days. At end of this time water-seal and set in a cool spot for 6 months. Draw off into a fresh cask and let stand for another 6 months before bottling.

Parsnip Wine 2

Parsnips	Cream of tartar
Water	Yeast
Sugar	

Use 4½ lbs. of parsnips to every gal. of water. Clean thoroughly, but do not scrape off skins, and split each parsnip into 3 or 4 parts. Boil in an uncovered pan until soft. This should require about 2 hours and boiling should be gentle, not vigorous. When they are tender, pour off water without bruising the parsnips, as no part of them must get into the wine. To every gal. of liquor add 2½ lbs. of good brown sugar, and to every 5 gals. allow 1 oz. of cream of tartar. Stir in well and start fermentation with yeast. Ferment for about 10 days in an open vat, skimming off the surface every morning. Water-seal in cask and bottle in March.

Parsnip Wine 3

Parsnips	Sugar
Water	Yeast

Clean well, but without scraping off the skins, 3 lbs. of firm parsnips and slice them quite thin. Boil in a gal. of water for 1½ hours, pour off water, and squeeze parsnips gently in a bag to secure what liquid remains. Strain all juice through a fine sieve or cloth, add enough water to restore original amount and boil again for ½ or ¾ hour. When lukewarm, pour into a vat and ferment with yeast. Stir daily and skim the surface without removing too much of the liquor. At the end of 10 days put in cask and water-seal. Bottle after a year.

Parsnip Wine 4

Parsnips	Cream of tartar
Water	Yeast
Brown sugar	Brandy (optional)

Clean thoroughly and slice thin 4 lbs. of parsnips and boil in 1 gal. of water for 1½ hours. Strain off liquor and dissolve in it 3 lbs. of best quality brown sugar and ¼ oz. of cream of tartar. Put in cask and start fermentation with yeast. When fermentation has completely stopped, bung up tightly and let stand until March, when the wine may be bottled.

If desired, brandy may be added in the amount of 1 qt. to every 5 gals. of wine at the time of bunging.

Peach Wine 1

Peaches	Cream of tartar
Water	Brandy (optional)
Sugar	

Dissolve in 9 gals. of water 15 lbs. of sugar and 1 oz. of cream of tartar, and let stand for a day. Now remove the stones from about 40 ripe but not overripe peaches, crush these and place in the liquor. Break open a dozen or so of the stones and add the kernels to the contents of the vat. Stir well and let the whole stand for 5 days after fermentation begins; then press out the liquor, strain, put in cask and water-seal. When fermentation has subsided for good, 3 or 4 qts. of brandy may be added if it is desired. In this case the wine should be allowed to remain in the cask for at least 2 months more before it is bottled.

Peach Wine 2

Peaches	Cream of tartar
Water	Yeast
Sugar	

Decide first how much it is desired to make, then allow 5 peaches to each gal. of water. Use only ripe fruit. Slice and stone it and mash in the vat. Break the pits of half the fruit open and throw the kernels and shells in with the crushed fruit. Add warm water in the proportion mentioned and let the whole stand for 36 hours. At the end of this time stir into the mixture 3 lbs. of sugar and ¼ oz. of cream of tartar for every gal. of water used. Ferment with yeast, and after a week strain off and put in a fresh cask. Water-seal at once and let stand until perfectly fine. It may now be bottled, but should remain for 2 or 3 months in glass before being served.

Peach Wine 3

Dried peaches   Cream of tartar
Raisins   Brandy
Water   Yeast
Sugar

Run through a meat chopper 8 lbs. of dried peaches and 3 lbs. of raisins, and place in a vat. Add 15 lbs. of sugar and 2 oz. of cream of tartar, and pour over the whole 8 gals. of boiling water. Stir well and when liquor is lukewarm start fermentation with yeast. Allow to ferment in open vat for a week, then strain into a cask, add 1 qt. of good brandy and water-seal. Rack off into a fresh cask at the end of a month, bung up tightly, and bottle after 4 months.

Pear Wine

Pears   Sugar
Water   Yeast

Grind a bushel of pears (preferably cored) by running through a meat grinder or any similar crusher. Press out the juice and allow to stand for a day. To every gallon of juice now add 10 lbs. of sugar, previously dissolved in 2½ gals. of water. Pour this into the pear juice and stir the mixture well. Let stand in the fermenting vat for four or five days, stirring daily. Dissolve two cakes of yeast in a bit of warm water. Add this to the mixture and turn the whole into a cask or carboy. Water-seal and let stand for 4 or 5 months.

Pineapple Wine 1

Pineapples   Water
Sugar   Yeast

Shred or cut into small pieces a quantity of ripe pineapples and over every gal. of the measured fruit pour 1 gal. of hot water. Let stand for 3 or 4 days, stirring frequently. Then draw off the juice, press the pulp dry, and after straining all the liquor obtained, put it in a clean vat with 2½ to 3 lbs. of sugar per gal. and start fermentation with yeast. In a week's time strain again, turn into a cask and water-seal. Bottle when brilliantly clear.

Pineapple Wine 2

Pineapples   Yeast
Sugar

Where the fruit is plentiful, undiluted juice may be used. To every gal. of juice add 1½ lbs. of sugar and ferment with yeast. The entire process of fermentation may be carried out in a cask. When the wine comes perfectly fine, it may be bottled.

Plum Wine 1

Plums   Cream of tartar
Water   Yeast
Sugar

Stone 4 gals. of ripe plums before the flesh has become mushy, crush them in the vat, and pour upon the pulp 5½ gals. of warm (not hot) water. Stir vigorously for a few minutes, and let stand for 6 hours. Press out juice, strain, and set aside until next day. Now stir in it 15 lbs. of sugar and 2 oz. of cream of tartar. Start fermentation with yeast. During this process keep suspended in the liquor the kernels from 1 gal. of the fruit. Water-seal when the violent stage has passed, and bottle after 4 months.

Plum Wine 2

Plums   Brown sugar
Water   Yeast

Pour 5 gals of boiling water upon 40 lbs. of sound ripe

plums and let stand for 2 days. At the end of this time press out and strain liquid into a cask. Now stir in for 10 minutes 2½ lbs. of brown sugar for every gal. Start fermentation with yeast and water-seal after violent stage has passed. Bottle in 5 monhs.

Pomona Wine 1

Cider   Brandy
Sugar

Dissolve 10 lbs. of sugar in 5 gals. of fresh apple cider which has been strained through a flannel bag or cloth. Turn into a cask as soon as sugar is thoroughly dissolved and let ferment, keeping filled to the top. When fermentation begins to grow weaker, lower a bit, add 1 qt. of good brandy and water-seal. If set aside in September or October, this will be ready for bottling in May or June.

Pomona Wine 2

Boil a good-quality cider until it is reduced to half, then strain through flannel or several thicknesses of cheesecloth 3 or 4 times. Put in a cask and leave bung open for 3 or 4 days. Then seal up with water-seal and allow to stand for 2 years.

Pomona Wine 3

Another pomona wine can be made as follows. Make a fairly thick syrup of sugar and cider. To every gal. of new clear cider add 1 pt. of this syrup. Place in a cask, water-seal, and put in a cool place to ferment. Ready after a year.

Potato Wine

Potatoes   Sugar
Raisins   Yeast
Water

Scrub clean and dice 12 lbs. of potatoes and put them in the vat with 12 lbs. of raisins which have been run through a meat chopper. Pour upon them 6 gals. of warm water and stir well. Now dissolve in the liquor 12 lbs. of sugar and start fermentation with yeast. Allow to remain in the vat for 10 or 12 days, stirring each day, and at end of that time strain off into a clean cask and water-seal. Bottle when fine.

The flavor of the wine may be improved by throwing a handful of cracked cherry, plum, or peach pits into the wine just before sealing it.

Primrose Wine

Use 1 pt. of gently packed but not bruised flowers per gal. of water and follow directions given in recipe for Cowslip Wine 1.

Prune Wine 1

Prunes	Cream of tartar
Water	Yeast
Sugar	

Stone, and crush in the vat 8 gals. of sound, ripe prunes and pour upon them 10 gals. of warm water. Stir vigorously for a few minutes and then set aside. The following day, press out juice and dissolve in it 15 lbs. of sugar and 3 oz. of cream of tartar. Add 5 or 6 handfuls of cracked pits and start fermentation with yeast. Strain into a cask after 8 or 10 days and water-seal. Bottle at the end of 5 months.

Prunes may be substituted in the recipes given for Damson Wine.

Prune Wine 2

Prunes	Sugar
Water	Yeast

Over every gal. of ripe but sound fruit pour 1 gal. of

boiling water and let stand for 2 days; then pour off the liquor, pressing fruit well to get it all. Add to this 3 lbs. of sugar per gal. and ferment in a cask with yeast. Water-seal at proper time and allow to remain in the cask until brilliantly fine before bottling. The wine will be ready for serving when 6 months old.

Improve the flavor by throwing in a handful of cracked kernels just before sealing it in.

Quince Wine 1

Quinces	Lemons
Water	Yeast
Sugar	

Run through a vegetable grinder or mash to a pulp 100 good ripe quinces which have previously been cored and cut into pieces. Put the crushed fruit in 5 gals. of water at boiling point and allow to simmer for 20 minutes; then strain off liquor, pressing pulp dry. Turn this into the vat and add the juice of 6 lemons and 10 lbs. of sugar. When lukewarm, start fermentation with yeast and let stand for 2 days, stirring 2 or 3 times each day; then strain once more, put in cask and water-seal. After 6 months this should be fine and ready for bottling. Age helps quince wine.

Quince Wine 2

Quinces	Sugar

Select quinces that are fully ripe, but make sure that they are not decayed, or, at least, that all decayed spots have been removed. Mash or grind them and press out juice. To each gal. of this add 2½ lbs. of sugar, stirring well until it is dissolved. The early working may be allowed to take place in either the vat or a cask. After the wine has been sealed in, it should be left until the month of March or April before it is bottled.

Raisin Wine 1

Raisins
Water
Sugar

Cream of tartar
Brandy (optional)

Over 28 lbs. of finely chopped Malaga raisins pour 3 gals. of hot water. Stir well and let stand 12 hours; then squeeze out all liquid and strain through cloth bag. Pour 2 gals. of hot water on the pressed remains, mix well and let stand again for 12 hours. Press out and strain this juice as before and add to that already obtained. Now stir in well 3 lbs. of sugar and 1 oz. of cream of tartar. Cover the vat and let ferment for a few days, stirring daily. When violent fermentation has ceased, turn into cask and water-seal. The wine may be advantageously racked into a fresh cask at the end of 3 months. Time spent in the wood helps this wine and it is better if not bottled before the end of a year.

Brandy, if desired, may be added at the time of first racking.

Raisin Wine 2

Raisins
Water

Sugar

Over 6 lbs. of chopped raisins pour 2 gals. of hot, but not boiling, water. Let stand for 15 minutes and then stir, taking care to break up all lumps. Strain off liquor and press husks well to get all they contain. Now pour over the pressed remains 2 gals. more of hot water and proceed as before. Repeat this process a third time. All the liquor obtained is put into a vat and to each gal. of it is allowed 1 lb. of sugar. Stir daily for about 10 days, then turn into a cask and water-seal. Bottle after 10 months.

Raisin Wine 3

Raisins   Lemons
Water   Yeast
Sugar

Place in the vat 6 lbs. of finely chopped raisins, the
rind of 5 lemons and the juice of 1 doz., and 6 lbs. of
sugar. Boil 6 gals. of water for 30 minutes, skim and
pour over the contents of the vat, mixing all together.
Start fermentation with yeast and keep it the vat, which
should be covered with a cloth or newspaper. Stir daily
for 6 or 7 days, then turn into a cask and water-seal.
Bottle when brilliantly fine.

Raisin Wine 4

Raisins   Oranges
Water   Brandy
Sugar

Grind 20 lbs. of seeded muscat raisins and put them
into a vat. Over them pour 5 gals. of water. Cover and
allow to stand for a month, stirring once every day. At
end of this time strain into a cask and water-seal. Let
the wine stand for another month. Now rack off into a
fresh cask and to every gal. of liquor add ¾ lb. of
sugar and the juice and thin peel of one California
orange. When sugar is thoroughly dissolved, water-seal
once more. Bottle after 3 months.

Raisin Wine 5

Raisins   Lemons
Apple cider   Brandy
Sugar

Run through meat chopper 15 lbs. of Malaga raisins
and place in the vat with 10 gals. of apple cider. Add
2 lbs. of sugar and stir well until this is dissolved. Drop
in the liquor the thinly pared rinds of 3 lemons. Fer-

ment in a cask. After a week add 1 qt. of brandy and water-seal. It is ready for bottling after 6 months.

Raisin Wine 6

Raisins	Sugar
Water	Yeast

Allow 5 lbs. of chopped raisins to simmer gently for an hour in 5 gals. of water. Strain through a sieve into the vat, rubbing raisins through with the hands. Add now 10 lbs. of sugar and stir well. Start fermentation with yeast and let stand in the vat for 4 days, stirring daily. Now strain into a cask and water-seal. Bottle in a year.

Raisin Wine 7

Raisins	Sugar
Water	

Pour 5 gals. of water upon 10 lbs. of raisins. Stir daily, and when violent fermentation has passed, pour into a cask and water-seal. Bottle when fine, or let stand in the cask for a year.

Raisin and Elderberry Wine

Raisins	Sugar
Elderberry juice	Yeast
Water	

Run 30 lbs. of muscat raisins through a meat chopper, place in a vat, and pour over them 5 gals. of boiling water. Cover and let stand for 10 days, stirring every day. At end of this time add 5 qts. of juice pressed from fully ripe elderberries, and start fermentation with yeast. After a week strain into cask and water-seal. The wine may be bottled in 6 months, but a year in the wood will improve its quality.

Raspberry Wine 1

Raspberries	Egg-white
Water	Currant juice (optional)
Sugar	Whiskey (optional)

To every gal. of ripe red raspberries add 1 gal. of boiling water and let stand in an open vat for a day, stirring frequently. Press out juice and for each gal. add 2 lbs. of sugar. When this is thoroughly dissolved, turn into cask, and when violent stage of fermentation has passed, water-seal. When all active fermentation has stopped, remove seal and stir in the well-beaten whites of 2 eggs for every 5 gals. of wine. Re-seal and let stand for 3 months before bottling.

The wine wine may be touched up a bit by substituting a gal. or two of currant juice for an equal amount of water.

An additional flavor, which is pleasing to many people, may be imparted to the wine by adding 3 or 4 qts. of good whiskey after it has stood for a month. Let stand for 2 months more before serving.

Raspberry Wine 2

Raspberries	Oranges
Water	Cream of tartar
Sugar	Brandy
Lemons	Currant juice (optional)
Apple cider	

Crush well in the vat 6 gals. of ripe berries and let stand for 3 or 4 hours; then press out juice. Pour upon the pressed remains 5 gals. of water and allow this to stand for 12 hours. Press out again and add to the liquor already obtained. Now add to this 4 gals. of apple cider, 15 lbs. of sugar, 2½ oz. of cream of tartar, and let the whole ferment in the vat. Very early in the process throw into the mixture the juice and rinds of 2 lemons and 2 oranges. When violent fermentation has subsided, strain through sieve and put in cask. Water-seal and when all activity has stopped, remove seal and stir in 2 qts. of brandy. Bottle after 4 months.

This wine may be given additional flavor by the substitution of a gal. of currant juice for a gal. of water.

Raspberry Wine 3

Raspberries	Sugar
Water	

Mash well 1 gal. of ripe raspberries in the vat and pour over them 1 gal. of cold water. Let stand for 24 hours, stirring often. Press out and strain liquor. Add 4 lbs. of sugar to each gal. and ferment in cask. Bottle after 4 months.

This wine may be made less sweet by reducing the amount of sugar used.

Rhubarb Wine 1

Rhubarb	Water
Sugar	Lemon

Mash rhubarb to a pulp and for every 5 lbs. allow 1 gal. of cold water. Stir well and let steep for 3 or 4 days, mixing 2 or 3 times daily. Press off juice and put it into the vat and dissolve in it 3 lbs. of sugar for each gal. of juice. Now drop in the liquor the parings of 1 lemon, and let the whole ferment for a week. Skim off crust and pour into a fresh cask and water-seal. Bottle in February or March.

Rhubarb Wine 2

Rhubarb	Allspice
Water	Nutmeg
Brown sugar	Cloves
Cinnamon	

Cut into small pieces 4 lbs. of rhubarb stalks and

pour over them 1 gal. of boiling water. Let stand for 24 hours with frequent stirrings, and then press out and strain juice. Dissolve in it 4 lbs. of brown sugar to every gal. and mix in well ¼ oz. cinnamon, ¼ oz. of allspice, ⅛ oz. of nutmeg, 3 bruised cloves, and let the whole ferment in a cask. Water-seal when violent activity has stopped and let remain for 3 months before bottling. Serve the folowing spring.

Rhubarb Wine 3

| Rhubarb | Sugar |
| Water | Lemon |

Cut several lbs. of rhubarb stalk into small pieces and to every gal. thus prepared allow 3 lbs. of sugar, and the thin parings and juice of 1 lemon. Pour over the whole 1 gal. of boiling water and let stand in an open vat for 10 days with daily stirring. At end of this time strain off and put in a fresh cask and water-seal. It may be bottled when perfectly fine, but should not be served until it has spent several more months in either the wood or the bottles.

Rhubarb Wine 4

| Rhubarb | Sugar |
| Water | |

Prepare rhubarb by cooking until tender, and then mash into a pulp and press out juice. To each gal. of this allow 1 gal. of soft, or boiled water and 7 lbs. of brown sugar. Put in cask to ferment. When the liquor is through working, it may be bottled immediately, or it may be bunged up tightly and left in the cask until spring. Be sure cask is full before bunging.

Rhubarb Wine 5

It often happens in truck-garden districts that growers have large quantities of rhubarb left on their hands when the market season is over or has passed its peak. Here is a method for helpful disposal of part of this surplus.

Fill a barrel with chopped or ground rhubarb stalks. Over the contents of a 50-gallon barrel pour 100 lbs. of white sugar and stir well. Now put on barrel head and drill in it a small hole through which the escaping gas may pass (water-sealing will do as well). Let stand until next spring when the wine is ready to serve or bottle or both.

The barrel should stand on end and a spigot should be inserted near the bottom before the rhubarb is put in it.

Rhubarb normally gives about ¾ of its weight in juice, a fact which should make it easy to determine the amount of sugar to be used with barrels of varying size.

Rice and Raisin Wine

Rice	Sugar
Raisins	Yeast
Water	

Place in the vat 12 lbs. of rice and 12 lbs. of chopped raisins and pour upon them 6 gals. of warm water. Stir for several minutes to assure that all lumps will be broken. Now add 12 lbs. of sugar and stir again until all sugar is dissolved. Ferment with 2 cakes of yeast. Let stand in a covered vat 10 to 12 days, stirring once each day. At end of this time strain off and turn into a cask and water-seal. The wine will be ready for bottling in 3 months.

This wine may be nicely touched up by placing in the vat during the stage of violent fermentation 3 or 4 handfuls of walnut leaves, or by placing in cask just before sealing, a handful of cracked cherry, plum, or peach pits.

Rose Wine

Use sweet, odorous blossoms, allowing 1 pt. of gently pressed flowers per gal. of water. Follow recipe for Cowslip Wine 1. Wild roses will do very well.

Rue and Fennel Wine

Rue	Honey
Fennel root	Water

Boil together for 45 minutes 1 gal. of water, 3 sprigs of rue, a fair-sized handful of fennel root, and 3 lbs. of honey. At end of this period boiled water may be added to restore original amount. Now strain the liquor well and boil for 2 hours more, skimming the surface frequently. Again make up for water lost through evaporation by adding more that has been well boiled. Turn into cask and water-seal. Bottle when a year old.

Sugar may be substituted for honey by allowing 3 lbs. per gal. In this case reduce second boiling period to 30 minutes.

Sage Wine

Green sage	Sugar
Raisins	Yeast
Water	

Put 1 bu. of green sage in a large vat with 10 lbs. of raisins which have been run through a meat chopper and 8 lbs. of sugar. Now pour upon this 5 gals. of boiling water and stir well for 5 or 10 minutes. When lukewarm start fermentation with a cake of yeast. Stir twice daily for a week, then strain off into cask and water-seal. Bottle when thoroughly fine. A few months of age will improve this wine.

Sarsaparilla Wine

Sarsaparilla leaves	Lemon
Water	Raisins
Sugar	

Over every lb. of sarsaparilla leaves and stems pour 1 gal. of water. Now add to the liquid ¼ lb. of chopped raisins, 2 lbs. of sugar, and 1 lemon sliced. Fermentation should be started with yeast and allowed to continue in an open vat for 5 or 6 days, then put the wine under water-seal until it is quite fine, at which time it is ready for bottling.

If sarsaparilla leaves and stems are not available, 1 gal. of sarsaparilla syrup may be substituted for every lb. of leaves and stems. If syrup is used, be sure to omit the sugar from the above recipe.

Scuppernong Wine

Use recipes for Muscadine Wine.

Sloe Wine

Sloes	Sugar
Water	Brandy

Mash 5 gals. of sound, ripe fruit in the vat and pour over it 5 gals. of boiling water. Stir daily for a week, or better yet, use hands to separate skins, pulp, and stones. At end of this time add 18 to 20 lbs. of sugar and allow to stand for another week with daily stirrings. Now press out juice, strain, and turn into a fresh cask. Add 2 qts. of brandy and water-seal. Bottle after 9 months.

The flavor may be enhanced by throwing in a handful of cracked cherry or plum pits at the time of sealing.

Sorghum Wine

Sorghum molasses	Hops
Water	Yeast

Mix together equal portions of sorghum molasses and water, and to every gal. of the mixture allow 1 oz. of hops. Boil the whole for 20 minutes, then skim well and remove from fire. When the liquor has cooled to lukewarmness, start fermentation with yeast. Turn into a cask on following day, and when sludge no longer rises through opening, water-seal and set aside until perfectly fine. This wine will improve somewhat with age.

Spice Wine

Make Sugar Wine as per recipe below and add essence of spice just before sealing.

Essence of spice is a strong concentrate and not much is required (see recipe for Spruce Wine). It is necessary to determine by experiment the amount to be used. Keep stirring into a gal. of warm water small quantities of essence of spice, or of any particular spice. When the taste imparted to the water is satisfactory, multiply the amount of essence added by the number of gals. of wine desired.

This wine should stand for 2 or 3 months after making, either in the cask or in the bottle.

Spruce Wine

Essence of spruce	Cream of tartar
Water	Grape leaves
Sugar	Yeast

Dissolve 4 lbs. of sugar in 1 gal. of water which has been boiled for 45 minutes. Add ¼ oz. cream of tartar and a handful of grape leaves or tendrils. Ferment in a vat with yeast, and when this process is over, pour in a cask and add ¼ oz. essence of spruce to each gal. of wine. Stir in well, water-seal and let stand for 2 months before serving.

Strawberry Wine 1

Strawberries	Lemons
Water	Cream of tartar
Brown sugar	Brandy (optional)
Cider	

Mash 6 gals. of ripe strawberries in the vat and pour upon them 6 gals. of apple cider and 7 gals. of water. Stir well and let stand for 3 days in a fairly warm basement. Press out liquor and strain through fine sieve or coarse cloth. Now add 16 lbs. of brown sugar, 3 oz. of cream of tartar, and the thin parings and juice of 2 lemons. Mix all together, stirring well to make sure that the sugar is completely dissolved. Pour in cask and allow to ferment for 3 days, then add 2 qts. of brandy and water-seal. Do not bottle before 2 months.

Strawberry Wine 2

Strawberries	Oranges
Water	Cream of tartar
Cider	Brandy
Sugar	Currant juice (optional)
Lemons	

Mash in the vat 6 gals. of strawberries and allow them to stand for 3 hours, then press out the juice and pour upon the pressed remains 5 gals. of water and let stand for 12 hours, stirring only ocasionally. Press out this liquor and add it to the juice already obtained. Into the mixture now put 4 gals. of apple cider, 15 lbs. of sugar, 2½ oz. of cream of tartar, and the juice and rinds of 2 lemons and 2 oranges. Let ferment until the violent stage has passed, then pour into a cask and keep under water-seal until fermentation has stopped completely. Now stir in the wine 1 gal. of brandy and bung up tightly for 4 months. At end of this time the wine should be fine and ready for bottling.

The substitution of 2 or 3 gals. of currant juice for equal amounts of water will add to the flavor of the finished product.

Strawberry Wine 3

Strawberries	Lemon
Water	Orange
Sugar	Whiskey (optional)

To every gal. of crushed fruit add 1 qt. of water, stir well and let stand for 24 hours. Press off liquor, strain, and dissolve in it 2½ lbs. of sugar to each gal. Turn into cask to ferment. While the fermentation is in process, keep suspended in the wine in a small cloth bag the rinds of 1 lemon and 1 orange. Water-seal after 2 or 3 days, and when fermentation has completely subsided, remove the bag containing the parings, and add 1 pt. of good quality whiskey for every gal. of wine. Now bung up tightly and set aside for 2 months before bottling. The whiskey need not be used unless desired.

Strawberry Wine 4

Strawberries	Orange
Water	Cream of tartar
Sugar	Brandy (optional)
Lemon	

Mash in the vat 5 gals. of ripe strawberries and pour over them 5 gals. of water. Let ferment for 3 days, and then press out juice and strain. To the quantity obtained add 13 lbs. of sugar, the thin parings and the juice of 1 lemon and 1 orange, and 1¼ oz. of cream of tartar. Stir well and pour into a fresh cask. After 2 or 3 days, water-seal. If brandy is desired, 2 qts. should be added just before sealing the cask. The wine should be fine and ready for the bottle after 3 months.

Strawberry Wine 5

Strawberries   Sugar
Water

Mash well a quantity of good ripe strawberries and press out the juice at once. To each gal. of this add 1 gal. of water and 4 lbs. of sugar. When the violent stage of fermentation has passed, turn into a cask and water-seal. Bottle after 2 months.

Strawberry Wine 6

Strawberries   Sugar
Water

Mash in the vat 3 gals. of ripe fruit and let stand for 3 hours. Press out juice and add 1 gal. of water and 4 lbs. of sugar. Mix well and ferment in cask. Water-seal after the violent stage has passed. If the wine is thoroughly fine at the end of 6 weeks, it is ready for bottling.

Sugar Wine

Though this wine cannot be recommended for its flavor, of which it has little, it is, nevertheless, worth knowing how to make, for it can be made to serve as a base for many others. Various spice wines may be made by adding a sufficient quantity of spice or essence of spice just before sealing in cask. Also, many flower wines can be had by pouring the syrup described below over the blossoms while it is still hot.

Dissolve 3 lbs. of sugar in 1 gal. of boiling water. Add 1 lb. of honey, ½ oz. of cream of tartar, and, if they can be got, a handful of grape leaves or tendrils for their tannin (or dry tannic acid from the drugstore, in the proportion of 1 gm. to every 5 gals. of liquor, will do just as well). Ferment in a warm place. If this is slow in coming, start with yeast. Seal in cask when fermentation has stopped, and bottle when perfectly fine.

Sycamore Wine

Draw sap when it is running and follow the recipe given for Birch Wine.

Tomato Wine 1

Tomatoes	Salt
Sugar	

Mash well a quantity of tomatoes and allow them to stand for 24 hours. At the end of this time press out all juice and dissolve in it 4 lbs. of sugar for every gal. Ferment in the vat covered with a light cloth, skimming off scum as it rises. The wine may be fermented out in the vat, or it may be turned into cask after 10 days and allowed to complete its fermentation under water-seal. It is ready for bottling when fine.

Though it is not necessary, 1 or 2 tsp. of salt added to every gal. while fermentation is in process will improve the quality of the wine.

When served, this wine may be diluted with sugar and water to suit the individual taste.

Tomato Wine 2

Tomatoes	Brown sugar

To each gal. of tomato juice add 4 lbs. of brown sugar. When this is thoroughly dissolved, turn into a cask to ferment. After a few days water-seal and let stand for 4 months. Like most wines made with brown sugar, this improves with age.

Tomato Wine 3

Tomatoes	Sugar
Water	

Mash thoroughly a quantity of small tomatoes, press out juice and strain at once. To every gal. obtained, add ½ gal. of water and 2½ lbs. of sugar. Start fermentation in the vat, then strain into cask and water-seal. Do this before the wine has completely stopped its fermentation. When this has subsided entirely, remove water-seal, fill cask to bunghole and bung up tightly. Bottle when it comes fine.

Turnip Wine 1

Turnips	Cream of tartar
Water	Yeast
Brown sugar	Brandy (optional)

Use turnips in the proportion of 4 lbs. to 1 gal. of water. Wash turnips well and cook in water until tender. Press out all liquor and strain through a cloth. To every gal. obtained add 3 lbs. of brown sugar and ¼ oz. of cream of tartar. Start fermentation in a vat with yeast and turn into a cask after 3 or 4 days. When scum no longer rises through bunghole, lower surface about 2 inches and water-seal until the wine has ceased wholly to work. Then fill cask, bung up tightly and let stand until March or April before bottling.

Brandy, if desired, may be added at the time of bunging in the proportion of 2½ qts. for every 5 gals. of wine.

Turnip Wine 2

Turnips	Brandy
Sugar	

Pare and cut into thin slices a large quantity of good sound turnips. Put in the vat, sprinkle with sugar, and let stand for 2 days. Now press out juice through a cloth bag, strain and place in a cask. Allow 3 lbs. of sugar per gal. of liquor, and when this is thoroughly dissolved, mix in 2 qts. of brandy and water-seal. Bottle after 4 months. This wine improves with age and will be better after a year has elapsed.

Turnip Wine 3

Turnips	Cream of tartar
Water	Yeast
Sugar	

Boil 3 lbs. of turnips, previously washed clean, in 1 gal. of water until they are very tender. Pour off the liquor carefully taking care not to bruise the turnips, and add enough boiling water to restore the original gallon. Now add 3 lbs. of sugar and ¼ oz. of cream of tartar. When lukewarm pour into a vat and start fermentation with yeast. Stir every day for 10 or 12 days. At end of this time place in a cask, water-seal, and let stand for 4 months, when it should be racked into a fresh cask. Set aside for 6 months more and then bottle.

Verbena Wine

Use verbena blossoms and follow recipe given for Clary Wine.

Vervain Wine

Same as Verbena Wine.

Violet Wine

Use flowers while still fresh in the proportion of 1 pt. of violets to 1 gal. of water, and follow recipe for Cowslip Wine 1.

Walnut Leaf Wine

Walnut leaves
Water

Honey (or sugar)
Yeast

Gather 150, or a few more, black walnut leaves which are entirely free from scale or wilt. Allow 5 gals. of water and 17 lbs. of honey. Boil together for 1 hour, skimming off carefully all but the leaves. Restore original amount of water and put in a vat. When lukewarm, start fermentation with yeast. Within 24 hours after the yeast has been stirred in, mix well once more, strain, and turn into cask. Water-seal and hold until 3 months have elapsed before bottling.

If sugar is used instead of honey, allow 3 lbs. per gal. of liquor. Boil same length of time.

Wheat Wine 1

Wheat
Raisins
Potatoes

Water
Sugar
Yeast

Place into a vat 4 lbs. of wheat, 4 lbs. of chopped raisins, and 8 or 9 medium-size potatoes scrubbed clean and diced, and pour over the whole 6 gals. of warm water. Stir well, then dissolve in the mixture 18 lbs. of sugar. Start fermentation with yeast in a vat. Stir daily for 10 days. At the end of this time turn into a clean cask and water-seal. It is ready for bottling at the end of 2 months.

Wheat Wine 2

Wheat
Raisins
Water

Yeast
Sugar

To 10 lbs. of wheat add an equal amount by weight of raisins which have been run through a meat grinder, and pour upon the whole 5 gals. of hot water. Mix well and add 10 lbs. of sugar. Stir until dissolved. Ferment with yeast in the vat for about 12 days, stirring daily. At the end of this time strain off, put into cask and water-seal. Bottle after 3 months.

The flavor may be improved by adding a handful of cracked pits from cherries, plums, or peaches at the time of sealing.

appendices

APPENDIX I

Figure 24. Copy of Form 1541, which must be filed by every home winemaker. Obtainable from Regional Offices.

Form 1541
U. S. TREASURY DEPARTMENT
INTERNAL REVENUE SERVICE
(Revised February 1962)

TAX-FREE WINE FOR FAMILY USE

TO:
DISTRICT SUPERVISOR,
Alcohol and Tobacco Tax Division,

....
(City and State)

FROM:

....
(Name)

....
(Street and number)

....
(City, postal zone, county, and State)
(Print or type your name and address)

...., 19..........

SUPERVISOR'S
STAMP
(Date received)

Notice is hereby given that on or about ...., 19........, I intend to commence the production of not more than 200 gallons of wine solely for my family use. The following information is submitted:

1. The wine will be produced and stored at ....
(Give address)

2. Are you the head of a family? ....
(Answer yes or no)

3. Are you single? .... If so, do any dependents live with you? ....
(Answer yes or no) (Answer yes or no)

4. Are you married? .... If so, do wife (husband) or other dependents live
(Answer yes or no)
with you? ....
(Answer yes or no)

5. I understand that the filing of this notice
(a) does not give me authority to sell the wine produced;
(b) does not give me authority to make wine in partnership with another person;
(c) does not give me authority to make wine for a person not a member of my family.

6. I also understand that if I sell any of the wine or otherwise do not observe the limitations stated on the reverse side of this form, I will be subject to the penalties imposed by internal revenue law.

....
(Signature)

ATTENTION

Both copies of this form must be sent to the District Supervisor, Alcohol and Tobacco Tax Division, at least 5 days before commencing production of wine. One stamped copy will be returned to you. When the wine has been produced, you must show the following information on such retained copy:

I produced .... gallons of .... wine during ...., 19.......
(Number) (Grape, blackberry, etc.) (Month)

CAUTION

It is unlawful to produce wine for family use without filing this notice. If you cannot meet requirements for the tax-free production of wine for family use, or if you desire to produce more than 200 gallons of wine, or if you desire to produce any quantity of wine for sale, you must (before producing wine) obtain a permit from the District Supervisor, Alcohol and Tobacco Tax Division, file a bond, and meet other requirements for the operation of a bonded winery.

(SEE REVERSE SIDE) 16—10160-8

APPENDIX II

Addresses of Assistant Regional Commissioners, Alcohol and Tobacco Tax

North-Atlantic Region
Internal Revenue Service
90 Church Street
New York, New York
   10008

Midwest Region
Internal Revenue Service
35 E. Wacker Drive
Chicago, Illinois   60601

Mid-Atlantic Region
Internal Revenue Service
2 Penn Center Plaza
Philadelphia, Pennsylvania
   19102

Central Region
Internal Revenue Service
6503 Federal Office
   Building
Cincinnati, Ohio   45202

Southeast Region
Internal Revenue Service
275 Peachtree St. NE
Atlanta, Georgia   30303

Western Region
Internal Revenue Service
870 Market Street
San Francisco, California
   94102

Southwest Region
Internal Revenue Service
1114 Commerce Street
Dallas, Texas   75202

Address the Assistant Regional Commissioner, Alcohol and Tobacco Tax, of the region in which you live and ask for duplicate copies of Form 1541, "Registration for Production of Wine for Family Use." This form must be filed in duplicate with the Assistant Regional Commissioner, Alcohol and Tobacco Tax, of your region five days before commencing the manufacture of wine.

APPENDIX III

Where to Buy Accessories

Suppliers of Equipment for Home Winemakers (write for catalogs):

The Amateur Wine Shop, 1705 Dollard Avenue, Wille LaSalle, Quebec, Canada

Blythe Vineyards, Box 389, La Plata, Md. 20646

Budde & Westermann, P.O. Box 177, Montclair, N.J.

Chateau Guillaume, 18 N. Central Ave., Hartsdale, N.Y. 10530

The Compleat Winemaker, P.O. Box 2470, Yountville, Cal. 94599

Continental Products, Inc., P.O. Box 26034, Indianapolis, Ind. 46226

Ferrett Products, P.O. Box 1355, Winnipeg 1, Manitoba, Canada

M. J. Gelpi, 408 Harwood Road, Cantonsville, Md. 21228

Herter's, Inc., Waseca, Minn. 56093

Interstate Products, Inc., P.O. Box 1, Pelham, N.H. 03076

Jim Dandy Wine Supplies, P.O. Box 30230, Cincinnati, Ohio 45230

Kraus Company, P.O. Box 451, Nevada, Missouri 64722

Leslie Edelman, Inc., Route 463, Horsham Road, Horsham, Pa. 10944

Milan Laboratory, 57 Spring St., New York, N.Y. 10012

Mark D. Miller, Benmarl Vineyards, Marlboro, N.Y. 12542

Old Dominion Winemaker, 4708 Ponderosa Drive, Annandale, Va. 22003

Oreco, 615 N.E. 68th Ave., Portland, Oregon 97213

Presque Isle Wine Cellars, 9440 Buffalo Road, North East, Pa. 16428

Rockridge Laboratories, P.O. Box 2842, Rockridge Station, Oakland, Calif. 94618

J. H. Schiner Co., 683 Bryant St., San Francisco, Calif. 94107

Semplex of U.S.A., P.O. Box 7208, Minneapolis, Minn. 55412

F. H. Steinbart Co., 526 S.E. Grand Ave., Portland, Oregon 97214

Tarula Farm, Creek Rd., R.R. 1, Clarksville, Ohio 45113

Vino Corporation, 961 Lyell Ave., P.O. Box 7885, Rochester, N.Y. 14606

Wine Art of America, 4324 Geary Blvd., San Francisco, Calif. 94118. *(Fifty branches in U.S.A. and Canada.)*

Wine Cellar Supply House, Bethlehem and Butler Pikes, Ambler, Pa. 19002

The Winemakers Shop, Bully Hill Road, Hammondsport, N.Y. 14840

Wine Record Co., 847 Woodstock Rd., Olympia Field, Ill. 60461

Wine Unlimited, P.O. Box 458, Essex, Ontario

A. R. Zacher Co., P.O. Box 1006, Fresno, Calif. 93714

ACID INDICATOR PAPERS (for testing the acidity of wine)

Semplex of U.S.A.

ASBESTOS (for filtering)

Budde & Westermann
Milan Laboratory
Semplex of U.S.A.

BARRELS, KEGS, AND CASKS

F. H. Steinbart Co.

Semplex of U.S.A.

The following are manufacturers or distributors:

Allied Drum Service, Inc., N. 25th & Duncan Streets, Louisville, Ky. 40212

Binder Cooperage Co., Front & Dickenson Streets, Philadelphia, Pa. 19147

Buckeye Cooperage Co., 3800 Orange Ave., Cleveland, Ohio 44115

Michigan Bag and Barrel Co., 4827 Russell Street, Detroit, Mich. 48207

BOTTLES (The following distributors and manufacturers
   have indicated their willingness to remain on this list.
   The winemaker should write them, asking where their
   products may be obtained or if they will ship quantity
   orders directly to him.)

W. Braun Co., 300 N. Canal Street, Chicago, Ill.   60606
Brockway Glass Co., Brockway, Pa.   15824
Continental Glass Co., 843 W. Cermak, Chicago, Ill.
   60608
Diamond Glass Co., Royersford, Pa.   19468
Fairmont Glass Works, Inc. 1501 S. Keystone Ave.,
   Indianapolis, Ind.   46203
Glass Containers, Inc., 3601 Santa Fe Ave., Los Angeles,
   Calif.   90058
Hazel-Atlas Glass Co., 1535 Jacob Street, Wheeling,
   W. Va.   26003
Knox Glass Co., Knox, Pa.   16232
Liberty Glass Co., Sapulpa, Okla.   74066
Northwestern Glass Co., 5801 E. Marginal Way South,
   Seattle, Wash.   98134
Reed Glass Co., Inc., 860 Maple Street, Rochester, N.Y.
   14611

BOTTLE BRUSHES

Budde & Westermann (for 5-gallon size bottle)
Herter's, Inc.
Leslie Edelman, Inc.
Milan Laboratory
Semplex of U.S.A.

BOTTLE CAPS (See also Screw Caps and Jug Caps)

Herter's, Inc.
Leslie Edelman, Inc.
Milan Laboratory
Semplex of U.S.A.

BOTTLE CAPPERS

Herter's, Inc.

Leslie Edelman, Inc.
Milan Laboratory
Semplex of U.S.A.

BOTTLE CORKING MACHINES

American Wood Working Co., Montello, Wis.   53949
Budde & Westermann
Milan Laboratory
Semplex of U.S.A.

BUNG STARTER (Mallet)

Milan Laboratory

BUNGS

Milan Laboratory
Semplex of U.S.A.

CAPSULES (Foil for covering cork end of bottle)

Semplex of U.S.A.

CARBOYS

F. H. Steinbart Co.
Herter's, Inc. (plastic)
Leslie Edelman, Inc. (plastic)
Semplex of U.S.A.
And from any chemical- or laboratory-supply house.

CASKS (See under Barrels, Kegs, and Casks)

CHALK (precipitated)

Milan Laboratory
Semplex of U.S.A.

CONCENTRATES (grape)

Herter's, Inc.
Leslie Edelman, Inc.
Semplex of U.S.A.

CORKING MACHINE (See Bottle Corking Machines)

CORKS (bung)

Milan Laboratory

CORKS (wine)

Milan Laboratory
Semplex of U.S.A.

CORKSCREWS

Milan Laboratory
Semplex of U.S.A.

CRIMPING RING (for applying foil capsules, giving the

bottles a professional look)
Semplex of U.S.A.

CRUSHERS (See under Fruit Crushers)

DISCS (for champagne bottles)

Milan Laboratory

EHRLENMEYER FLASK

Any chemical- or laboratory-supply house. Your drugstore may be willing to order for you.

EXTRACTS (for flavoring)

Milan Laboratory
Semplex of U.S.A.

FAUCET (See under Spigot)

FILTER AIDS

Budde & Westermann
Milan Laboratory
Semplex of U.S.A.

FINING MATERIALS (Clarifiers)

> Milan Laboratory
> Semplex of U.S.A.

FRUIT CRUSHERS

> Milan Laboratory
> Semplex of U.S.A.

FUNNELS

> Budde & Westermann
> Milan Laboratory
> Semplex of U.S.A.

GELATIN (for fining)

> Milan Laboratory
> From any chemical- or laboratory-supply house. Have your druggist order for you.

GRAPE CRUSHERS (See under Fruit Crushers)

GRAPE VINES

> Henry Leuthardt Nurseries, Inc., Montauk Highway, East Moriches, Long Island, N.Y. 11940

HOODS (See under Wire Hoods)

HOPS

> F. H. Steinbart Co.
> Semplex of U.S.A.
> Also, any store selling home brew supplies.

HYDROMETER JAR

> F. H. Steinbart Co.
> Herter's, Inc.
> Leslie Edelman, Inc.
> Milan Laboratory
> Semplex of U.S.A.

ISINGLASS (for fining)

Semplex of U.S.A.

JUG CAPS

Budde & Westermann
Herter's, Inc.
Leslie Edelman, Inc.

LABELS (for wine bottles)

Milan Laboratory
Semplex of U.S.A.

LEAD FOIL CAPS (for champagne bottles)

Milan Laboratory
Semplex of U.S.A.

MAGAZINE

Semplex of U.S.A. is agent for the *Amateur Winemaker,*
a monthly magazine catering to the interests of the
home winemaker.

MALT

Herter's, Inc.
Leslie Edelman, Inc.
Semplex of U.S.A.

MEASURING GLASS

Milan Laboratory

NUTRIENTS (See under Yeast Nutrients)

PLASTIC BOTTLES (large)

F. H. Steinbart Co.
Herter's, Inc.
Leslie Edelman, Inc.

POTASSIUM METABISULPHITE

Milan Laboratory

PRESERVATIVES (to keep wine from spoiling)

Milan Laboratory

PRESSES (Fruit, Grape, Cider)

Budde & Westermann (ratchet press)
Herter's, Inc. (basket press)
Leslie Edelman, Inc. (ratchet press)
Milan Laboratory (basket, single ratchet, and double ratchet)
Semplex of U.S.A. (basket and ratchet)

RACKS (for storing wine)

Budde & Westermann

RUBBER HOSE

Milan Laboratory

SACCHAROMETER

Budde & Westermann
F. H. Steinbart Co.
Herter's, Inc.
Leslie Edelman, Inc.
Milan Laboratory
Semplex of U.S.A.

SCREW CAPS

Budde & Westermann
Herter's, Inc.
Leslie Edelman, Inc.
Milan Laboratory
Semplex of U.S.A.

SEALING WAX

Milan Laboratory

SIPHON

Greenland Studios, 375 Greenland Bldg., Miami, Fla.
33147
Semplex of U.S.A.

SODIUM METABISULPHITE

Herter's, Inc.
Leslie Edelman, Inc.
Semplex of U.S.A.

SPIGOT

Milan Laboratory
Semplex of U.S.A.

STOPPERS

Budde & Westermann
Milan Laboratory
Semplex of U.S.A.

SULPHUR STRIPS

Milan Laboratory
Semplex of U.S.A.

TANNIC ACID

Milan Laboratory
Semplex of U.S.A.

TARTARIC ACID

Milan Laboratory

THERMOMETER

Buy at any drugstore.

TUBING (rubber)

Milan Laboratory

VINOMETER (for measuring alcohol by volume in dry,
not sweet, wines)
Semplex of U.S.A.

WATER-SEAL

Budde & Westermann (called fermentation tube. Write
for description.)
Herter's, Inc.
Leslie Edelman, Inc.
Milan Laboratory
Semplex of U.S.A.

WINEMAKING KITS

The Vino Corporation, Box 7885-22, Rochester, N.Y.
14606

WIRE HOODS (for champagne bottles)

Milan Laboratory
Semplex of U.S.A.

YEASTS (wine)

Budde & Westermann
F. H. Steinbart Co.
Herter's, Inc.
Leslie Edelman, Inc.
Semplex of U.S.A.

YEAST NUTRIENTS

Semplex of U.S.A.

APPENDIX IV

The Home Winemaker's Equipment

(Almost all items listed are available from the supply houses mentioned in Appendix III.)

barrel. Nothing smaller than the 50-gallon size if it is to be used as a fermenting vat. (But see under *crock, vat,* and *plastic trash container*.)

beeswax. For use with paraffin in sealing bottles after filling.

bottle caps. Use only screw-on variety.

bottles. Use only round bottles. Wine bottles are best.

brushes. Almost essential for proper cleaning of used bottles; a scrub brush is needed for scouring the vat and the cask, and a small paint brush for applying paraffin.

bung. Wooden bungs are always needed after the water-seal has finished its usefulness. Large corks may be used.

candles. For candling (testing the clearness of) wine and to use as a substitute for paraffin.

carboy. It comes in handy for making relatively small quantities. When several are used large amounts of wine can be made.

cask. Of white oak or redwood. Nothing smaller than the 10-gallon size is worthwhile.

corks. For bottling. Large corks come in handy as bungs for the cask and in making home-made water-seal, or for stopping up the carboy.

cotton. For plugging the flask in which the yeast starter is made.

crock. A crock, or stone jar, used as a fermenting vat, is a good substitute for the 50-gal. barrel in making small quantities of wine.

cylinder (glass). See under *hydrometer jar*.

dipper. Has many uses. Should be of plastic, enamel, or tin.

faucet. See under *spigot*.

filtering aids. Bag, paper, asbestos pulp. For use in clearing and fining wine.

funnel. For filling bottles. Should be of plastic, glass, or enamelware.

hydrometer. See under *saccharometer.*

hydrometer jar. For use with saccharometer in determining the sugar content of a liquid. Buy a jar of the following size: 325 × 38 mm.

jugs. Glass jugs of one-gallon size are very convenient for holding surplus quantities of wine or juice to be used in refilling cask or carboy.

keg. Five-gallon size is not of much use. For larger size see under *cask.*

labels. All bottles should be marked with the fruit from which the wine is made and the year of manufacture.

measuring cup. Always useful for measuring liquids. Should be of glass or plastic.

meat grinder. Has many uses in making false wines.

plastic trash container. Makes a convenient fermenting vat. Comes in various sizes up to 32 gallons.

potato masher. Very convenient for crushing small quantities of fruit. This is a household article.

press. Essential to the making of white wines. A small basket press will serve the home winemaker.

saccharometer. Buy only Brix or Balling scale. Its only, but very important, use will be in measuring the sugar strength of liquids.

siphon. A five-foot rubber tube makes an excellent siphon.

spigot. Necessary if the wine is made in a cask.

spoons. Of glass, wood, or enamel.

stirring rod. Should be of glass or wood. Can be made at home.

stoneware. See under *vat* or *crock.*

stoppers. Should be either regular wine corks (No. 9, one and one-half inches long), or screw caps.

strainer. This article, found in every home, will find many uses in the winemaker's hands.

sugar meter. See under *saccharometer.*

thermometer. One for measuring the temperature of liquids, and another for measuring the temperature of the room. Bought at drug- and hardware stores.

tubing (glass). For making home-made water-seals.

vat. Thirty-gallon size makes an acceptable home fermenting vat. A 15-gallon vat is convenient for working with small quantities.

vinometer. An instrument for measuring the percentage of alcohol in dry wines. Will not work with sweet wines.

APPENDIX V

Chemicals and Other Materials Used in Winemaking

alum. Powdered alum is used in some cider wines. (At the drugstore.)

cream of tartar. For addition to fermenting juices that are short in tartaric acid. (Buy at drug- and grocery stores.)

charcoal (animal). For decoloring white wines. (At all drugstores.)

egg-white. For fining wines. (Wherever eggs are sold.)

fish glue. See under *Russian isinglass.*

gelatin. The kind to use is pure leaf gelatin, though the ordinary kitchen gelatin will do. (The former at drugstores, the latter at grocery stores.)

leek seed. For correcting sourness in wine. (At the drug- or grocery store.)

lime (unslaked). For cleaning and purifying casks and for temporarily correcting slight acetic acidity in wine. (At hardware stores and lumber companies.)

marble chips. Sometimes used to correct very slight acetic acidity in wine. (At marble or monument works.)

milk (skimmed). For fining wines. (From the local dairy.)

mountain ash (berries of). For treating ropiness, a disease of wine. (At the drugstore.)

olive oil. For correcting "caskiness" in wine. (At the grocery store.)

potassium bitartrate. For treating slight acetic acidity in wine. (At the larger city drugstores.)

potassium metabisulphite. For preparing grape juice before adding the yeast starter. (At the drugstore.)

potassium tartrate. For neutralizing an excess of malic acid in wine. (At the drugstore.)

Russian isinglass. For fining white wines. (Rather hard to get. Try the drugstore and the hardware stores.)

salt. For treating moldy casks.

soda. For cleaning the cask.

sugar. For raising the sugar content of a weak juice.

sulfur. For sulfurating a cask. (At drug- and hardware stores.)

tannic acid. Used in the making of white wines, or to restore tannin to a wine which has lost this substance when fined; and for treating ropiness in sick wines. Buy only dry tannic acid. (At drugstores.)

tannin. Same as tannic acid.

tartaric acid. See under *cream of tartar.*

yeast. For starting fermentation. (At grocery stores.)

APPENDIX VI

Making Red Wine

Consult text at every step of the process

1. Secure grapes a day or so before processing.

2. If a yeast starter is to be used, prepare it now.

3. Pick over grapes.

4. Crush grapes.

5. Test juice immediately for sugar content and record reading.

6. If juice is to be diluted, mix equal parts of juice and water and test with saccharometer. Record reading.

7. Put crushed grapes into vat, skins and all.

8. If yeast starter is to be used, add it now and cover vat with newspaper or cloth.

9. Stir twice daily for 8 or 10 days.

10. Remove juice from vat, pressing all skins.

11. If necessary, raise sugar content in accordance with reading already taken under 5 above.

12. If the juice is to be diluted, add water here and raise sugar content in accordance with reading taken under 6 above.

13. Turn the juice, or the mixture of water and juice, into a cask.

14. Let wine work until impurities are no longer discharged through bunghole.

15. Water-seal, spreading melted wax or paraffin over all junctures.

16. Rack into a clean cask in late November or early December.

17. Rack for second time by middle of February in the South or during first week in March in the North.

18. Rack for third time in June.

19. If wine is to be fined, now is the time.

20. Rack for fourth time in October.

21. Bottle after October racking.

22. Cork or cap bottles.

23. Store bottles on their sides in a cool place.

APPENDIX VII

Making White Wine

Consult text at every step of the process

1. Secure grapes a day or so before pressing, as for red wine.

2. If a yeast starter is to be used, prepare it now.

3. Pick over grapes.

4. Press grapes.

5. Test juice immediately for sugar content and record reading.

6. If juice is to be diluted, mix equal parts of juice and water and test with saccharometer. Record reading.

7. Put juice directly into clean cask.

8. Raise sugar content, if necessary, in accordance with the reading already taken under 5 above.

9. If juice is to be diluted, add water here and raise sugar content in accordance with reading already taken under 6 above.

10. If a yeast starter is to be used, add it now.

11. Add tannin.

12. Let wine work until impurities no longer rise through bunghole.

13. Water-seal, spreading melted wax or paraffin over all junctures.

14. If wine is to be decolored, add animal charcoal after all fermentation has stopped.

15. Rack into a clean cask late in November or early in December.

16. Rack for second time by middle of February in the South or during first week in March in the North.

17. If wine is not brilliantly clear, now is the time to fine it.

18. Rack for third time in June.

19. Rack for fourth time in October.

20. Bottle after October racking.

21. Cork or cap bottles.

22. Store bottles on their sides in a cool place.

APPENDIX VIII

Glossary

acetic acid. A colorless, pungent substance which is the chief ingredient of vinegar.

acidity. As applied to wine, this usually refers to its content of tannic and tartaric acids; less frequently it may refer to its acetic, or vinegar-like, quality.

alcohol. An important by-product of the fermentation process. Yeasts working upon the sugar contained in a liquid transform it into carbonic acid gas and alcohol.

aroma. The agreeable odor or smell of a wine, including the bouquet, but designating specifically its grape or fruity fragrance.

astringent. Applied to a wine that puckers the mouth with its high tannic and tartaric acid content.

Balling. A scale graduation for a hydrometer, or saccharometer, used to read the specific gravity of liquids or their sugar content.

blending. The mixing of two or more wines to achieve a better product or a special result.

body. The "extract content" of a wine, that is, the soluble, non-sugar solid it contains, such as tannin, tartaric and malic acids, and others which exist in minute proportions. Those having less than 2 percent of these solids are light wines. Heavy-bodied wines have 3 percent or more.

bond (in bond). An alcoholic liquor on which the internal revenue tax or duty has not yet been paid is said to be "in bond." It is under government control until the tax or duty has been paid.

bottle. A wine bottle contains from 23 to 26 ounces.

bouquet. The fragrance of a wine produced by the combination of its volatile acids and its essential oils with the alcohol. It is not identical with aroma, which is rather the smell of the grape or fruit from which it was made.

Brix. A scale graduation for a hydrometer, or saccharometer, used in reading the specific gravity of liquids or their sugar content.

Burgundy. A wine made in the Burgundy region of France. The reds are usually heavy-bodied.

carbonic acid gas. One of the important by-products thrown off by yeasts as they convert sugar into alcohol during fermentation.

carboy. A large glass bottle having a capacity of several gallons.

cask. A barrel-like container for wines, usually made of wood.

caskiness. A flavor imparted to wine by certain essential oils which remain in a cask that is not thoroughly clean.

cellar. As a wine term, this means the place where wine is stored.

Chablis. A light, dry wine from the Burgundy region of France.

Champagne. A white sparkling wine made in a well-defined region of France, formerly the province of Champagne.

Claret. Strictly a red table wine from the Bordeaux region of France. Commonly, a light-bodied red table wine.

clarify. To clear up a wine by causing a settlement of the minute particles that make it cloudy or unclear.

cloudiness. A state often characteristic of wines of low alcoholic content in which some albuminous substances refuse to settle.

colloidal suspension. A state that exists in liquids when certain semi-solid and albuminous particles remain suspended.

cordial. A sweet, aromatic beverage, usually of high alcoholic content—a liqueur.

corkiness. An unpleasant flavor imparted to wine by a defective cork or by defective stopping of the bottle with a cork.

corks. Wine bottle stoppers made from the bark of a tree known as the cork oak. The best corks come from Spain.

cream of tartar. A purified form of tartaric acid.

dago red. A term commonly used to refer to cheap, home-made wines of low alcoholic content, often sour, and which seldom keep well.

decant. To pour wine from one vessel into another; to pour a wine off its dregs, or deposit.

deposit. The normal sediment of microscopically fine particles precipitated by wine as it matures in the bottle.

dregs. The lees or sediment precipitated by a wine fermenting in the cask. Loosely applied to the deposit in the bottle.

dry. A wine term meaning *not sweet,* or the opposite of *sweet.* Wines containing less than 2 percent of sugar are dry.

essential oils. Volatile oils that give distinctive odor or flavor to plants, flowers, and fruits. In wines they combine with the alcohol to help determine its bouquet.

false wines. Wines not made from grapes.

fermentation. The chemical process by which the sugar in a liquid is broken down by yeasts into alcohol, carbonic acid gas, and some other by-products.

fermentation lock. See *water-seal.*

fifth. A liquid measure equal to one-fifth gallon.

fine. As a verb, fine means the process of clarifying wines by natural or other methods. As an adjective, it means brilliantly clear when applied to wines, and, loosely, of high quality.

fine wine. A wine in which all the properties necessary for the best wine are in perfect balance. This is usually the work of Nature and most fine wines are the product of those years in which Nature behaves "just right." Some blended wines, however, are fine wines—Sherry, for example.

fish glue. A substance prepared from the viscera of certain fish and used in making gelatin, in fining white wines, etc. See under *isinglass.*

flatness. A condition of wines due to insufficient alcohol.

flowers of wine. A ferment which forms on the surface of wine and oxidizes the alcohol. It is a disease and can be recognized by the small, whitish particles, or "flowers," on the surface of the wine.

fortified wine. A wine whose alcoholic content has been increased (usually to between 18 and 21 percent) by the addition of brandy.

fox grape. The *Vitis labrusca*, a native American grape found almost universally throughout New England and the North Central States.

foxy (foxiness). Terms used to describe the characteristic flavor and smell of the wine made from several American grapes of the species *V. labrusca*, the fox grape. Nobody really knows why it is called the "fox" grape. A long time ago, one William Bartram, influenced by the already existing name of the grape, wrote that this same name was due to the smell of the ripe fruit, which, he said, was like "the effluvia arising from the body of the fox."

fruity. A term used to indicate the flavor of the grape in the finished wine.

gallon. A liquid measure containing, in the United States, 128 ounces.

greenness. A defect of wine deriving from the use of unripe fruit and characterized by harshness of taste due to excess of malic and tartaric acids.

harshness. A condition due to lack of age, or to the same causes as "greenness." If the wine is healthy, it will often pass with age.

heavy wines. Wines having more than 3 percent of soluble, non-sugar solids. See under *body*.

Hock. An English abbreviation for the German *Hochheimer,* a type of Rhine wine, and loosely applied to any Rhine wine which is not Moselle.

hydrometer. An instrument, much like the saccharometer, for measuring the density of liquids.

hydrometer jar. A tall glass cylinder for holding liquids to be read by a hydrometer or saccharometer.

isinglass. A substance prepared from the viscera of certain fish and used in the manufacture of gelatin, in the fining of white wines, etc. *Russian isinglass* is a superior grade obtained chiefly from the sturgeon.

jerk wine. Wine made by pouring water on the remains of grapes whose juice has been pressed out for other wine. The alcohol is obtained by adding sugar. (See recipe for Grape Wine 9, pages 205–06.)

keg. A small cask.

lees. The sediment which settles to the bottom of a cask of fermenting wine.

light wines. Wines having 2 percent or less of soluble, non-sugar solids. See under *body.*

liqueur. A sweet, aromatic beverage, usually of high alcoholic content—a cordial.

malic acid. An acid occurring in certain fruits, among which are apples and grapes.

marc. The skins or husks and seeds which remain after the pressing of the grapes.

mold. A fungus that sometimes develops in wines deficient in alcohol.

Moselle. A light, delicate, and usually dry wine made in Germany in the valley of the Moselle river.

must. Unfermented juice of the grape.

musty. A term used to describe a moldy taste or smell acquired by wines that have been faultily prepared or bottled.

natural fermentation. Fermentation carried on under normal conditions and producing an alcoholic strength not greater than that which can be obtained from the sugar in the juice under the conditions of fermentation.

natural wines. Wines produced by natural fermentation, that is, made naturally, as distinguished from fortified wines.

ordinary wine. A common wine for everyday use as distinguished from superior or great wines. Also *vin ordinaire.*

pasteurization. The process, discovered by the French scientist Pasteur, of arresting or stopping ferments in wine, beer, milk and other liquids, by heating for a period of time to a temperature of between 144° and 149° Fahrenheit.

pips. Seeds.

Port. A heavy red wine from the Douro region of Portugal. It is made by stopping fermentation of the grape juice by the addition of brandy. This is Ruby Port. After it has aged for many years and much of the coloring matter has settled, it becomes Tawny Port.

quart. Liquid measure of 32 ounces.

rack. To draw the wine off its lees into a fresh container.

red wine. A wine with any red coloring, as distinguished from white wine.

Rhine wine. Any of a number of light, dry wines made in the Rhineland region of Germany.

ropiness. A disease of wine characterized by viscosity due to lack of astringent matter, chiefly tannic acid.

saccharometer. An instrument for measuring the sugar content of liquids.

Sauternes. A sweet, white wine from any of the five parishes of the Sauternais region of France. There is no such thing in France as a "dry" Sauternes.

scud. A mold which attacks white wines deficient in alcohol. Easily recognized as particles of matter which dart about at the slightest movement of the bottle.

sediment. The natural deposit thrown by wine as it matures.

Sherry. A fine fortified wine from southern Spain, usually characterized by a nutty flavor which American winemakers try to obtain by "baking" or "cooking."

siphon. An apparatus, usually consisting of a tube, by which liquids may be transferred to a lower level over an intervening barrier or elevation.

sour. Often loosely used to mean "dry" or "not sweet."

sourness. A sour condition of the wine not due to acetic acid.

sparkling wine. Wine which retains some of the carbonic acid gas thrown off by the yeasts during fermentation.

spigot. A faucet, or cork, usually made of wood and which fits in a hole in the end of a cask. It is used to draw off the contents of the cask.

still wine. Wine from which all the carbonic acid gas

produced by yeasts during fermentation has escaped. The opposite of sparkling wine.

sweet wine. Wine which contains 3 percent or more of sugar after fermentation.

tannic acid. See under *tannin.*

tannin. An astringent acid necessary to the proper maturing and keeping of wines.

tartaric acid. An acid found in several fruits, and especially in grapes. In its purified form it is known as cream of tartar.

Tokay. A very sweet, fortified Hungarian wine made from the Tokay grape.

vat. The container in which grape juice, or any liquid from which wine is to be made, is put to undergo its primary fermentation.

ventilating bung. See under *water-seal.*

viniculture. The theory and practice of winemaking.

vinosity. The "winey" quality of wine, especially as regards flavor, body, and bouquet.

vinous. Having a wine-like quality, or pertaining to wine.

vintage. The harvesting of the grape crop and the making of wine. Freely used to mean just wine.

vintage wine. Wine of certain regions that is the product of exceptional years only, usually bottled with the date and place of growth, manufacture, and bottling.

vintner. Wine seller.

viscidity. A disease of wine which causes it to become viscous or stringy, and due to lack of astringent matter, especially tannic acid.

viticulture. The theory and practice of grape growing.

Vitis vinifera. The European grape family.

volatile oil. An oil that readily vaporizes. Volatile oils give their distinctive odors and flavors to plants, flowers, and fruits.

water-bung. See under *water-seal.*

water-seal. An apparatus which seals a cask or other container of fermenting liquor from the air while permitting the carbonic acid gas to escape through water.

water-valve. Same as *water-seal.*

white wine. Wine without any trace of *red* coloring matter. White wines may run from deep brown to a
very light straw yellow or green.

wine. Strictly speaking, the fermented juice of the grape.
In a broader sense, and as used in this book, it is
the fermented juice of any fruit or a liquor prepared
by natural fermentation from any other substance,
but which is not brewed or distilled.

index

index

If you are tempted—but scared to begin trading for big profits in commodities —this book was written for you.

Commodities trading is a fast-moving, risky game. But if you are an emotionally stable person who likes to use money to make money, *you can make money 10 to 20 times as rapidly as you could in stocks.*

Stanley W. Angrist's SENSIBLE SPECULATING IN COMMODITIES: OR How to Profit in the Bellies, Bushels and Bales Markets is the first practical step-by-step book on commodities trading for the layman. In clear, simple language, it will show you exactly how the market works...how to get into it...the basic winning techniques of market analysis and trading.

What You Will Learn About Commodity Trading

- What is traded—and where
- The mechanics of trading
- How to forecast future prices
- How to open a trading account
- The beauty of short selling
- The 8 Commandments of sensible speculation in commodities

At your bookstore or mail this coupon for 14-day free examination

SIMON AND SCHUSTER, DEPT. 63, 630 5th Avenue, New York, N.Y. 10020

Please send me SENSIBLE SPECULATING IN COMMODITIES by Stanley W. Angrist. If I am not convinced that it can help me make money in commodities, I may return the book within 14 days and owe nothing. Otherwise, I will send only $7.95 plus mailing costs as payment in full. (Please Print)

Name_____

Address_____

City_____State_____Zip_____

☐ SAVE. Enclose $7.95 now and publisher pays mailing costs. Same 14-day return privilege with full refund guaranteed. 21342

S 77/3

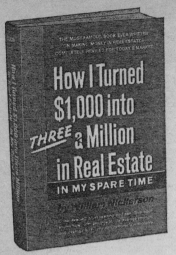

THE MOST FAMOUS BOOK EVER WRITTEN ON MAKING MONEY IN REAL ESTATE COMPLETELY REVISED FOR TODAY'S MARKET

How I Turned $1,000 into THREE a Million in Real Estate IN MY SPARE TIME by William Nickerson

"Is it still possible today to make a million by my formula?"

People are always asking me this question. And in spite of tight money and high taxes, I answer, "Yes— more than ever!" The new updated edition of my book *(How I Turned $1,000 into Three Million)* shows you how.   by William Nickerson

In my book I reveal—and tell how to use—these 4 basic principles of traveling the surest road to great fortune still open to the average person:

1. How to harness the secret force of free enterprise—the pyramiding power of borrowed money.

2. How to choose income-producing multiple dwellings in which to invest your own (and your borrowed) capital.

3. How to make your equity grow.

4. How to virtually eliminate the "tax bite" on your capital growth.

▼ AT YOUR BOOKSTORE OR MAIL THIS COUPON NOW FOR FREE 14-DAY TRIAL ▼